Dedication to John Muir

In the history of environmentalism one man stands out as the prophet of the international conservation movement: the Scots-born American naturalist, John Muir (1838–1914).

He was born at Dunbar in East Lothian and in 1849 his family emigrated to America. In his unfinished autobiography, *The Story of my Boyhood and Youth* (1913; Canongate Classics, 1987) Muir recalled his dawning awareness of the beauty of nature:

When I was a boy in Scotland I was fond of everything that was wild, and all my life I've been growing fonder and fonder of wild places and wild creatures. . . . With red-blooded playmates, wild as myself, I loved to wander in the fields to hear the birds sing, and along the seashore to gaze and wonder at the shells and seaweeds, eels and crabs, in the pools among the rocks when the tide was low.

After his arrival in America he spent ten years carving a farm from virgin forest. He described this time as one when he was his father's unpaid 'well-digger, plough-boy and lumberjack'. Later he was offered the chance to study at Wisconsin University, where he invented a number of remarkable machines; but in 1867 he was temporarily blinded in an industrial accident, and thereafter concentrated his attention on natural history, exploring the American west and especially the Yosemite area which he described in *My First Summer in the Sierra* (1908; Canongate Classics, 1988) and *The Mountains of California* (1911). He made fundamental discoveries about the nature of glaciation in the High Sierras and Alaska, and suggested that glaciers had carved out the great mountain valleys (see Chapter 1) – a view that was ridiculed at the time by academics. As a botanist he collected hundreds of plants.

He became deeply concerned about the threats facing the Yosemite Valley in the 1880s. Sheep had destroyed virtually all the wildflowers and seedling trees in Yosemite; the lumber companies were felling the giant redwoods and other trees along the watershed that surrounds the valley.

Muir campaigned tirelessly to save the valley from further desecration; and his efforts were apparently successful when, in 1890, Congress approved a bill making the Yosemite a State Park. But it was only after a further decade of campaigning that a much enlarged Yosemite was created America's first National Park in 1905.

In 1892 Muir founded the Sierra Club which is now one of the world's most powerful environmental bodies. He influenced Theodore Roosevelt, whose presidency (1901–12) saw the designation of thirty-three National Parks and 230,000 square miles of American National Forests, as well as twenty-three National Monuments, such as the Grand Canyon.

America has honoured John Muir by naming more than 200 natural areas after him, including Muir Beach and Muir Woods near San Francisco, Muir Glacier in Alaska and the John Muir Trail in the High Sierras.

By contrast in Scotland, the land of his birth, the name of John Muir is virtually unknown. But he has been honoured by East Lothian District Council who created the John Muir Country Park near Dunbar, and restored his home in Dunbar as a museum. The John Muir Trust was founded in Scotland in 1984 with the aim of 'conserving and protecting wild land for future generations while respecting the needs and aspirations of people living in such areas', and has so far purchased more than 3,000 acres (1,200 ha) of the wildest mountain land in Scotland.

John Muir's vision has inspired generations of conservationists and nature-lovers all over the world:

When one contemplates the whole globe as one great dewdrop, striped and dotted with continents and islands, flying through space with all the other stars, all singing and shining together as one, the whole universe appears as an infinite storm of beauty . . . this grand show is eternal. It is always sunrise somewhere; the dew is never all dried at once; a shower is forever falling; vapour is forever rising. Eternal sunrise, eternal sunset, eternal dawn and gloaming, on sea and continents and islands, each in its turn as the round earth rolls.

John Muir has not yet been accorded the place in the pantheon of great Scots which he deserves, but in retrospect he is arguably Scotland's greatest contribution to the global environmental movement, as the prophet whose ideas and spirit are being given renewed emphasis in the land of his birth. This book is dedicated to his memory and achievements.

THE NATURE OF
SCOTLAND

To Barbara and Ward,
with all best wishes.

Dunbar, July 1997.

Graham

THE NATURE OF
SCOTLAND

Landscape, Wildlife and People

Edited by
MAGNUS MAGNUSSON
and
GRAHAM WHITE

CANONGATE
·
SCOTTISH POST OFFICE BOARD

First published in Great Britain in 1991 by Canongate Press PLC,
14 Frederick Street, Edinburgh EH2 2HB

The Editors and Publishers gratefully acknowledge the contribution of the Scottish Post Office Board in the initiation and development of this book. It was they who recognised the need for a wide ranging work on Scotland's environment and without their considerable enthusiasm and support for this enterprise it would not have become a reality.

The publishers further wish to thank the trustees and staff of the Environment Centre for their guidance and generous assistance in the publication of this book.

The Publishers gratefully acknowledge copyright permission granted from the following sources for the right to reproduce photographs in
The Nature of Scotland.

John MacPherson *1, 2, 6, 8, 16, 17, 28, 41, 42, 46 top, 48, 51 top, 86, 102, 104, 105 foot, 106, 108 right, 115, 116 top, 116 foot, 117, 118, 121 top, 121 right, 127 top, 128 foot, 136 top, 137, 138, 139 top, 140, 142 top, 142 foot, 144, 146, 147, 158, 162 top, 182, 189 foot, 190 top, 192, 195, 200, 202, 203, 204, 205, 206, 207, 208, 209 top.* Laurie Campbell *40, 46 foot, 50 left, 52 top, 52 foot, 57 top, 58, 61 top, 62, 66 right, 68, 69, 101 mid, 123 top, 136 foot, 139 foot, 159, 160, 163 foot, 165 top, 165 foot, 167, 179 top, 185, 194.* Graham White *19, 22, 26, 50 top, 56 top, 96, 97, 99 top, 99 foot, 100 top, 101 top, 119 right, 149 foot, 163 top, 170/1, 174 top, 175 top, 175 foot, 177, 178, 181 foot, 210 top.* Mick Sharp *10, 87, 88 top, 90 top, 90 left, 91 right, 93, 94 foot, 95 top, 95 foot, 107, 135 foot, 210 foot.* National Galleries of Scotland *25, 27, 76, 127 foot, 150 right, 153, 157, 168, 174 foot, 198 top.* Sam Maynard *52/53, 108 left, 109 top, 109 foot, 110, 111, 119 top.* Dave Gowans *59, 72 top, 74, 75, 164, 187.* Alex Gillespie *34 foot, 36, 38, 150 left, 151 top.* T. Norman Tait *79 right, 80 foot, 81, 82, 83.* Lorne Gill/CCS *125, 184 top, 189 top, 190 foot.* RSPB *66 left, 71 top, 71 right, 73.* W. S. Paton/Natural Selection *64, 67 top.* W. S. Paton/RSPB *70, 72 foot.* Dick Balharry *54, 60, 123 foot.* Pater Maitland *141 foot, 141 top, 145.* Glasgow Museums & Art Galleries *21, 132, 196.* Gerald Rodway *79 left, 80 top, 84.* Bobby Tulloch *33, 91 top, 211.* Heather Angel *57 foot.* Heather Angel/Biophotos *57 mid.* Dr Michael Coates *20, 23.* Andrew Kitchener *56 foot, 67 foot.* Murdo MacLeod *114 top, 114 foot.* Oxford Scientific Films *31, 32.* Mike Scott *44, 45.* Sue Scott *30, 30 mid.* SMC Collections *199 foot, 199 right.* STB/Still Moving Pictures *112, 129.* Kevin D'Arcy *179.* P. J. Banks *56 mid.* A. Barbour *143.* Colin Baxter *188.* Amanda Brewis *49.* John Buckingham *51 foot.* Tim Clifford/NCCS *184 foot.* Douglas Corrance *176.* CSWT *122 left.* Stephen Dalton *170 foot.* William Daniel/National Library of Scotland *131.* Bob Davis *181 top.* Roy Dennis *171 right.* Edinburgh Butterfly World *85.* The Edinburgh Room *173.* Peter Hinson *151 foot.* Historic Scotland *94 top.* Paul Kay *63.* Angus King *37.* Paul Morrison/Natural Selection *47.* Alan Mowle *120.* National Remote Sensing Centre *161.* National Trust for Scotland *209 foot.* New Lanark Trust *149 top.* NHPA *180.* David Octavius Hill/Glasgow Museum & Art Galleries *130.* Peter Parks/Oxford Scientific Films *33.* David Paterson *122 top.* The Post Office *135 top.* Tom Prentice *201.* Graham Ritchie *88 foot.* J. Robinson *61 foot.* Royal Botanic Gardens *172.* Glyn Satterley *24.* Scottish Development Department *128 right.* Scottish National Portrait Gallery *18.* Scottish Nuclear Ltd *156.* Scottish Wildlife Trust *162 foot.* Tim Sheldon *19.* Stirling & Trossachs Tourist Board *126.* Douglas Stronach *166.* Richard Sutcliffe *76.* Charles Tait Photographic *89.* John Twidel *152.* Chris Tydeman/Natural Selection *191.* Wade Cooper Associates *155.* George Washington Wilson *133.* George Washington Wilson/Aberdeen University Library *34 top.*

British Library Cataloguing in Publication Data
The nature of Scotland: landscape, wildlife and people.
I. Magnusson, Magnus II. White, Graham
941.1

ISBN 0862413338

Jacket and book design by James Hutcheson, Edinburgh
Typeset by Hewer Text Composition Services
Colour origination by Colourscan (Overseas) Ltd
Printed and bound in Great Britain by
Butler and Tanner Ltd.

Contents

Foreword   9

Introduction   11

1   The Laying of the Foundations   17
    GEORGE FARROW AND IAN ROLFE

2   The Seas of Plenty   29
    JOHN HAMBREY

3   The Flowering of Scotland   43
    MICHAEL SCOTT

4   The World of the Mammals   55
    ANDREW KITCHENER

5   The Birds and their Habitats   65
    DAVID MINNS

6   The Beauty of Butterflies   77
    RICHARD SUTCLIFFE

7   The Coming of Man   87
    GRAHAM AND ANNA RITCHIE

8   The Farming of the Land   97
    ALEXANDER FENTON

9   The Way of Crofting   107
    FRANK RENNIE

10 The Managing of the Land   117
    ALAN MOWLE

11 The Paths of Progress   127
    JOHN HUME

12 The Streams of Life   137
    PETER MAITLAND

13 The Power of Scotland   147
    JOHN BUTT AND JOHN TWIDELL

14 The Conservation of Nature   159
    ALASTAIR SOMMERVILLE

15 The Greening of the Cities   169
    GRAHAM WHITE

16 The Protection of the Land   183
    JOHN ARNOTT

17 The Playground of the Future   197
    ROGER SMITH

Bibliography   212

Index   213

Foreword

ONE BY ONE MANY OF THE WORLD'S UNSPOILED POCKETS OF paradise have been destroyed; but now most people understand that our future depends on the way we deal with the environment.

Of recent years, concern about our environment – where we live our lives of work and leisure – has been edging ever more clearly and forcefully into our consciousness. We are now increasingly aware of the choices and challenges that face us if the very real pleasures of Scotland's nature and landscape are to be passed on to future generations and our children are to be able to see the country as we have known it.

We initiated the idea for this book, seeking a publication which would both establish an authoritative work of reference for environmental matters in Scotland and, of course, reflect the important role which The Post Office has in the provision of its services from the busiest city centre to highland glen or to the most remote island.

Under the editorship of Magnus Magnusson who, quite unbeknown to us when we sought his agreement, was to become Chairman of the Nature Conservancy Council for Scotland and Chairman designate of Scottish Natural Heritage, we have a book in which most aspects of the nature of Scotland are covered with scholarship, with clarity, and, above all, with splendid readability. Our thanks to him, his assistant editor, Graham White and to the publisher Canongate.

We hope that this book makes a positive contribution to the ongoing national and international debate about our environment. Certainly, the nature of Scotland is our greatest national heritage and one to be cherished and enjoyed by all.

KENNETH GRAHAM
Chairman, Scottish Post Office Board

The Ballochroy standing stones, Kintyre in Argyll. In the distance the sun sets over the Paps of Jura.

Introduction

MAGNUS MAGNUSSON

Scotland small? Our multiform, our infinite Scotland *small?*
Only as a patch of hillside may be a cliché corner
To a fool who cries 'Nothing but heather!' where in September another
Sitting there and resting and gazing around
Sees not only the heather but blaeberries
With bright green leaves and leaves already turned scarlet,
Hiding ripe blue berries; and amongst the sage-green leaves
Of the bog-myrtle the golden flowers of tormentil shining;
And on the small bare places, where the little Blackface sheep
Found grazing, milkworts blue as summer skies;
And down in neglected peat-hags, not worked
Within living memory, sphagnum moss in pastel shades
Of yellow, green and pink; sundew and butterwort
Waiting with wide-open sticky leaves for their tiny winged prey;
And nodding harebells vying in their colour
With the blue butterflies that poise themselves delicately upon them,
And stunted rowan with harsh dry leaves of glorious colour.
'Nothing but heather!'–How marvellously descriptive! And incomplete!

Nearly fifty years ago, Hugh MacDiarmid, that giant of modern Scottish poetry, brilliantly expressed in his autobiography, *Lucky Poet* (1943), the universality to be found in every Scottish microcosm of nature.

This book, by many distinguished hands, is intended as a celebration of the Nature of Scotland: a celebration of Scotland's natural heritage on many levels. But the Nature of Scotland is not just nature in the sense of wildlife and countryside; it is also the quintessential nature of the country Scotland has become as expressed in its people and their history. This book is about the Nature of Scotland in the broadest sense, and tries to illuminate its natural history in the context of its history proper.

It is obviously impossible within the covers of a single book to do full justice to the immense diversity and wealth of Scotland's natural heritage. What Graham White (my assistant editor) and I have tried to do is to bring together a collection of informed essays to provide an integrated picture of the way Scotland's natural heritage is today, the way it came about, and the ways in which we ought to address the pressures and problems facing it.

I should first of all declare an interest here. This book was commissioned and planned before I was appointed to my present position as chairman of the new Nature Conservancy Council for Scotland and chairman-designate of Scottish Natural Heritage, which comes into being in 1992 as a merger of the NCC for Scotland and the Countryside Commission for Scotland. Working on the book in its formative stages was a happy adumbration of the wider responsibilities which, unknown to me at the time, I was about to be asked to undertake; and talking to the contributors whom we had identified as the right specialists to address the fundamental factors that have helped to create the Nature of Scotland was in itself an education for those new responsibilities.

It goes almost without saying that the opinions expressed in the individual chapters are entirely those of the authors.

Our contributors were not asked to present a coherent policy blueprint for Scottish Natural Heritage. But taken as a whole, what they have to say forms a powerful plea to all of us, the people of Scotland and all those concerned with the future of Scotland's natural heritage, to take better care of it for the sake of the unborn future.

One common philosophical theme that informs much of their environmental thinking is the concept of 'sustainability' as enunciated by the *World Conservation Strategy* (1980): the sustainable development of renewable resources – sustaining Hugh MacDiarmid's 'patch of hillside' not just as a reserve for nature lovers or Sunday strollers, but as an infinitely valuable biological complex of universal significance.

In order to give shape and purpose to the book, the chapters were conceived in a roughly tripartite form: the past, the present and the future. And within each individual chapter the many aspects of Scotland's natural history have been given the same kind of historical perspective: yesterday, today and tomorrow.

The opening chapter, *The Laying of the Foundations* by George Farrow and Ian Rolfe, forms the bedrock of the book and gives the underlying geological story of Scotland's landscape and environment. It describes how Scotland was formed and assembled from separate parts of the earth's crust like a huge three-dimensional jigsaw puzzle that has been gradually drifting into place for hundreds of millions of years – and which is still on the move. The 'Scotland' we know today, seemingly anchored since the beginning of time in the northern hemisphere, actually started out in the southern hemisphere: Edinburgh's friendly neighbourhood volcano, Arthur's Seat, erupted from tropical seas when 'Scotland' was on the equator of the planet, some 400 million years ago.

Indeed Scotland has drifted across the surface of the planet like a great Ark, constructed of rock rather than of wood; moreover, this vessel floated not on water but on the ocean of molten rock buried deep within the planet's crust. This composite Ark did not contain just one collection of plants and animals, as did Noah's in the Bible story, but over hundreds of millions of years it has carried an ever-evolving population of exotic creatures and plants on an unending journey through aeons of time.

There is an obvious and striking correlation between geology and the rich diversity and variety of Scotland's scenery. But there is much more to it than that. The rocks which are the very foundations of the land not only influence the flora and fauna we find in different parts of the countryside, but also shape and frame the lives of the human communities that live there. The underlying geology of Scotland has determined our agricultural present, but the rocks and minerals have also shaped our industrial past – it was the abundance of coal and shale-oil deposits below the Central Belt that literally fuelled the Industrial Revolution in Scotland, with all the environmental consequences which we see to this day.

The opening chapter, conceived as a series of snapshots in geological time, peels away the layers of landscape beneath our feet to reveal the story of Scotland's evolution which lies hidden in the rocks.

From there it is a natural step to the next chapter, *The Seas of Plenty* by John Hambrey. Scotland's coastal waters are among the richest in the world; yet our marine environment is relatively uncharted, and the problem of how best to conserve it is still unresolved. For too long we have taken the sea for granted, treating it as a bountiful cornucopia that would never run dry. But modern times, modern demands and vastly improved fishing technologies have put our traditional marine resources under increasing pressure. The world beneath the sea is now as threatened as is the natural heritage of the land.

Scotland can boast a wonderful variety of dramatic and attractive plants, especially in the arctic-alpine species of the mountainous areas. Some of them are extremely rare – and all the more precious for that; but many of them are under severe threat from human activities and from climatic change. In *The Flowering of Scotland*, Michael Scott gives a historical overview of what happened in Scotland as the last Ice Age receded, 12,000 years ago; what kind of plants and ground cover the new human colonists found waiting for them; what effects the development of settled farming communities and climatic change have brought; and what the picture is today.

Scotland is also renowned for its rich and varied wildlife, and for the great diversity and beauty of its wildlife habitats. Today Scotland is a vital staging post, or an important last refuge, for many species that were once common throughout Europe. Among the more famous and important of its current inhabitants are the wildcat, the red squirrel, the pine marten and the otter, as well as magnificent birds of prey such as the golden eagle, the osprey and the peregrine falcon.

But birds and animals do not happen by chance. They do not exist in splendid isolation. They are found in particular 'habitats' (another word for 'living places') which they share with a whole community of other plants and animals, including human beings. We cannot consider an animal or plant outside the context of the habitat which supports it.

In *The World of the Mammals*, Andrew Kitchener shows how changing habitats have gone hand in hand with changing wildlife, so that today's animals and plants are altogether different from those which our ancestors knew.

On land, for instance, we have lost animals such as the giant deer, the wild horse, the reindeer, the lynx, the moose (elk), the beaver, the wild ox (also known as the aurochs or urus), the brown bear, the wild boar, the wolf, the polecat – and, most recently, the St Kilda house mouse. All down the ages there have been comings and goings of mammal species in Scotland. Some have failed to adapt to a changing climate, some have been hunted to extinction; others have arrived as stowaways or colonisers, or have been deliberately introduced or re-introduced by humans for their own purposes.

Basically, Scotland's natural heritage is not 'natural' at all; for however 'wild' or scenic the countryside, it has largely been shaped and contoured by human exploitation. Today, Scotland's wildlife is still being affected by land-use and other environmental changes;

so it is vital that we accept full responsibility for the wildlife habitats and the creatures which live in them, for the enrichment of Scotland's countryside heritage and for the future benefit of us all.

In *The Birds and their Habitats*, David Minns gives an overview of the special nature of four groups of internationally important birds for which Scotland is justly celebrated as a special place: seabirds, waders and wildfowl, birds of prey and pinewood birds, Some birds, such as starlings, chaffinches, blackbirds, pigeons and gulls, are very catholic in their choice of habitats; others are much more selective, and if their chosen habitat is altered or destroyed, then their very survival is endangered.

Insects are not normally given much prominence in general nature books. Yet butterflies are perhaps the most enchanting creatures you can see on a summer's day, dancing on iridescent wings from flower to flower, little miracles of fragility. 'To break a butterfly upon a wheel', in Alexander Pope's memorable phrase, has become synonymous with the destruction of beauty by brute force. How such creatures manage to survive at all in our rough world is itself little short of miraculous. But survive they do, if only just. Butterflies are a sort of litmus paper of the general health of our ecology; when the harsh winds of environmental change begin to rise, they are the first to be blown out of existence. In *The Beauty of Butterflies*, Richard Sutcliffe shows how their presence and/or disappearance are often prime indicators of the loss of habitat and other factors, such as pesticides, which are adversely affecting the environment.

The Coming of Man, by Anna and Graham Ritchie, heralds the arrival of the creature who would have the most profound impact on Scotland's environment, and signals the start of the social history section of the book. In geological terms Man has only lived in Scotland for the blink of an eye; but ever since the first human hunting groups began to move into Scotland towards the end of the last Ice Age, Man has had an increasingly marked effect. The Ritchies trace the story of the waves of incomers who followed, from the first settled farmers to the Celts, the Romans, the Britons, the Picts, the Angles, the Scots, the Vikings and the Normans.

Man's later impact has been even more profound. In *The Farming of the Land*, Alexander Fenton charts and analyses the immense changes in the forms of land-use that Scotland has seen over the last 300 years up to the Second World War, first in the Lowland farming areas and subsequently, in modified form, in the Highlands and Islands. The powerful environmental forces that have radically altered the landscape and the environment of farming in Scotland, and the local communities dependent upon it, are still operating. They inform and illuminate Scotland's recent social history – nowhere more so than in the so-called Crofting Areas of the Highlands and Islands, where (as Frank Rennie points out in *The Way of Crofting*) the Clearances gave rise to a crofting subsistence economy which is both romanticised and rubbished with equal fervour but is now being recognised as a significant means of achieving the universally desired aim of the sustainable use of renewable resources.

In *The Managing of the Land*, Alan Mowle takes up the post-war story of the two major uses to which the land is put – farming and forestry – and likens Scotland's countryside to a garden that has to be managed and tended if we are to halt the inexorable decline of the countryside and sustain the wildlife heritage, the beauty of the landscape and the productive capacity of the land.

The development of transport and communications has also had a profound effect on the nature of Scotland, both directly and indirectly. It is not merely a matter of visual impact: with every advance in sophisticated community living, Man's ingenuity and aspirations for a more comfortable and prosperous way of life have involved ever greater demands on the natural resources of the environment. In *The Paths of Progress*, John Hume shows how improved methods of transport have changed the face of Scotland and provided the means of changing the physical patterns of life in Scotland: transport not only met people's needs, but created new ones – and the ways to satisfy them.

Transport by river and canal was a major factor in this revolution; and the lochs and rivers of Scotland are given separate treatment in *The Streams of Life* by Peter Maitland. Scotland is fortunate in having vast amounts of high quality water; yet although we value and constantly celebrate Scotland's fresh waters for their beauty, we often undervalue them as a key national resource.

Water is only one of Scotland's diverse energy resources. In *The Power of Scotland*, John Butt and John Twidell survey the story of the discovery and exploitation of these resources and their environmental consequences: the application of sun, wind, water and tide for example; the exploitation of the ancient fossil fuels of coal, shale-oil, oil and natural gas; the use of the biological energy sources of peat and timber, now augmented by the potential of domestic waste for fuel and of gas derived from landfills; the splitting of the atom and the creation of the 'friendly enemy', nuclear power.

The third section of the book is devoted more specifically to the problems and challenges of nature conservation: how we can safeguard and enhance the diversity and balance of nature in the face of ever-increasing pressures from economic exploitation and environmental pollution. In *The Conservation of Nature*, Alastair Sommerville takes an in-depth look at current conservation issues and suggests ways in which we can all become involved in conserving and protecting Scotland's natural heritage.

The remote uplands may be the most fragile parts of our ecological heritage; but to four-fifths of the population, it is the nature within and around towns that they experience for most of their lives. In *The Greening of the Cities*, Graham White argues that we must look again at our stereotypes of 'nature', 'town' and 'countryside' and realise that nature does not begin somewhere out beyond the green belt but right here in our streets, parks and gardens. We must promote environmental education where nature actually begins, from the heart of the inner cities outwards. If we want children to become adult conservationists who care about rare species in the Hebrides, we must start by involving them in caring for the local pond, the trees in their street, the blackbird in the park. In this chapter he suggests that only by adopting a more holistic environmental ethic, in which we look at the quality of environment of Scotland's towns as well as our wildlife habitats, can a truly broadly-based environmental movement be created in Scotland.

The penultimate chapter, *The Protection of the Land*, by John Arnott, considers the many ways in which significant parts of Scotland are protected. Most of the countryside is in private hands and all of it is used in one way or another, whether it be for farming and hill-sheep grazing, forestry, sporting activities, water catchment, amenity or recreation. All of it has been protected for these purposes, sometimes exclusively. But there is in addition a somewhat confusing system of more than forty designations of one kind or another, and innumerable controls and incentives: NNR (National Nature Reserve), NSA (National Scenic Area), SSSI (Site of Special Scientific Interest), LFA (Less Favoured Area) and so on, imposed or desired by the main official and voluntary bodies involved in the countryside. The would-be conservationist will appreciate this comprehensive guide through the thicket of acronyms that has sprouted over the years.

The final chapter of the book, *The Playground of the Future* by Roger Smith, tells the story of the manifold development of recreation in Scotland – shooting, mountaineering, rambling, skiing, tourism, 'leisure' resorts and sports. He highlights the conflicting demands which need to be resolved if the Nature of Scotland is not to be irrevocably damaged in the coming years.

So there, in summary, is the outline and thrust of this book. In addition, in special boxes throughout the text, we have focused on the great Scottish pioneers in various fields who have inspired the way in which we think about the environment: men like James Hutton, the 'father of modern geology'; Hugh Miller, the great populariser of geology; Sir Charles Lyell, the prophet of the theory of 'continental drift'; Sir Frank Fraser Darling, one of the pioneers of the ecological and environmental movement in Scotland; and above all the man to whose memory this book is dedicated, John

Muir, the Scots-born American explorer and naturalist who is increasingly regarded as the prophet of the international conservation movement.

I mentioned earlier the key concept of sustainability: the sustainable development of renewable resources. It's a lovely rolling phrase but already it is in danger of becoming a cliché. Yet it is more than just a buzz-word. It is a blueprint for a way of life, an achievable dream which we and our children must clothe in reality. It can

Sunset over the Isle of Rhum from Cleadale on the Isle of Eigg.

provide a framework on which all of us can build, whether we be farmers, foresters, crofters, conservationists, land owners, tourists, sportsmen, local authorities or development and enterprise bodies: a framework in which local communities can survive and prosper through the sustainable use of their natural resources.

In this concept of sustainable development, the greatest renewable resource of all is Man. Scotland is nothing without its people. But the people of Scotland are nothing without Scotland – and our aim must be to ensure that this Scotland of ours continues to be worth living in. The heritage and stewardship of nature is ours; and it is the duty of us all to hand that inheritance on to future generations in even better shape than when it was given into our care.

Magnus Magnusson, April 1991

*Buchaille Etive Mor and the
river Coupall, Glencoe.*

16

The Laying of the Foundations

GEORGE FARROW and IAN ROLFE

Dr George E. Farrow has done extensive fieldwork both in Scotland and abroad, especially on shell-sands. He lectured at Glasgow University for thirteen years and has worked for Britoil and the Royal Museum of Scotland in Edinburgh. He is now senior geologist with Croft Exploration in Glasgow.

Dr W.D. Ian Rolfe is the Keeper of Geology at the Royal Museum of Scotland and is an authority on fossil arthropods.

Most people have probably never met a geologist and may have little idea of just what they do, but geologists are in a unique position to throw light on the nature of Scotland and its origins in the distant past. It is easy to look at the mountains, valleys and plains of the Scottish landscape today and think that it has always looked like this; but geologists see the present landscape as merely the latest evidence of a series of massive and unending series of transformations of the Scottish scene. They can help people to understand these barely imaginable changes by revealing the story of Scotland's evolution which lies buried in the rocks. We are going to try to describe these changes for you in a rather unusual way.

We have put the story of Scotland's origins together as a series of 'snapshots' in geological time, like a family album, depicting the stages of the land's evolution. Starting with today's landscape, which everyone thinks of as 'the real Scotland', we shall peel away the layers of rock beneath our feet, going further and further back in time with each layer, to reveal the ancient, buried landscapes of Scotland's distant past.

In order to do this we have to set our geological clock to record the passage of 800 million years during a single twenty-four hours; on this scale, one hour represents 33 million years, a minute would be 550,000 years and a mere second would last almost 10,000 years. If we take the present moment to be midnight on our twenty-four-hour clock, then the story of Scotland's origins begins at the previous midnight, twenty-four geological hours and 800 million years ago.

THE BIRTH OF LOCH LOMOND, 10,000 YEARS AGO: 23:59.59 HOURS

Loch Lomond is the largest freshwater lake in Britain and, although it may seem to be 'as old as the hills', in fact on the timescale of our geological clock it was created barely a second ago.

Loch Lomond appeared on the scene just 10,000 years ago, at the very end of the last Ice Age. As the last of the melting glaciers retreated, they dumped vast quantities of rock which had been embedded in the ice, leaving behind piles of rubble which clearly mark the farthest point to which the glaciers advanced. These piles of glacial rubble show us that the last spreading of the ice, termed by geologists the 'Lomond Readvance', finally stopped just short of Dunblane. To the south, beyond the edge of this great ice cap the land was barren, permanently frozen tundra.

The area around Loch Lomond, with its recently acquired covering of thin soils and trees, thus gives us a glimpse of what a late-glacial landscape looked like. When you next drive past it, remember that you are looking at the most recent effects of a glacier (see Chapter 12, Box 1).

RIVERS CHANGE DIRECTION, 50,000 YEARS AGO: 23:59.55 HOURS

At the height of the last Ice Age, glacial erosion removed vast amounts of rock from the landscape, carving out the great valleys, leaving the planed and smoothed mountain tops standing proud above them. These glaciers also caused some intriguing changes in our river systems; the direction in which some rivers flow is certainly very odd in parts of Scotland, particularly around the Campsie Fells, towards Drymen.

Back in the middle of the last Ice Age, about 50,000 years ago, a colossal sheet of ice ground its way relentlessly south, past Ben Lomond, moving at a rate of between 9 and 180 metres a year and gouging out the rocky trench of Loch Lomond to a depth of 200 metres below sea level. As it moved southwards this ice-sheet cut across a series of rivers which had previously run eastwards to the Forth estuary. When they were dammed by the ice, these rivers were diverted and eventually burst out to flow westwards into the Clyde as the result

Loch Lomond is the largest body of fresh water in Great Britain

Ancient rivers which once flowed eastwards were diverted to the west by the last advance of the glaciers.

1. SIR CHARLES LYELL (1797–1875)

Sir Charles Lyell, the prophet of the theory of 'continental drift', was born in Kinnordy, the son of an eminent mycologist (a specialist in fungi) who was also a Dante scholar. He was brought up in England and studied law at Oxford, but his career changed dramatically when he attended some lectures in 1819 by William Buckland, who was then the Reader in mineralogy there. Lyell promptly dropped law, switched to geology, toured and studied in Europe, and during 1830–33 published his *Principles of Geology*, which had a profound impact on scientific thought in the nineteenth century.

His thesis was that the greatest geological changes had been produced by natural forces that were still at work; and he went on in *The Geological Evidence of the Antiquity of Man* (1863) to relate the evolution of the planet to Darwin's theory of evolution (*The Origin of Species by Means of Natural Selection*, 1859).

Lyell was particularly struck by the evidence of massive changes in climate which the rock records reveal. He was a century ahead of his time in acknowledging large-scale movements of the earth's surface and thus anticipating the modern theory of 'plate tectonics', the now-accepted fact that the continents are continually moving around the surface of the planet on the rocky 'plates' which make up the earth's land surface and the ocean floors. In 1875, the year of his death, he made this stunningly prophetic statement:

> Continents, therefore, although permanent for whole geological epochs, shift their positions entirely in the course of ages.

It would be almost a hundred years before modern geologists found the conclusive evidence for the new science of plate tectonics which Lyell's mind had envisaged.

of the gigantic forces of nature's ice-engineering.

THE 'OLD COURSE' LAID DOWN, 500,000 YEARS AGO: 23:59.05 HOURS

It is hard to find any aspect of the Scottish scene that has not been created or shaped by the last Ice Age . This even includes the eighteenth green at St Andrews, the celebrated 'Old Course', which in common with many of our golf links is located on a 'raised beach'. But how did the Ice Age help create the Old Course?

Some 500,000 years ago, Scotland was like a laden cargo ship carrying an incredibly heavy sheet of ice, over one kilometre thick, on her decks. Under this crushing burden Scotland actually sank into the deep plasticky subsurface of the planet by a depth of several metres; as the ice melted, the weight was removed from the 'ship' and Scotland rose again. We see the evidence of this in 'raised beaches' around our coasts, which are several metres above current sea levels.

In contrast, the south-east of England was never covered by ice; the land was never crushed under the weight of the glaciers and we see no raised beaches there. In fact the south-east coast of England is actually sinking slowly, as opposed to Scotland, which is still rising. Given the current concerns over the 'greenhouse effect' and rising sea levels, it would seem that a Scottish golf course could well be the safest place to be!

WESTERN SCOTLAND OVERRUN BY LAVA, 60 MILLION YEARS AGO: 22:12 HOURS

Our first three geological 'time snapshots' showed Scotland buried under a kilometre-thick shroud of ice, and in fact there were at least five Ice Ages during the last three million years. But Scotland was not always a land of cold and ice. If we dig further down through the rock record to 60 million years ago, we find Bunessan, on the island of Mull, basking in tropical sunshine.

The fossils we find in the rocks of this period tell us that Mull would have looked something like today's Florida. Close relatives of the Californian giant redwoods grew alongside trees similar to those found in the Far East, which now need the heat of Glasgow's Kibble Palace to keep them alive. Beautiful lotus flowers floated in warm lakes on the lava rock surface, and magnolias, the most primitive of flowering plants, lent a splash of vivid colour. It really is a shame that we are 60 million years too late to enjoy it all, since this is only a

The Old Course at St Andrews is laid out on an ancient raised beach.

fossil snapshot, alas!

The landscape of Mull was made up of beds of lava rock, 1800 metres thick, which had poured from giant volcanoes over the previous three million years. This intense volcanic activity happened because the North Atlantic was opening up, as North America slowly split away from Scotland. Volcanoes rose along the line of the north-east/south-west split and their outpourings of lava forced the two rocky plates apart, creating the Atlantic Ocean. The volcanic islands of Iceland and the Azores show the line of the split. The Atlantic is still widening, at the same rate as your finger nails are growing; if your nails grew for 60 million years they would reach from Glasgow to New York!

There are only two possible solutions to the puzzle of Mull's tropical fossils: either the whole world was much warmer at that time, or Scotland must have been located much further south on the planet (Box 1) – or perhaps both were true; we shall discover the answer later on.

The basalt columns of Staffa and Fingal's Cave were formed by intense volcanic activity in the region of Mull over sixty million years ago

Icthyosaurs and nautilus witnessed the submarine earthquakes and tidal waves which devastated Helmsdale.

SCOTLAND IS A DESERT, 260 MILLION YEARS AGO: 16:10 HOURS

The Burrell Collection in Pollok Park, Glasgow, is filled with precious historical objects and paintings of world importance. But it is also a work of art itself in which the combination of fine sandstones, glass, light and space has produced a gallery of international repute. As you enter the Burrell you are surrounded by stone blocks cut from the New Red Sandstone beds of Scotland, which were formed from the sand dunes of a 260–million-year-old desert (Box 2).

At the time when the New Red Sandstone was formed, great geological fault lines were very active in Scotland. Vast geological troughs like the North Minch and the Sea of the Hebrides were let down like 100–mile-long trapdoors in the rocks along the Minch Fault. At that time, 260 million years ago, there was no sea to fill these troughs and, as they collapsed below sea level, they formed sand deserts with their own drainage basins like Death Valley in California today. Cut off from moisture-bearing winds they would have had rare rainfalls and flash floods, as Death Valley occasionally has.

2. NEW RED SANDSTONE QUARRY (CORNCOCKLE MUIR)

Quarries producing New Red Sandstone in the Dumfries area have been worked for more than a hundred years. Corncockle Muir quarry produced the superb fossilised reptile tracks which are now displayed in the Royal Museum of Scotland in Edinburgh. Another at Locharbriggs is still working the stone today; much of the New Red Sandstone used in Glasgow's buildings came from a deep quarry at Mauchline in Ayrshire (now closed, alas). If you are walking in Glasgow you may notice that buildings of New Red Sandstone tend to be later in date than those made of the honey-coloured carboniferous sandstone: 'New Red' buildings became more common after 1900.

HELMSDALE: EARTHQUAKES AND TIDAL WAVES, 120 MILLION YEARS AGO: 20:20 HOURS

If we go even further back in time and look at the east coast of Scotland 120 million years ago, life was very different from the tropical paradise of Mull described above. The northern coast of the Moray Firth, near Helmsdale, had a submarine equivalent of the San Andreas Fault in California. The Helmsdale Fault was an underwater earthquake zone which produced terrific shocks, bringing down boulders the size of houses. Tidal waves created by the quakes broke huge heads off the coral which grew in the seas and swept them into deep water, along with mature trees from the land, forming fossils on the sea bed. The fossilised corals give us another clue that the climate was warmer than it is today, since they are of a type now found no further north than Bermuda. We also find fossils of more than sixty species of sub-tropical plants in the area, which also point to the area's tropical climate.

Deserts like those of California's Death Valley once covered much of Scotland.

If Scotland had such great deserts, we can deduce that the country must have been located much further south than it is today; in fact, it probably lay about 15°N of the equator, in line perhaps with today's Khartoum in the Sudan or Madras in India. Scotland was far from green at that time! Scotland's deserts of this period were slowly acquiring the distinctive red sands which we now see compressed and shaped into the stones of the Burrell Collection, as red iron oxide began to cement together the perfectly round, wind-blasted sand grains of our desert past.

Artist's diorama of the Fossil Grove which was unearthed in Glasgow's Victoria Park.

3. QUARRYMEN REVEAL THE FOUNDATIONS

The first tarmacadam road surface was laid in 1845 and since then the demand for good road-stone has never ceased. More than a hundred years ago, quarrymen working in the outskirts of Glasgow accidentally uncovered the famous 'Fossil Grove' of stone trees in what is now Victoria Park. Although they did not realise it at the time, they were revealing a fundamental chapter in Scotland's geological and climatic story. Geologists now reckon that these fossil trees are more than 300 million years old.

Although it is hard for us to accept, these fossils prove that, at that time, Scotland was not actually located where she is today; she stood on the equator, in the tropical rain forest belt. Scotland was then covered in dense rain forest and was far greener than she is today.

21

TROPICAL SWAMPS COVER THE CENTRAL BELT, 300 MILLION YEARS AGO: 15:00 HOURS

If we dig even further, another 40 million years deeper into the rock layers, we find evidence that Scotland was actually on the equator (Box 3). Instead of the hot deserts of the New Red Sandstone era we find Scotland covered in equatorial rain forest, with 100 (250 cm) inches of rain a year and a steamy humidity.

These rain forests girdled the planet from mid-America to Russia, via what is now Cowdenbeath! Central Scotland marks the southern edge of a long-vanished supercontinent called 'Laurentia', which covered all of what is now the Atlantic Ocean with dry land.

Occasionally the ancient southern ocean invaded the swamps of Laurentia's river deltas, depositing a blanket of sea muds that hardened over millennia and creating the fossils which we now find at Cowdenbeath, Bearsden and Bathgate. These river deltas on the ocean edge must have been very flat, and the animals and plants which lived there must have been very much like those of today's Florida Everglades. However, two-metre-long millipede fossils show us that these creatures were far larger than their modern equivalents.

But surely we're imagining things to picture Cowdenbeath on the equator with a tropical rain forest climate similar to today's Florida? It seems impossible; but don't forget that we are allowing over 300 million years to shift Scotland from the equator to her current position at 56°N, a distance of at least 3,500 miles (5,600 km). It hardly seems possible that forces exist which can move an entire country with all its mountains and rocks for such a distance. But they do, and they did!

The power that moves continents around and builds mountains is driven by the huge volcanic forces operating deep within the earth. The rocky plates which make up the surface of the planet are really just a thin crust, floating on a semi-molten sea of lava or magma. People may find it hard to imagine just how great an impact volcanoes have had on Scotland's past. If we go back another 30 million years deeper into the rock record, beyond the Amazon swamps of Scotland, we find that the sites of modern Glasgow and Edinburgh were deluged by vast lava flows.

These rivers of lava didn't just come from conical volcanoes like Arthur's Seat (Box 4); they also seeped from cracks and fissures, creating flat lava beds and plateaux such as those we find in Iceland today. Over 1,000 volcanic vents from the carboniferous era have been mapped in what is now Scotland's Central Belt in addition to more typical volcanic remnants such as Arthur's Seat and the Bass Rock.

Things were also still bubbling away below the surface of the rocks, even when no actual lavas were being erupted. We know that there was a lava plateau on the site of today's Bathgate in West Lothian, which had hot springs feeding a shallow warm-water lake. The ancient creatures that lived near these lakes have been preserved as fossils which have recently become the centre of world attention, as a result of the pioneering excavations of professional fossil-hunter Stan Wood

4. EDINBURGH'S VOLCANO

Arthur's Seat, Scotland's most famous volcano, dominates the landscape of central Edinburgh. It erupted 340 million years ago – but not where Edinburgh stands today. The volcano actually rose from the tropical seas of the equator, and the red-hot lava flows were quenched by tropical thunderstorms. Since that time the whole continental plate on which Scotland sits has drifted north, carrying Arthur's Seat along with it.

We can trace at least thirteen lava flows on the southern slopes of Arthur's Seat. However, the cliffs of Salisbury Crags on the north-facing slopes are not a lava flow from the volcano at all, although they might appear to be so; they are in fact a solidified slab of magma, formed deep in the earth millions of years after the volcano had ceased erupting.

Salisbury Crags were actually buried beneath a kilometre-thick layer of other rocks but most of these have been removed by erosion since the ground was tilted and broken by large-scale earth movements. During the last Ice Age about 150 metres of rock were stripped off by the glacier ice as it ground across the volcano towards the east. However, far more rock was gouged out from the softer rocks on either side of the hard volcanic core. This glacial erosion also affected the rocks of Edinburgh Castle as the glaciers carved out the troughs of the Grassmarket and Princes Street Gardens on either side of the Castle rock; this can be seen distinctly along the line of the fault which lies below the main platform of Waverley station on the left of the picture.

(Box 5). These fossils include metre-long land scorpions; the ancestors of today's frogs; the world's earliest known reptile and a newly discovered fossil tree that has been given the scientific name of Stanwoodia.

This landscape of lava beds and tropical hot springs eventually sank beneath a shallow tropical sea which covered central Scotland, and the waters of Bearsden were invaded by strange and bizarre sharks whose fossils have been found locally.

SCOTLAND SOUTH OF THE EQUATOR, 400 MILLION YEARS AGO: 12:00 NOON

Beneath the lavas described earlier we find a second layer of red sandstone rocks, similar to the New Red Sandstones of the Burrell Collection; however, these lower layers are much older and consequently are called the 'Old Red Sandstone', a title immortalised in the writings of the Scottish author and amateur geologist, Hugh Miller (Box 6). Whereas the New Red Sandstone was formed north of the equator, we know that the Old Red was formed some way south of the equator. This period was also highly volcanic, and evidence of this can be found in the Ochil Hills, where the lavas contain some of the finest agates in the world.

It appears that at this time Scotland was once again a dry desert conspicuously lacking rain forests and tropic-al swamps. This geological period is very early in the story of life on the land; as such we find only a few fossils of primitive plants and spiders which were carrying out a patchy colonisation of the land from the seas. Most of the land suffered from a semi-arid climate and the sandy deserts provided little encouragement for pioneering land plants and animals. However, we know that there was some water about during this period of sandstone formation, since these sandstones of the 'Old Red' period were laid down in river beds, as opposed to the younger 'New Red' Sandstones, which were created from wind-blown sand dunes.

The animals in the lakes of this period were preyed upon by fearsome armoured fish, whose fossils we find preserved in the sandy flagstone rocks of Orkney and Caithness.

SCOTLAND AND ENGLAND SEPARATE, OVER 400 MILLION YEARS AGO NEARLY 12:00 NOON

During our travel down through the rocks, 400 million years backwards in time towards noon on our geological clock, it has not been too difficult to find the evidence for Scotland's northward drift from south of the equator to her present position in the far north. However, even further back in time, beneath the Old Red Sandstone, lies a jumbled stack of highly eroded and contorted layers of rock. These layers were laid down as the bed of an ancient ocean which geologists call 'Iapetus'.

This ocean covered southern Scotland and separated

Stan Wood pictured in his workshop.

5. STAN WOOD (1940–)

More than 200 years after James Hutton (Box 7) made Scotland the birthplace of the science of modern geology, a former merchant seaman and insurance salesman has thrust Scotland into the limelight of international geology once again.

Stanley Purdie Wood was born and brought up in Edinburgh. He is essentially a self-made and self-taught man (he took an Open University degree in 1986). He first developed an interest in fossils when he saw fossil tree stumps in a coal merchant's yard in 1965; and six years later, in 1971, he found his first fossil fish.

After that there was no stopping him. He became a full-time fossil hunter, opening up quarries, diverting streams, and hiring mechanical diggers and JCBs. Over the next few years he discovered some of the best-preserved fossil sharks in the world, on the foreshore at Granton in Edinburgh and at Bearsden in Glasgow. He also unearthed the oldest fossil reptile found anywhere in the world, at Bathgate.

In 1983, after training with Glasgow University's Business Enterprise programme, he established his own small business collecting and preparing rare fossils for sale to museums all over the world. Stan Wood has revolutionised our knowledge of the evolution of Scotland's natural heritage. Without his discoveries, our ideas about the evolution of reptiles would, quite simply, be wrong by a factor of over 38 million years!

it from England, which lay 1000 miles to the south. James Hutton (Box 7) was the first geologist to realise what these jumbled-up rock layers represented, when he observed them at Jedburgh and at Siccar Point on the Berwickshire coast. Spectacular evidence of the existence of the Iapetus ocean comes from rocks on the Ayrshire coast around Girvan and Ballantrae. The green 'pillow lavas' which we find there are only formed when hot lava is extruded into water; these rounded 'pillows' prove that submarine volcanoes were erupting on the floor of an ancient ocean. These eruptions confirm the role volcanoes have played in forming Scotland's landscape down the ages, as we have seen in the Inner Hebrides, Edinburgh, Glasgow, the Ochils and now Ayrshire.

The fossilised remains of the animals that once lived on the Scottish shores of the Iapetus Ocean provide evidence of how wide it must have been at one stage in its past. These fossils are more similar to those found in rocks in North America than they are to those found in the English Lake District. The geological union of England and Scotland only took place much later, when Scotland and Northern Ireland closed on to England, Wales and southern Ireland in a pincer-like movement, which squeezed the Iapetus Ocean out of existence.

SCOTTISH ASSEMBLY II, 450 MILLION YEARS AGO: 10:30 HOURS

It has often been remarked that Scotland has more varieties of rock within its boundaries than many larger countries do. This geological richness occurred because large geological slices of the planet, each with its own different rocks, gradually converged, ground into one another and fused into one rocky plate along the fault lines we can still see today in Scotland. Geologists call these huge sheets of rock 'terranes'; the blocks which make up the Grampian mountains and the northern Highlands are distinct geological terranes which slid in along lines of weakness like the Great Glen Fault, colliding and fusing together more than 400 million years ago. These fault lines are still active in Scotland and are quite capable of causing earthquakes as the huge sheets of rock grind past each other; the Solway earthquake on Boxing Day, 1979, shows us that Scotland is still an earthquake zone.

SCOTTISH ASSEMBLY I, 700 MILLION YEARS AGO: 03:00 HOURS

If we go back even further in time, deeper through the rock layers, beyond the bed of the Iapetus Ocean, we discover a very bleak picture of Scotland. This layer of rocks was formed long before plants and animals invaded the land, when the only green things visible on the land surface would have been moist patches of blue-green algae and microbial sludge. The older rocks of Islay, Jura, Scarba and the Garvellachs reveal an even bleaker picture. They show us that about 700 million years ago, Scotland suffered no fewer than seventeen successive Ice Ages! Although Scotland was then far down in the southern hemisphere, these Ice Ages do not imply that it was in the Antarctic. Rather, it seems that these periods of glaciation were world-wide, with ice covering much of the planet. It also seems that these Ice Ages were separated by sixteen periods of global warming: an extraordinary scenario of rapid climatic change and temperature reversals at a time before land plants had yet evolved.

GLACIERS EXHUME A BILLION-YEAR LANDSCAPE: 00:00.01 HOURS

On the Isle of Lewis we find one of the oldest and toughest rocks existing anywhere on earth; it is known as Lewisian Gneiss (pronounced 'nice'). It is little wonder that it is a hard rock, because it was formed 2,500 million years ago, under incredible pressure, at a depth of 12 miles (19 km) beneath the crust of the earth.

The staggering truth is that up in the north-west of Scotland we can actually stand on a piece of the earth's lower crust, the very foundation of all the rocks, which has been pushed upwards to the surface through a distance that is twice the height of Mount Everest.

We know that these rocks broke through to the surface at least 1,000 million years ago, because the pink sandstones of the Torridon region were deposited on top of this Lewisian rock by ancient rivers flowing across the landscape at that time. Within the last 25,000 years, huge glaciers carved valleys through these Torridonian sandstone beds, grinding down through thousands of feet of rock to reveal the Lewisian Gneiss beneath.

These recent glaciers carved out the valleys between the great mountains of Suilven and Canisp, leaving these eroded sentinels to watch over an exhumed, billion-year-old landscape which was once entirely devoid of plants and animals. It would be a very, very long time before Scotland became as green as she is today.

6. HUGH MILLER (1802–56)

One of the first geological best-sellers was a collection of articles written by an extraordinary Scotsman and entitled *The Old Red Sandstone*. First published in 1841, it ran to no fewer than twenty-six editions and placed Scotland's superb fossil heritage at the centre of the world stage.

Hugh Miller was a remarkable man in every way: stonemason, journalist, churchman, social philanthropist, author and amateur geologist. Born in Cromarty in the north of Scotland, his father was lost at sea when Hugh was only five years old. After a rebellious school career in various academies he was apprenticed as a stonemason at the age of sixteen, but he retained a burning desire to become a man of letters. He devoted his winter months to reading, writing and the study of natural history; and in 1829 he published *Poems written in the Leisure Hours of a Journeyman Stonemason*, followed by *Scenes and Legends of the North of Scotland* in 1835.

Working as a craftsman with stone for seventeen years had aroused in him a passionate interest in fossils; and for the church periodical, *The Witness*, he wrote a series of geological articles which formed the basis of *The Old Red Sandstone*. He pioneered popular science books, but was acutely aware of the irreconcilable conflict between the biblical account of the creation of the earth and the geological evidence for an immeasurably greater

timescale indicated by the fossils he found in the rocks. In particular, he disputed the Darwinian evolutionary theory with his book *Footsteps of the Creator* (1850). *The Testimony of the Rocks* (1857) and *Sketchbook of Popular Geology* (1859) were both published posthumously.

Tragically he shot himself in the chest on Christmas Eve, 1856; four doctors concluded 'from the diseased appearances found in the brain . . . that the act was suicidal under the impulse of insanity'.

The thatched cottage in Cromarty in which he was born is now preserved by the National Trust for Scotland.

Hugh Miller (1802–56): stonemason, fossil collector and populariser of geology.

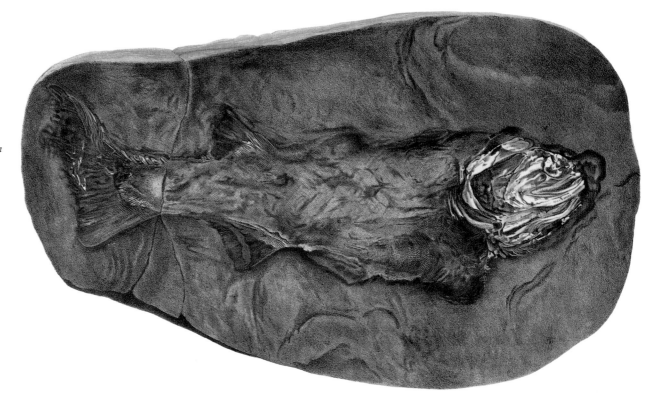

Fossil of armoured fish from the rocks of Caithness.

The mountains of Torridon were carved from beds of sandstone by recent glaciers, only 25,000 years ago.

7. JAMES HUTTON (1726–97)

Edinburgh-born James Hutton is now universally recognised as the 'father of modern geology'. He not only accumulated scientific facts through observation and research but also recognised the connections between different aspects of the natural world and showed how they are bound together in cycles of destruction and renewal.

He was the first person ever to grasp the nature of the immense age of geological time. After studying rock formations at Siccar Point on the Berwickshire coast, he had a dramatic and intuitive insight into the nature of the forces which had formed them and the incredible passage of time which must have been necessary. He wrote: 'My mind seemed to grow giddy by looking so far back into the abyss of time'.

It should be remembered that the dominant Bible-based viewpoint of the society in which Hutton lived held that the Book of Genesis was literally true and that the earth was only a few thousand years old.

Hutton first qualified as a doctor, but never practised medicine. Instead he spent some time in Norfolk learning about new agricultural methods there before settling on a small farm in Berwickshire. His interest in geology had begun during his early years as a farmer when he made the first of many journeys on horseback through England, Wales and Scotland. He observed that many rocks are made up of the debris of other rocks and he suggested that sediments derived from rocks on the surface of the earth are compacted and consolidated on the ocean floor and then raised up as dry land by heat from within the earth. From these insights he made the huge imaginative leap which tied together the erosion of mountains and the formation of sedimentary rocks. Hutton recognised that the process was a cyclical one in which the surface of the earth was continually being created and destroyed.

His theory of the igneous origin of many rocks was first expounded to the newly-formed Royal Society of Edinburgh in 1758 and expanded into book form in 1795 as *Theory of the Earth*. This book ranks alongside Darwin's *The Origin of Species*, which was published much later, as one of the greatest scientific contributions of all time.

But he was more than just the world pioneer of geology. He was also a prophet of the unborn science of ecology. He was concerned with the physiology of plants and animals as well as the broad sweep of the earth's history. In his view the cyclical process of earth formation had a clear purpose: it was, he said, 'contrived in consummate wisdom by a Supreme Being... a world beautifully calculated for the growth of plants and the nourishment of men and animals'.

He also wrote:

> Man has the disposal of nature so much at his will...he must, by studying nature, learn what will most conduce to the success of his design. No part [of the surface of the earth] is indifferent to man.

It could almost have been a modern environmentalist speaking.

James Hutton (1726–97), the father of modern geology.

Sandwood Bay, Sutherland

The Seas of Plenty

JOHN HAMBREY

Dr John Hambrey is a consultant ecologist who has specialised in rural development, fisheries and fish farming in Scotland; he is currently working on giant clam farming in the Solomon islands.

Scotland's coastal waters are among the richest in the world. From them we harvest half a million tonnes of wild fish caught each year. Into them we release a staggering volume of sewage and industrial effluent. We use these waters for sailing, canoeing, swimming and diving, and our children play on the beaches that fringe them. We pour in food, chemicals and drugs to raise 30,000 tonnes of farmed salmon; we risk releasing massive quantities of oil, nuclear waste and toxic chemicals from accidental spills. So far the sea has been remarkably forgiving, and we have been very lucky. But we cannot rely on luck for much longer.

An intricate coastline more than 6,000 miles (10,000 km) in length; the ebb and flow of powerful tides; a great upwelling and mixing of ocean currents on the continental shelf to the west of the Outer Hebrides; shallow sand banks fertilised by the bodies of falling plankton: these are the factors that create the wealth of Scotland's marine environment.

Where the North Atlantic Drift swells up over the continental shelf around Rockall and St Kilda an explosion of marine life is produced (Box 1). It is here that the warm surface waters, depleted of nutrients as marine life dies and falls into the ocean depths, become mixed with cold, nutrient-rich waters from below, providing ideal conditions for the growth of the micro-scopic plants and animals of the plankton. Several other ocean currents replenish the waters around Scotland by bringing a constant supply of nutrients and they also have a major effect on our climate.

Twice a day a great tidal wave sweeps clockwise around the Scottish coast carrying the enriched water into the sea lochs of the west coast and across the shallow banks of the North Sea. As the tide passes, the water is sucked to and fro, and, where it meets obstructions, powerful tidal streams are created. In places these streams become rapids, pouring and breaking over sand and rocks at speeds of up to eight knots, churning the food and nutrients and sending them flooding into quiet pools and lochs where they nourish sea urchins, anemones, barnacles and scallops, and all the creatures of the sea.

Thus the ocean currents bring nutrients and clean water, and exotic creatures from the tropics; the tides keep the solution well mixed and the summer sun powers the production of millions of tonnes of sea life in our coastal waters.

THE PLANKTON

When we gaze down into the clear waters of a sandy bay on the west coast of Scotland the sea seems almost empty of life. But in reality this crystal-clear water is a thin soup of microscopic creatures. They are called 'plankton', a Greek word meaning 'that which is made to wander or drift', because they are at the mercy of ocean currents and tidal streams. They serve as the grasslands and forests of the sea, since these tiny plants and animals, low in the food chain, are food for all the fish and mammals which we harvest. It is on the plankton that the fish, the mammals, the birds and the fishermen of Scotland ultimately depend.

To enter and understand the world of the plankton requires a shift in perspective and scale. If we could make ourselves very small and enter the sea we would experience a very different world: half dream, half nightmare. At first sight everything would appear slow and benign; strange animals and plants drift by, or float and sink gently. Occasionally there is a flash of light, or a rapid contraction of tentacles: a struggling fish, a strange mass of sounds from near and far.

We would see creatures resembling green and amber crystal caskets turning and tumbling until they stop, caught in a web of glistening protoplasm cast around their delicate silica sphere. There would be creatures with long spines and red eyes, with intricate shells carved by the genius of evolution; or shrimp-like creatures whose legs bear little beacons of light scurrying through a dim world, black below, brilliant above. We would feel the vibrations as we struggled through a fluid far thicker and more viscous than the water we remember. A sudden flash and our shrimp-creature is gripped in the fangs of a slender transparent arrow. We could drift on past snails with delicate wings flying

Jewel anemones blossom in the crystal waters of St Kilda.

Scottish sunstar.

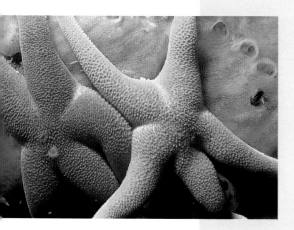

Starfish on sponge, Berneray Sound, Western Isles.

1. THE UNDERWATER WORLD

Sinking slowly to the seabed 100 ft below our survey vessel, there is the usual sense of anticipation: probably no human eyes have looked here before – what will we find this time? We land gently on a sandy seabed, and start to explore. Smooth rocks loom ahead of us like sleeping Leviathans in this mysterious twilight world.

Our torch beams transform the grey rocks, illuminating a crust of purple-pink studded with a million cup corals, each one less than three centimetres across. Their delicate green and orange tentacles are expanded over a hard white skeleton to catch even smaller creatures in the water currents. Although cup corals are true corals we are not on a tropical reef, but in the cold Atlantic waters which bathe the west coast of Scotland.

On the crest of the rocks are more stunningly coloured creatures. Featherstars perch with ten arms held upwards, the tip of each arm slightly rolled under like a newly-expanding fern. Some are a rich, dark red; others orange banded with white. Our torchlight makes their arms curl in discomfort, and we move on.

A tall white anemone tops the next boulder with a powder-puff head of tiny tentacles – pretty, but deadly to small crustaceans. Beneath the boulder a dark blue lobster sits at the entrance to his burrow, tasting the water constantly with two long red antennae. One antenna touches my hand, and he comes towards me with claws outstretched. He is only partly bluffing and I keep my fingers out of range. Beside him an orange cushion starfish edges slowly towards yellow and white soft corals, ready for his next meal of their fluffy white tentacles. Soft corals, like tiny cup corals, are abundant in Scottish waters, especially in strong currents.

Cuckoo wrasse, lovely, colourful inquisitive fish with their own territories on boulder slopes, come to check out these noisy, lumbering visitors and peer at us through our masks. Shoals of silvery fish flit past, coming close as we hold our breath but scattering as our exhaled bubbles disturb their peace. We cannot stay too long in their deep-water environment because our bodies will absorb too much nitrogen as we breathe under the great pressure of the water above. We move upwards into a sand-filled gully.

My companion has found another attraction, a little octopus which prickles indignantly and eyes him warily, shuffling across the sand with its coiled, suckered arms. He changes colour from red-brown to white and back again, eventually losing his nerve and jetting off backwards at great speed. We look for him but without success, because he is a master of disguise and has probably changed colour again to match his background.

Now we are in shallow water and shafts of sunlight filter down through an eerie underwater forest, turning the water beyond into a beautiful greenish-blue. The woodland 'trees' are kelp, a giant brown seaweed which forms dense forest in shallow water all around Scotland. Its thick stalks are covered with red seaweeds, fluffy white corals and orange featherstars, and are topped with a palm-like frond. On the rocks below the kelp, urchins graze the seaweeds and multicoloured anemones line rock crevices.

Eventually we reach the surface after forty minutes of total absorption, delighted with the underwater creatures and scenery. How on earth can we share this with people who have never been diving? I have described only a single site and only a small sample of its diverse inhabitants. Scotland's long and complex coast has many different habitats, all with their own characteristic marine communities.

The sea lochs of the west and north coasts, in particular, are a Scottish speciality. Essentially 'fiords', with deep sheltered basins, they harbour communities of plants and animals not found elsewhere in diveable depths in Britain. Imagine a forest of tall white feathers, three ft high, growing out of the deep mud in the peaty gloom 100 ft down. These are strange animals called sea pens; just one of the extraordinary inhabitants of sea lochs.

Unfortunately not all our dives are so exhilarating. On a survey at the entrance to Loch Nevis, for instance, three pairs of divers, at separate sites, reported wire hawsers littering the seabed, and the unmistakable devastation after the dragging of scallop trawls: wide lifeless tracks on the seabed, with broken and smothered marine life piled into the ridges between. A whelk crawling along the seabed without its protective shell is a sad sight. In other places we saw smashed cup corals and broken sea fans – thirty years' growth destroyed in a few seconds.

In the past we could perhaps plead ignorance;

Microscopic foraminiferans use the equivalent of hooks and lines to ensnare their prey among the plankton

the surface of the sea was a great barrier to knowledge and understanding. The marine life hauled up in dredges or washed up on the shore was nothing more than a curiosity, and a poor shadow of the animal or plant in its natural habitat. With the great advances in underwater exploration in the 1980s (diving, submersibles, photography and video) it should now be obvious that, on our doorstep, we have a treasure: an underwater wildlife wilderness to be conserved and enjoyed, not treated as a dump for unwanted refuse from the land, or raped by destructive fishing methods.

Sue Scott

slowly through the dim light, while others parachute through the water beneath sheets of silver mucus. A huge object with transparent bells ejecting jets of water, and rose-coloured petals trailing behind, suddenly envelops us. . . .

But this is no dream. All these creatures exist. Indeed most of them could be found in a bucketful of ordinary Scottish sea water. A single bucket might hold as many as four million tiny plants, animals and bacteria. These would be of immense variety, drawn from every major group or phylum, including several which are not represented on the seabed or on the land.

The 'phytoplankton' is made up of bacteria, single-celled and small multi-celled plants which use the sun's energy to create food just as plants on the land do. In a sense they represent the 'pastures of the sea' and they are grazed upon by a great variety of 'zooplankton' (Box 2), the tiny animals which eat both the phyto-plankton and each other.

Among the plankton there are some tiny creatures that the Greeks named the 'copepods' or 'oar-footed ones', which are vital to the larger animals in the marine food chain. These shrimp-like crustaceans, ranging from pinhead to matchhead in size, make up as much as 90 per cent of the zooplankton; they are the staple food of other marine creatures, and may be the most abundant of all multicellular animals living on earth. In recent years some larger species, known collectively as the Antarctic 'krill', have been harvested by Japanese

Medusa jellyfish.

and Russian factory ships for use as human food.

Plankton are also eaten by fish such as the sand eel and the herring, which are in turn food for salmon, cod, puffins, cormorants, seals, and ultimately Man. So the smallest creatures in the sea, the plankton, are the basis for all other life forms, just as the plants on the land sustain all the other creatures of the earth.

SAND EELS

In recent years people have been made aware of the sand eel's immense importance to the ecology of our waters. Everyone has seen pictures of puffins with rows of sand eels stacked in their beaks, and anyone living by the coast will almost certainly have seen these little fish, especially in sheltered bays where huge shoals sometimes gather. Occasionally, if mackerel are hunting them, the sand eels leap from the water in great silver showers.

If the water is clear one can look down and see thousands of the sand eels flashing as they twist and strike at tiny plankton. These fish are food for almost everything in the sea that is bigger than themselves, including herring, salmon and seals, seabirds and, increasingly, Man. Thus, they are a critical link in the food chain between the tiny plankton and the larger creatures of the sea.

It is only since 1974 that significant quantities of these fish have been taken by Man from Scottish waters, but by 1982 some 63,000 tonnes were being landed at Scottish ports. Some experts have cited the disastrous breeding failure of seabirds in Orkney and Shetland over the last four years (see Chapter 5) as evidence of overfishing of the sand eel, which is the principal food of many seabirds there. Other scientists have suggested that the sand eel has simply changed its behaviour, that it is swimming deeper and thus harder to catch. There is no agreement and little hard evidence, although urgent scientific research and survey is now under way; but it seems self-evident that the sudden competition from Man for a major food item must have had some ecological consequences. It is merely the scale of the effect which is in doubt.

THE SILVER DARLINGS

Of all the fish taken from Scottish waters the best known are the herring, 'the silver darlings', which have had a great influence on the evolution of Scotland's fisheries, economy and culture .

Vast shoals of these fish migrate around our coasts every year feeding for most of the time on plankton, especially a shrimp-like crustacean called *Calanus*, which is the most common copepod in Scottish waters. The herring's gills are especially adapted with 'rakers' to comb the tiny plankton from the water; however they also take larger food such as sand eels, which make up almost half the diet of adult herring.

There is evidence of a commercial fishery for herring off East Anglia as early as the sixth century AD. The growth of the Hanseatic towns of the Baltic in the twelfth century was founded on a major herring fishery using seine and drift nets. As has happened repeatedly in the history of herring fisheries, the shoals dwindled in the sixteenth century and fishing effort moved to the northern North Sea.

By the seventeenth century the Dutch were working a large distant-water herring fishery, centred on Orkney and Shetland; they had about 2,000 boats or 'busses' of around 80 tonnes each, each with a crew of fifteen or so men. Each boat could bring home 70 tonnes of fish, since herring were barrelled and cured on board. It is reported that in the year 1614 a total of 150,000 tonnes of herring was exported from Holland, and by 1669 some 450,000 people – a fifth of the entire Dutch population – were employed in the herring fishery and associated businesses. The herring economy was thus crucial to the development of Dutch sea power. It has

been said that Amsterdam was built on a foundation of herring bones; needless to say, they were Scottish herring bones.

The Dutch fishery declined during the Napoleonic wars, which enabled Scots fishermen to exploit their home market. They were also helped by the increasing demand for fish in the industrial boom towns of Britain, whose markets were made more accessible through the rapid development of railways (see Chapter 11). The government saw an opportunity for economic expansion and, from the late eighteenth century, support

Sand eels landed by commercial trawler.

2. ZOOPLANKTON, 'THE ANIMAL PLANKTON'

One of the most remarkable and plentiful of the smaller animals in the plankton is *Oikopleura*. This small tadpole-like animal is a member of the *Chordata*, the great phylum of backboned animals to which we ourselves belong.

This extraordinary animal builds a disposable 'house' around itself, in which it installs a complete filtering and plumbing system. At one end it creates two entrance doors across which it stretches a coarse net to keep out the larger, more dangerous animals. From these water intakes, two funnels are stretched which join to form a single tube, passing through a corrugated filter of the finest material. Stationing itself in the main channel, *Oikopleura* wags its tail to create a flow of water, which draws tiny plankton into the filter. Plankton collects at

the end of the filter and is conveyed by yet another tube to the mouth of the little creature. Every five hours or so the filtering system clogs, whereupon the remarkable engineer simply discards it and builds a new one.

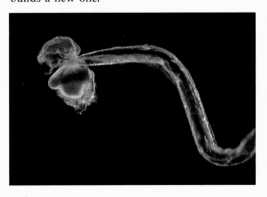

Herring boats at Fraserburgh.

Herring landed at Mallaig, West of Scotland.

grants were offered for boat construction, in addition to subsidies for the number of barrels of herring cured.

Scotland was slow to realise the massive potential of its waters, although there had been a small commercial herring fishery in East Fife from as early as the twelfth century, which culminated in the 'Lammas Drave' (Box 3). There were similar herring fisheries in the Clyde and in Loch Fyne. However it was not until the late eighteenth century that the 'Great Summer Fishery' of the east coast began to develop. At first this was based along the shores of Caithness, but it became centred on Wick in the early nineteenth century and reached its high point in the early 1880s around Peterhead, Fraserburgh and Aberdeen.

The 'Great Summer Fishery' began as local enterprises and were purely seasonal. In the winter crofters did a little line fishing for haddock or ling or worked the land. But the money to be made in the short herring season encouraged investment in bigger boats and more nets. But it was pointless for them to lie idle for most of the year, so the fishermen began to sail to more distant fishing grounds, following the shoals and seeking new stocks to exploit. They sailed to Lewis and Barra in May, to Shetland in June, to the Scottish east coast in late summer, and down the English coast to East Anglia for the late autumn. A whole troupe of camp followers went with them, including the gutters or 'fishwives', the curers, agents and dealers. When the fleet landed a good catch the activity was frantic, for herring 'go off' rapidly and speed was at a premium.

It was perhaps inevitable that this great fishery should founder in a crisis of over-production and slumping prices. By the late 1880s there was widespread unemployment and poverty in all the fishing communities.

In the early part of this century the sailing drifters were replaced by the steam drifters and the North Sea herring fishery catch settled at around 650,000 tonnes annually, with a relatively stable market. Ironically the use of modern technology led to greater instability in the fishery. In 1963 the Icelanders and the Norwegians began to use vast purse-seine nets, measuring around 60 metres deep by 600 metres long, which were soon adopted by the Scots in 1965. As a result, over the next few years the North Sea herring catch jumped to a staggering 1.3 million tonnes; the market was flooded and fish stocks were rapidly depleted. International attempts to agree on catch restrictions failed; politics and short-term economics dominated decisions, and quotas were adopted which were consistently higher than those recommended by scientists. In the mid 1970s the stocks of herring collapsed; the fishery was partially closed from 1976 and completely closed between 1978 and 1980 as a drastic conservation measure. Everyone suffered as unemployment hit entire communities and boats were sold off. Modern technology had finally conquered the silver darlings, and they have never quite recovered.

THE WHITE FISH

Cod, haddock, ling and related species are known as 'white fish' because of the colour of their flesh. They are very different from the herring since they are exclusively carnivorous, feed in deeper water (often on the bottom) and do not shoal, except at certain times of year.

White fish seem to have been hunted by man at an earlier stage than herring; perhaps the hook was invented before the net. The bones of cod, ling, saithe, turbot, and even a 40lb halibut, have been found at ancient sites in Orkney, suggesting that hook and line fishing from skin-covered boats was going on as early as 5,000 years ago. The large middens of limpet shells at these sites imply that limpets were probably used as bait for fishing rather than as human food. With so much fine fish available it seems unlikely that these early hunter-gatherers would have eaten limpets, which have tough and unpalatable flesh and little food value. Unfortunately no early hooks, boats, nets or fish traps have survived, and we can only assume that these were swept away or have decayed. Perhaps they will turn up one day preserved in the muds of the sea bed.

There have been commercial line fisheries for white fish in the distant waters of the Arctic and the Grand Banks of Newfoundland since the sixth century, but fishing for white fish round Scottish coasts remained a subsistence affair until the close of the last century. At that time trawling, which had been used by the Dutch since the seventeenth century and by the English since

By the 1950s, Forth fishermen could no longer fish for herring.

3. THE LAMMAS DRAVE

'Lammas' is a Celtic festival beginning on the first day of August, associated with the Feast of St Peter ad Vincula. The name was given to an impressive summer fishery, or 'Drave', which took place close to the Fife coast in the mouth of the Forth estuary. An important fishery for herring existed here as early as the twelfth century, and by the seventeenth century around 20,000 people (including many foreigners) gathered for the season. We can only guess at how much herring they caught but it must have been a huge amount to sustain such a number of people.

The fishery reached its modern peak in 1860 when around 300 boats fishing a relatively small area centred off Pittenweem and Anstruther landed 14,000 tonnes; and on the remarkable night of 21 August 1860, 140 small boats averaged 11 tonnes of fish each. Sadly, this fishery declined rapidly in succeeding years, either because of damage caused to the stocks or spawning grounds, or simply because the herring chose to go elsewhere.

White fish on the dock at Mallaig, West of Scotland.

undersized haddock are netted along with the whiting and then thrown dead into the sea. This is conservation madness and, since the discarded haddock are not recorded, it makes a mockery of the scientists' attempts to make predictions about the fishery.

THE SALMON

When Pliny the Elder, the first-century Roman natural historian, named the salmon 'salmo' in his *Historia Naturalis*, he did not intend it as an obscure scientific name. To a Latin reader the name simply meant 'the leaper', and Pliny used it to describe a common but beautiful fish.

The Atlantic salmon, *salmo salar*, has such a powerful homing instinct that it migrates 1,000 miles (1,600 km) from Greenland waters to the Scottish rivers of its birth. It can survive the transition from a saltwater to a freshwater environment in a matter of days, which few species have managed in millions of years of evolution. Once home, it will swim and leap 60 miles (96 km) or more from the sea to the small burns and headwaters of our rivers to spawn and then die.

The salmon faces many dangers on its journey. In the open sea it is hunted by men in trawlers, as well as by seals and dolphins. Offshore it runs the gauntlet of invisible nylon drift nets; off rocky headlands, along loch shores and in river estuaries it must thread its way among a maze of stake nets and traps. As it struggles upstream it must ignore the tempting fly of the angler during the day and evade the blazing lights, gaffs and spears of the poacher at night. But it is probable that none of these factors is the main cause for the decline of the salmon; their enormous reproductive power means that only a few adults need to survive and spawn in order to maintain the fish stocks. Salmon were once abundant throughout Europe and the North Atlantic as far south as the Iberian peninsula. However in the last two centuries they have almost vanished from Portugal, Belgium, the Netherlands, Germany, Switzerland, and Czechoslovakia, while they have been severely depleted in Spain, France, Denmark, the United States and Poland.

In England they were once plentiful but are now restricted to just a few rivers. Ranulf Higden, a monk of St Werburg's monastery in Chester in the fourteenth century, noted in his *Polychronicon* that salmon were so cheap that they were fed to pigs. In Scotland they were even more plentiful and were exported to England and the continent by the thirteenth century. Richard Franck, a soldier in Cromwell's army, wrote at Stirling that 'the river Forth relieves the country with her great quantity of salmon' and noted that the Burgomasters are 'compelled to reinforce an ancient statute that commands all masters not to compel any servant or apprentice to feed upon salmon more than thrice a week'.

the eighteenth century, became far more efficient because of technological developments. Larger steel boats radically improved catching efficiency, along with the introduction of steam power, steel cables and power winches. By 1982 a modern fleet, equipped with powerful diesel engines, lightweight nylon nets and electronic fish finders, was landing 55,000 tonnes of cod and 113,000 tonnes of haddock at Scottish ports.

As with the herring fishery it seems that such catches simply cannot be sustained. The fish stocks are now in very poor shape, following five years in which few young fish have entered the fishable stock, and the prospects look bleak indeed. The fishermen themselves agree that the situation is serious, but some are still prepared to fish illegally because they feel they have no choice. With perhaps £500,000 invested in a vessel and its gear, with high interest on loans, they simply have to fish to the limit; if this means they have to break the rules some will undoubtedly do so, since the alternative is bankruptcy.

One of the modern controls on fishing is particularly perverse. The most obvious way to manage the fishery is to use nets with larger mesh sizes, so that only bigger fish are caught and the young ones escape to breed and be caught later. Unfortunately much of North Sea white fishing is a 'mixed fishery', with several different sized species being hunted at the same time. Fish such as whiting are smaller than haddock and the mesh size of the net is therefore designed to catch the smaller whiting, causing undersized haddock to be taken accidentally.

In order to preserve stocks it is now illegal to land haddock which are below a certain size. However, instead of preventing the capture of small fish, the size regulations have simply meant that vast numbers of

Fish farm worker harvesting farmed salmon.

The value of salmon was recognised from the beginning, and laws to conserve stocks go back a very long way. As early as 1030 Malcolm II of Scotland introduced a close-season on fishing, from Assumption Day (at the end of August) to Martinmas (11 November); there have been laws governing the taking of salmon ever since.

It seems likely that overfishing had partially depleted the stocks of salmon by the beginning of the nineteenth century. However, stocks were still large: over 100,000 salmon and grilse (a young salmon on its first return to fresh water) were being caught on the River Tweed each year, and the River Tay produced only a few less. By the end of the century, however, the output from Scottish waters was a mere fraction of what it had been and salmon had disappeared entirely from many rivers. In England the situation was even worse.

The causes of the decline included pollution, dams and canalisation. Dams meant that fish could not ascend the rivers and spawning beds were buried in silt; pollution reduced survival and breeding success to critically low levels. All the major rivers were seriously polluted by the middle of the last century. Organic wastes from whisky stills poured into the River Spey, textile dyes were dumped into the Tweed, coal washings into the Nith, ammonia into the Don, bleach into the Tay, and great quantities of raw sewage from the expanding towns flooded most rivers. The salmon was quietly and insidiously being poisoned.

But increasing scarcity had its benefits, especially to those holding rights to exploit the remaining fish stocks. The economic value of salmon for food and sport soared as the food of servants became a dish fit only for lords, and this price rise triggered the dramatic development of salmon farming in recent years.

FISH FARMING

Over the last decade a remarkable change has taken place in some of the most isolated parts of Scotland. New life has been brought to declining communities, and for the first time in decades three generations of people may be found living together beside our wildest sea lochs; people are returning to the Highland coasts. The cause of this return has been the dramatic growth of salmon farming.

For more than a century, salmon smolts had been reared in hatcheries for the restocking of Scottish and English rivers. But it was not until the early 1970s that serious attempts were made by both government (the White Fish Authority) and industry (the Unilever subsidiary, Marine Harvest) to rear salmon to maturity in the sea. The industry got off to a slow start, following an impressive Norwegian lead, but it was helped by grants from the Highlands and Islands Development Board with research and training being offered by universities and government institutes.

During the 1980s the expansion was remarkable. By 1990 Scotland's salmon industry was producing around 30,000 tonnes of fish and employing around 2,000 people directly, with 10,000 more in processing and distribution. However, the rearing of salmon in floating cages among sheltered sea lochs, and the rapid expansion of the industry, has created conflicts of interest and environmental problems.

The first concern that arose related to the quantity of organic fish wastes being dropped from cages in the pristine sea lochs. Most animals are only about 10 per cent efficient in converting food into body weight; ten kilogrammes of food produce only one kilogramme of flesh. Salmon are no exception, and most of the fish pellets fed to them are voided into the water as fish wastes. The quantities involved are considerable: a fish farm producing 100 tonnes of fish each year releases into the surrounding waters around 10 tonnes of nitrogen and 3 tonnes of phosphorus, and around 80 tonnes (dry weight) of solid wastes, much of which will settle around and beneath the cages. It should be remembered that the lochs in which the cages are sited represent the cleanest and most unspoiled marine habitats in Britain, which is reflected in the richness of the wildlife found there.

The ecological impact of such discharges will depend on the rate of water exchange or tidal flushing in the loch, but in most cases severe effects of solid wastes are relatively local, mainly within 50 metres of the cage. It has proved impossible to evaluate the effect of dissolved phosphorus and nitrogen on the surrounding water and plankton since our understanding of the underlying processes is too limited. It has been suggested, however, that blooms of poisonous algae are related to nutrient levels in the water, and there have been some serious algal blooms in recent years in areas with high fish farming activity. The causal link cannot be proven, however, and our ignorance of planktonic systems is such that it may take a catastrophe to demonstrate one.

Fish farms also create pollution through the use of antibiotics and chemical pesticides. Dichlorvos or 'Nuvan' is an organo-phosphorus nerve poison currently used to kill parasitic sea lice, to which farmed salmon are particularly vulnerable. A chemical which kills sea lice will clearly kill other crustaceans and small creatures in the plankton. The extent of these effects in the surrounding water is presently being researched and is the subject of fierce debate. Early results from research by the Scottish Office Agricultural and Fisheries Department (SOAFD) suggest that there is indeed an effect, but that it is rapidly diluted and neutralised in the surrounding water. Clearly, however, the use of large quantities of these chemicals on big farms must affect nearby plankton, and also the larvae of crabs, lobsters, shrimps and shellfish. Research is currently going on (supported by the salmon farmers themselves) to develop biological control of sea lice using cleaner-wrasse – fish which feed on the sea lice. Early results are encouraging and, if successful, salmon farmers may be able to dispense with Dichlorvos altogether.

The killing of wild creatures which eat salmon has also raised concern. Not surprisingly seals, otters, cormorants, herons and many other fish-eating animals are attracted by cages full of salmon. Shooting does take place, sometimes illegally, but SOAFD may also issue licences to salmon farmers in severe cases. Shooting is often ineffective, and the use of predator nets around the cages has become almost standard practice.

There are also fears about the effects of escaped or released salmon on the wild genetic stock. Although farmed salmon are less fitted to the natural environment than wild fish, they may be released in such numbers that they successfully compete for food and are able to mate with the wild stock. Such competition could endanger the survival of wild salmon and introduce alien and ill-adapted genes to the local population. This is the subject of much debate but, given the poor state of our native salmon and their unique adaptations to different river systems, the dangers must be taken

Floating cages of salmon farm on Loch Leven.

seriously. In recent years there have been massive releases of fish, from both sea cages and freshwater hatcheries, and the threat should not be treated lightly, as it tends to be by some fish farmers.

There have also been complaints about fish farms from fishermen, yachtsmen, tourists, and professional conservationists, who in their different ways fear salmon farms may damage their recreation as well as destroying the scenic beauty of some of Britain's wildest areas.

The rate of expansion of salmon farming has now slowed as a result of market pressures and there is less danger of an imminent environmental disaster. But such concerns are valid and demonstrate a clear need for informed and impartial planning and control if the industry is to prosper in harmony with environmental and other interests. Fish farmers themselves are taking a positive attitude and have drawn up codes of practice after consultations with other interests. However, the present planning procedures are seriously flawed.

There are many other kinds of fish and shellfish farming. Not all are as controversial as salmon farming: shellfish for example require no artificial food and as yet are not subject to disease, so they represent an activity which is both economically and ecologically sound.

The best salmon feed is a pellet whose major ingredient is fish meal, usually made from sand eel, herring, Norway pout, or capelin. Given the inefficiency of food conversion it is evident that for every kilogramme of farmed salmon produced, perhaps ten kilogrammes of wild fish have to be processed as salmon pellets. This is why farmed salmon can only be produced at considerable cost; you have to catch ten kilos of sand eels or herring to make one kilo of salmon.

If salmon farming is a technical triumph it is also a supreme example of our short-sighted approach to natural resources. If we had managed the wild salmon fishery sensibly and kept our rivers clean, we would still have cheap wild salmon and unspoiled sea lochs. We would need only a net and some local fishermen to bring home the salmon. By contrast, industrialised salmon farming is staggeringly inefficient and capital intensive. It needs high technology hatcheries, storm-resistant cages, helicopter transport of young smolts and the pouring into the sea of massive quantities of food, of which 90 per cent is wasted.

Perhaps the most painful irony of all is that it was pollution that finally destroyed the salmon in many of our rivers; and now industrialised salmon farming is bringing pollution to our last unspoiled sea lochs.

THE HUNTING OF THE WHALES

People do not generally think of Scotland as a whaling nation, yet whale and walrus bones have been found at the earliest archeological sites in Scotland, where they were used to make tools and other artefacts. We do not know whether these bones come from whales that were stranded naturally, or driven ashore by hunters, as pilot whales were until recently in Shetland and the Outer Hebrides, and as they are to this day in the Faroe Islands.

Apart from the possibility of deliberate hunting, the accidental stranding of a large whale would have been a valuable windfall for early communities and we have records of this from historic times. In the sixteenth century the Swedish historian Olaus Magnus recorded in his *Historia de Gentibus Septentrionalibus* (1555) the stranding of a whale; it yielded over 300 wagon loads of meat, blubber and bones for fuel and building, as well as enough hide and skin to make forty sets of clothes. For a small community in Scotland such a stranding would represent a massive injection of wealth.

Between 1913 and 1926 more than thirty whales on average per year were stranded on British coasts, and we can assume that before whale hunting reduced the stocks there would have been many more. The River Forth and other estuaries acted as natural traps for whales, when the whales became confused among sand banks or were stranded by rapid changes in tidal levels. The bones of many great whales have been uncovered in the silted deposits of the Stirling Carse, well up the Forth estuary, showing that such accidents were indeed frequent.

Commercial whaling on a significant scale was first developed by the Basques in medieval times. At first they hunted along their own coasts in the Bay of Gascony, and later off Newfoundland where they also developed the white fishery. Apart from the driving of pilot whales in Shetland and the Hebrides, the Scots did not really join in until the opening up of the Arctic whale fishery of the seventeenth and eighteenth centuries, but they developed a major whaling industry in later times.

It was in 1758 that the first steam-powered whaling ship left Dundee for Arctic waters; it was steam (and later diesel-powered) ships, using explosive harpoons, which hunted many whale species to the verge of extinction.

Scotland had its own whale fishery around the Outer Hebrides and Shetland until the 1950s. In the years 1903–29 a total of 5,848 fin whales, 395 blue whales, 100 right whales, 95 sperm whales, 70 humpbacks, and 26 northern bottle-nose whales were taken in Scottish waters; this was before the serious decline of the whale stocks began.

However, from the beginning, there was little attempt at stock conservation in the whaling industry. The Newfoundland whale fishery of the Basques was ruined by the end of the seventeenth century and Spitsbergen was finished by 1720. As the century wore on, the whalers ventured into more distant Arctic waters as more accessible stocks declined. By the middle

Whale vertebrae on the beach at South Uist.

of the nineteenth century the industry would have collapsed due to the depletion of the stocks had it not been for the new technology which allowed them to catch the faster, heavier 'rorqual' species, such as the blue whale.

Soon these too had become scarce, and in 1892 four Scottish whalers headed south seeking new whaling grounds in the Antarctic to continue the plunder. These southern waters were hunted until the near extinction of many species in the 1950s and 1960s. Now, at last, some of the whale stocks are recovering, although it will be many years before they regain even a fraction of their former numbers.

MANAGING OUR MARINE RESOURCES

The story of fishing in Scotland has a thread running through it which begins with abundance and always ends in scarcity. Whether we look at the herring, the salmon, the cod, haddock or the great whales, the story is the same. Man has taken and taken, with short-term profit always uppermost in mind, until there was nothing left to take. But, as a hunter of fish in the sea, Man is a mere beginner when compared with even the most humble creatures in the sea, the plankton.

For example, the drift net was developed hundreds of millions of years ago by tiny planktonic *Foraminiferans*. The equivalent of long-lines with hooks can be found among *Siphonophores*, close relatives of the jellyfish. The filtering and plumbing system secreted by *Oikopleura* matches in subtlety and efficiency anything produced by Man. But as deadly and calculating hunters it is the squid and octopus, the cephalopods, who truly excel; in speed, disguise and ingenuity they make a mockery of Man's blunderings and splashings after his prey.

In the natural world each evolution of the hunter has been matched by defensive adaptation by the prey, or the balance has been redressed by the emergence of a new predator to eat the hunter in turn. The result has been a natural balance between prey and predator. The technology of human hunting, however, has developed so rapidly that Man has over-exploited the fish stocks, causing ecological crashes, and, in the case of several whale species, has almost exterminated them.

Ironically it was the shoaling behaviour of the herring, helping them to avoid predators, that made them vulnerable to human hunters with nets. The herring's habit of following the zooplankton to the surface waters at night made them easy prey for fishermen. Similarly the great size of the whale, which made it invulnerable to sharks, made it an easy target for the whalers. And the salmon, returning to fresh waters and migrating up the rivers en masse, were so easy to trap that even medieval kings saw the need to protect them.

Fortunately our seas are so productive, and the fish are so fertile and resilient, that although fishing may decimate stocks they will almost always recover; the greatest losers in the overfishing game are always fishermen themselves. Man the industrial hunter-fisherman has become lethally efficient, but has still not

learned to control his power for his own benefit. But there is room for optimism. The whalers did not quite exterminate the great whales, and these – the most vulnerable of creatures – are making a slow recovery. The herring, given their stunning fecundity, could recover fully in a few years if given the chance. The dangers to fish stocks from the human predator, although sometimes spectacular, are generally temporary; and although there are immense difficulties, there are at least mechanisms for controlling and managing our fisheries.

But the microscopic world of the plankton, and the entire pyramid of life that depends upon it, is much more vulnerable to invisible chemical and nuclear pollution. We have already lost the dragonflies and salmon from many of our rivers through pollution by sewage, pesticides and industrial effluents. Much of this pollution eventually enters the sea, where it accumulates in sediments and becomes more concentrated as it passes up the food chains. Man, as the top predator, is likely to absorb the final cumulative dose of pesticides, chemicals or radioactivity.

We have little idea of the likely environmental impacts of all these substances but they will generally affect the plankton in the first place. And although we understand virtually nothing about the processes governing the populations of these microscopic creatures, we do know that they are the basis for all the other life in the sea. They even play a vital part in controlling levels of atmospheric carbon dioxide, thereby regulating the so-called 'greenhouse effect'.

The sea is not an endless sink for all our wastes; it is a world of great beauty and complexity, made up of thousands of ecosystems which provide us with food, drinking water, aesthetic inspiration and simple recreational pleasure. It has a profound influence on our climate and even helps control the temperature of our planet.

We abuse it at our peril.

Seal at sunrise, Sangobeg beach, Durness, Sutherland.

The ridge of Liathac seen from Beinn Eighe.

The Flowering of Scotland

MICHAEL SCOTT

Michael Scott is a wildlife consultant, lecturer and broadcaster with extensive experience of fieldwork in Scotland and elsewhere. He is the Scottish Representative of the Conservation Association of Botanical Societies.

When the glaciers retreated at the end of the last Ice Age, about 12,000 years ago, they left behind a slate wiped clean of plants and animals. At its peak the ice was up to 8,000 ft (2,400 m) thick, almost twice the height of Ben Nevis; so it is highly unlikely that any islands of rock projected above the ice to provide a refuge for any flowers, or even the most resilient of lichens.

As the climate warmed and the glaciers retreated, they left a landscape stripped of soil and covered in a debris of rocks ground by the ice into gravel or boulder clay. This material was rich in minerals, but lacked the humus essential for plant growth. Today these so-called 'primitive soils' are found only in the Arctic, although in Scotland some of the highest mountains and most windswept hills have small areas of similar material.

Throughout the height of the Ice Age the south of England had remained glacier-free and the plants that survived there were now poised to extend their range, following the glaciers as they retreated. Mosses, liverworts and lichens were the first plants to arrive in Scotland; as they died they rotted to form thin soils which enabled small herbs and shrubs, adapted to the arctic climate, to gain a foothold. Their remains in turn added further humus to the soil and, as soil accumulated and the climate warmed, less well adapted southern and lowland species were able to colonise.

These were often ranker-growing and smothered the delicate arctic plants. They were followed, in turn, by taller shrubs and trees which completed the process. Increasingly the arctic plants were pushed out into areas where high altitude or northern latitudes created a climate similar to southern England during the Ice Age.

Many of these Ice Age survivors are found in Scotland today, usually in the high mountains where the climate is severe and late snow cover allows only a brief growing season. Most of these species also survive today high in the mountains of central Europe, or in Greenland, Iceland and the far north of Scandinavia, justifying the name for these plants: arctic-alpines.

Today the widest variety of arctic-alpines occurs at sites where the mineral rich rocks are so friable (crumbly) that they readily erode to produce rich, basic soils, like the primitive soils the glaciers left behind. The only Scottish endemics (species peculiar to Scotland) are a few hawkweeds and other so-called 'micro-species' – closely related species distinguished by experts on the basis of very fine details. However the precise mix of species in the Scottish hills is unique, with arctic plants almost at the south of their range and alpine flowers at unusually low altitudes. The resulting plant communities are therefore of international scientific interest, and merit the most careful conservation.

THE ARCTIC-ALPINES

Perhaps the most famous site in Scotland for its arctic-alpine flora is Ben Lawers, a National Nature Reserve (see Chapter 16) largely owned by the National Trust for Scotland. At 3,984 ft (1,214 m), Ben Lawers is the highest mountain for many miles and thus has a particularly severe climate. This, combined with an extensive outcrop of a rich and friable rock called Lawers schist, creates precisely the conditions in which arctic-alpines can flourish.

One stretch of cliff in particular probably holds more species of arctic-alpines in a small area than anywhere else in Britain. Its rarities include alpine gentian which, although often less than an inch high, is as intense a gentian blue as any of its larger relatives. Also here we find alpine forget-me-not, a widespread plant in the true Alps found at only one other site in Britain. Beside this grows the so-called alpine fleabane, a relative of the daisy, with tight purple flowerheads. Despite its name it is not found in the Alps but only in the Arctic, and Ben Lawers may well be the only site in the world where it grows side-by-side with alpine forget-me-not.

Despite the fame of Ben Lawers, outcrops of rock similar to Lawers schist occur throughout the Breadalbane hills. Many of these, as far west as Ben Lui, are almost as rich as Lawers itself, although the schist generally occurs at rather lower altitudes, excluding some of the most strongly montane species. Ben Lui does have one notable plant, apparently missing from Ben Lawers. This is alpine bartsia, a handsome plant with dark purple flowers reminiscent of toadflax. Apart from this area of the western Breadalbanes, this species is only found by the upper stretches of the River Tees in northern England, yet it is common and widespread in both the Alps and the Arctic – another mystery of Scottish plant distribution.

Eastwards of Lawers essentially the same band of lime-rich rock outcrops at a number of other very important sites. Ben-y-Vrackie, near Pitlochry, has a limited area of crag with a diverse arctic-alpine flora, including alpine milk-vetch with its delicate pale purple pea-like flowers. Further east the crags in Glen Lochy are one of only two sites for yellow oxytropis, another member of the pea family, with clusters of flowers the colour of parchment suffused with yellow and purple.

Continuing eastwards two attractive mountain grasses, alpine foxtail and alpine cat's-tail, flourish in snow-fed runnels beneath the imposing domed summit of Glas Maol. On the east side of the summit, dramatic crags plunge down into Caenlochan Glen, another rich site sharing many of the characteristic species of Ben Lawers. One acidic bluff of rock here is home for blue sowthistle, a tall member of the daisy family. In the Alps and Arctic it is a woodland species, but here deforestation and grazing by sheep and red deer have confined it to inaccessible mountain rock ledges.

In the north, many of the arctic-alpines creep lower down the mountain slopes. On Skye the richest montane flora is found on limestone west of Broadford, or on the slumped crags and pinnacles of the Trotternish ridge, usually below 1,000 ft (300m). At greater heights, one corrie in the Cuillin hills is the only British site for alpine rock-cress, otherwise widespread in both the Alps and the Arctic. The Invernaver National Nature Reserve, near Bettyhill on the north coast, has a rich montane flora almost at sea level, including the purple species of oxytropis, while mountain avens (Box 1) forms extensive heathland at low altitude near Durness.

Shetland has one particularly remarkable site: a low rounded hill on Unst called the Keen of Hamar, where the exposed climate and a severe soil create an unusual flora including a subspecies of arctic chickweed unique to this small area.

The granite mountains of the eastern Highlands, centred on the Cairngorms, produce poor, acid soils which support far fewer species. Plants flourishing in this harsh habitat include trailing azalea (recognised by its delicate pink flowers and narrow, leathery leaves) and dwarf willow, a miniature tree that grows to only an inch or two in height.

The high tops of the Cairngorms have the most arctic climate in Britain, with snow patches lasting through many summers on some north-facing corries. Several particularly demanding species are restricted to these areas, including arctic chickweed, Highland saxifrage and hare's-foot sedge, named after the appearance of its oval grey flowerheads.

Many other upland sites around Scotland, although less rich, support arctic-alpine species, from the higher hills of Dumfries and Galloway to many areas around the Highlands and Islands. Alpine lady's-mantle is often a useful indicator of rich sites, easily recognisable by its frothy yellow flowerheads and fingered leaves edged with silver hairs. The commoner mountain saxifrages may also occur here: purple saxifrage is the only one with purple flowers, which it produces soon after the snow has gone in March and April; starry saxifrage, with starry white flowers, often grows in mossy flushes

1. MOUNTAIN AVENS: A CLASSIC ARCTIC-ALPINE

Mountain avens (*Dryas octopetala*) is a low creeping shrub which hugs the ground to avoid the worst effects of the winter winds. The name of its genus, *Dryas*, honours the oak fairies, or dryads, and refers to the oak-like shape of its dark, deeply veined, evergreen leaves. Its showy white flowers are well over an inch across and have eight petals. They are pollinated by flies and bees which are attracted by nectar and partly by the warmth trapped inside the flowers, which follow the sun like miniature satellite dishes.

Mountain avens grows commonly throughout the Arctic, in the mountains of central Europe and in the Rocky Mountains of the USA. In Britain it grows only where the severe climate excludes other ranker-growing species. In gardens it will survive only if competing species are removed by weeding.

It is found mostly in lime-rich mountain areas in the north and west Highlands. It grows at altitudes of up to 3,400 ft (1,000 m) in the Cairngorms, but in the far north it can come down almost to sea level, because the climate there is relatively arctic, even at low altitudes.

where underwater springs enrich the soil; while yellow mountain saxifrage, which has yellow flowers and stems packed with narrow leaves, often grows beside mountain streams.

Many other species grace our Scottish mountains and reward the botanical hill walker. The best introduction to these is *Mountain Flowers*, by John Raven and Max Walters (1956). This describes a heady period in the early 1950s when three new mountain flowers were discovered in Scotland: diapensia in Inverness-shire (Box 2); Iceland purslane, a tiny relative of docks, on Skye; and Norwegian mugwort, looking like a withered daisy, on the hills of Skye and Wester Ross. While the decades since have been less productive, those remarkable finds suggest that more species may await discovery by the dedicated botanist in the Scottish hills.

THE FORESTS OF CALEDON

About 9,000 years ago, as the climate continued to warm, trees began to colonise Scotland, finally swamping the arctic-alpine plants of the lowlands. The woodland spread gradually, with temporary retreats in periods when the climate became colder.

The first tree to arrive after the ice melted was birch, which is also the tree growing furthest north in the arctic taiga forest today. The birch spread rapidly, forming low patchy woodland often mixed with juniper and willow. It was succeeded in turn by Scots pine, which arrived in Wester Ross about 8,000 years ago and spread south-eastwards from there.

Then, as the climate reached its warmest about 7,000 years ago, oak began to spread from the south to form extensive forests in most of southern Scotland and the west Highlands. Ash, elm and hazel grew among the oak, with birch, rowan and holly where the soil was poorer. Ash established locally in limestone areas, while alder grew in the wetter areas and beside rivers. But oak was not suited to all of Scotland. Pine remained the dominant tree over much of the central and eastern Highlands while, north of this, birch woodland persisted. Most of the far north of Caithness and Sutherland was never covered by trees but remained as open moorland, patterned with peat-stained bog pools known as dubh lochans – an area now celebrated as the Flow Country (see Chapter 5).

The loss of tree cover from most of the rest of Scotland occurred partly as a result of human activity and partly through natural processes. About 4,000 years ago a colder oceanic climate developed, bringing stronger winds and increased rainfall.

In many northern and western areas the climate became so wet that the bog mosses expanded beyond their wet hollows to form widespread blanket bogs, swamping and killing many trees that grew there. These bogs eventually turned to peat, and the preserved remains of so-called bog oaks and pines are still

unearthed from the peat today. Even where trees survived, the wet soil and strong winds killed any seedlings and, without young trees, the woods eventually died out.

Shortly after this change in climate the first signs of Man's farming activity appeared on the landscape (see Chapter 7) as our ancestors cut down large areas of forest for land on which to grow their crops. In the lowlands, deforestation began in the Bronze Age, about 3,000 years ago, but even in northern Skye and Sutherland the dominant birch and hazel woodland began to disappear about 2,500 years ago. This has been linked to Iron Age clearances for agriculture and charcoal production.

Nevertheless by the time the Romans arrived, most of Scotland was still forested; their Latin name for the country, 'Caledonia', means 'wooded heights'. By about AD 400, however, woodlands were being felled across most of Scotland. By the sixteenth century almost all the forests of the central Lowlands had gone and the western oakwoods were much reduced.

The pinewoods of the eastern and central Highlands

2. DIAPENSIA: AN ICE AGE RELICT

In 1951 a birdwatcher discovered an unfamiliar plant flowering on a windswept shoulder in the hills near Glenfinnan. Expert botanists identified it as *Diapensia lapponica*, a plant new to Scotland, in a family never before found in Britain.

Diapensia is a low cushion-plant related to heathers. It has narrow leathery leaves and creamy-white bell-shaped flowers. It normally flowers in May, although this can be delayed by bad spring weather. It is found throughout the Arctic but is restricted in Scotland to an acre or so of ice-shattered rock on a rather dull hillside. It was probably left behind there as the glaciers retreated, although the possibility of accidental or deliberate introduction by Man cannot be ruled out. It is a mystery why it does not grow anywhere else in Scotland, but perhaps other colonies await discovery elsewhere in the Scottish hills.

Rowan sapling at Creag Meagaidh National Nature Reserve.

3. THE PINE OF SCOTLAND

An ancient granny pine tree is as potent a symbol of Scottish history as any historic castle. Our oldest pines, over 400 years old, would have been mature trees when wolves still roamed the Highlands.

Scots pine (*Pinus sylvestris*) is easily recognisable by the reddish brown upper trunk, where the bark has peeled off to reveal the heartwood, which is sold commercially as 'red deal'. A mature straight tree can be up to 160 ft (49 m) tall, and it would take five people to circle its trunk with linked arms.

Scots pines and heather, RSPB reserve, Abernethy forest.

The paired needles of Scots pine are bluish and about an inch long. In springtime, oval yellowish clusters of male flowers produce abundant pollen which is carried by the wind to the female flowers, growing in crimson tufts at the tip of new shoots. These develop by the following summer into soft green cones which become hard and woody, splitting to release the seeds in the third summer.

'Scots pine' is perhaps an inappropriate name for the most widely distributed conifer in the world: it is found from the Sierra Nevada of Spain to north of the Arctic Circle in Scandinavia, and east to the Pacific coast of the USSR.

(see Box 3) survived rather longer, because of their remoteness. However, the introduction of sheep farming in the early eighteenth century accelerated their decline; the grazing of sheep and burning of undergrowth killed all young trees until eventually the wood died out.

The development of grouse moors in Victorian times further hastened this process. Modern grouse moors, dominated by ling heather, originated as the dwarf-shrub understorey of pinewoods. Such moors today are thus a totally artificial landscape, created by tree-felling and maintained by regular burning. In theory, pine trees could re-establish if the burning stopped, but in most areas there are no mature trees left to provide seed, and red deer browse off any seedlings that do sprout.

The timber demands of the Napoleonic wars and two world wars brought the final demise of our extensive native woodlands, so that today only tiny fragments remain of the old woods of Caledon; and even these are threatened by the fast expanding red deer population.

TODAY'S WOODLANDS

The area of relatively natural pine woodland left in the Highlands today is less than 42 square miles (108 sq km). Fortunately the best remnant woods are protected either as nature reserves or as Sites of Special Scientific Interest (see Chapter 16). The largest area under active conservation management is the Abernethy reserve owned by the Royal Society for the Protection of Birds, with a total area of almost 50 square miles (130 sq km), although by no means all of this is native pine forest.

Other pinewood remnants include the Black Wood of Rannoch on the south shore of Loch Rannoch; an area on the south shore of Loch Maree in the Beinn Eighe National Nature Reserve; parts of Rothiemurchus in Speyside, Mar Lodge, Glen Tanar near Braemar, and Glen Affric west of Drumnadrochit.

Many pinewood remnants gain extra appeal from the gnarled multi-trunked trees growing there – a natural variety of Scots pine called *condensata*. In a truly pristine wood they would be intermixed with other forms with straight, true trunks; but in most forests the straight trees have been selectively felled over the last three centuries for their high timber value. The pines we romantically admire as natural woodland may often be merely the rejects of forest harvesting.

The remnant pinewoods are characterised by pine trees of widely varying age, but also have birch, juniper and willow trees and a distinctive ground flora. Many of these typical flowers and mosses are soon lost if a wood is felled or heavily managed, and their presence is a strong sign of undisturbed woodland. They include creeping lady's-tresses orchid, and four species of wintergreen with oval glossy leaves and spikes of creamy-white flowers. Some of these pinewood plants also occur in birchwoods which, although often over-looked, were also an important component of the Old Caledonian Forest.

4. CORNCOCKLE: A VANISHING WEED

Corncockle (*Agrostemma githago*) was a common weed of arable crops in lowland Scotland during the late nineteenth century. However by 1983 the last remaining Scottish site where it was found was in Moray; this decline was caused by the use of cleaner seed corn early this century and through the increased use of herbicides.

Corncockle was well adapted as a cornfield weed. It thrived in the same soil as cereal crops, and had fruits that matured around harvest time, and its seeds were so similar to grain in size and weight that they could not be separated in the harvest. In 1920 almost two per cent of oat crops were contaminated by corncockle seeds which gave flour a bitter taste and were poisonous in quantity.

There were obvious benefits in eradicating the plant from cornfields, although in the process we lost an attractive plant. A relative of garden pinks, it has showy pink flowers up two inches (5 cm) in diameter and a tall stem with greyish, hairy, spear-shaped leaves.

It has apparently disappeared from the roadside verge on which it grew in Moray, but is now making a comeback elsewhere in Scotland. Increasingly, it is planted in wildflower gardens, both for its beauty and to attract butterflies.

Primroses and bluebells in the oak woods of Kinloch Castle, Isle of Rhum.

Semi-natural oak woodland is almost as rare as pine, with isolated examples in Kirkcudbrightshire, in the more inaccessible parts of the Upper Clyde Valley, on islands in Loch Lomond, and most notably around Loch Sunart in Ardnamurchan and Loch Sween in Kintyre.

Although we label them 'oak' woodland, such woods include a mixture of other trees and shrubs. Their ground flora is less typical than that of pinewoods, and many of the commoner species will also grow in plantations. Common species include dog's mercury, primrose, wood anemone, lesser celandine, dog violet, wild hyacinth (the bluebell of England), early purple orchid, bugle, wild garlic, wood cranesbill, wild strawberry, foxglove, and blaeberry (the Scots name for bilberry), together producing a glorious display in spring and early summer.

Many ferns also grow in these woods. Hay-scented buckler-fern is restricted to the far west, while filmy-ferns are only found in damp and shady, frost-free pockets of the same area. But perhaps the most important feature of these western oakwoods is the diverse and abundant growth of mosses, liverworts and lichens that grow on the trunks and branches of the trees, including several species unique to Scotland.

Although afforestation has been extensive in the Border and Highland hills since the Second World War, these plantations are a poor substitute botanically for the native woods. There are few places more dark and sterile than the floor of a thickly planted Sitka spruce forest. Even plantations of native Scots pine or broad-leaved trees have a less varied flora than natural woods, because dense even-aged planting leaves little space for other herbaceous species to move in, and the inevitable management work disturbs and restricts the flora.

PLANTS AND FARMING

Early farming actually benefited a few wild flowering plants. Some plants set seed at the same time as the grain crops, and had seeds of similar size and weight; such seeds could not easily be separated from the harvested grain, and were therefore sown with the following year's seed crop. Cornflower (a beautiful blue-flowered relative of scabious), corncockle (Box 4) and bindweeds flourished in this way, but today's cleaner seed corn and herbicides have all but eliminated them from our fields.

Herbicides also poisoned other cornfield weeds that had adapted to the regular disturbance of ploughing. Poppies and the yellow daisy-flowers of corn marigold both declined dramatically under the chemical farming regime, as did redshank (a straggly relative of dockens), bugloss (an attractive plant with blue flowers and densely hairy foliage) and fumitories, which scramble over the surrounding vegetation with weak stems and have attractive, tubular, pink flowers tipped with crimson. These are common today only in the crofting areas of the north-west and the machair farmland of the Western Isles, where the intensive use of chemicals is shunned (see Chapter 5).

The seeds of many of these species can survive for decades in the soil and occasionally reappear when, for example, farmland is ploughed and abandoned prior to construction work. Suddenly an unexpected blaze of colour will appear as the long-dormant seeds burst into flower.

Roadside banks also serve as a last refuge for many of these weed species. Scrub and coarse grasses must of course be kept down by occasional cutting, but if the mowing is delayed until late summer when the plants have set seed, this can help spread the seeds and maintain a wide variety of wildflowers.

One Scottish habitat that has disappeared almost completely is wet meadowland. Once, these were common in marshes and along riverbanks, but drainage and farm improvements have converted most of them to drier, less attractive, grassy swards.

Wet meadows were the home of plants such as globeflower (a relative of buttercups with shining yellow, globular flowers); wood cranesbill (with showy purple flowers); and melancholy thistle (perhaps the true thistle of Scotland), which has lance-shaped leaves, white felted on their underside and solitary swollen purple flowers. Today these survive only in the few remaining fragments of meadowland; elsewhere they have survived only on mountain ledges beyond the reach of deer and sheep.

But human activity has also enhanced our flora, for better or for worse, by introducing a wide variety of alien species either deliberately or accidentally. Many of our commonest trees, for instance, are introductions – not just the plantation conifers such as Sitka spruce (from western North America), European larch and Norway spruce (from the European mainland), but also common species such as sycamore (introduced in the fifteenth or sixteenth century).

While these were deliberately planted, others arrived

Poppies among the crops near Drem, East Lothian.

accidentally as seeds attached to sheep or their wool, which was imported as 'shoddy' for fertilising fields. Early this century Tweeddale was particularly famous for its short-lived flora of invaders from the southern hemisphere, and today seaports are the entry point for other invaders which rarely survive in our climate for long.

Most aliens, however, originated as garden escapes. Some of these can have a harmful effect by swamping native vegetation. Giant hogweed (Box 5), Himalayan and giant knotweed are particularly aggressive invaders. However, other alien plants have spread widely with little detrimental effect. Slender speedwell, with pale-blue flowers on thread-like stalks, is a native of the Caucasus but is now probably Scotland's commonest speedwell, while New Zealand willowherb, a low mat-forming plant with delicate pink flowers, was first recorded as a garden weed in 1904 and has already spread to the Outer Hebrides and Orkney.

THE COAST: A LAST WILD REFUGE

Seen in the context of the changes wrought by man in the landscape, the coast acquires a considerable importance as a natural habitat. This is especially so in Scotland. With the fiord-like sea lochs of the west coast and the myriad islands of the north and west, Scotland's coastline is estimated at more than 6,000 miles (10,000 km) in all, 65 per cent of the total UK coast.

Sea-washed coasts are a severe habitat for plant life. Paradoxically the main difficulty is often a shortage of fresh water. Rain drains quickly from rocky shores and sand, while tidal floods exclude fresh water from salt-marshes for long periods. Sea water itself is highly damaging to most plant life because it upsets the balance of salts inside and outside the cell, which is crucial to the process by which plants absorb water. Many coastal plants are therefore highly adapted to cope with this harsh environment. On exposed windy coastlines, where the soil is thin and plants are regularly doused with salt spray, trees have never established and the vegetation is similar to that found on the mountain tops. Thrift, whose tufts of pink flowers are such an attractive feature of rocky coasts in May, is also widespread on mountain tops, growing, for example, above 4,000 ft (1,200m) on Ben Nevis.

Similarly roseroot, a yellow-flowered relative of the stonecrops, which grows on rich ledges high in the mountains, is also found on sea cliffs around Scotland. It has thick fleshy leaves with a bluish waxy coating, which protects it both from icy mountain winds and coastal spray. Sea campion, common scurvy-grass, buck's-horn plantain, sea-spurrey, and sea-lavender are all widely distributed on sea cliffs, as are many lichens and ferns.

As its name suggests, Scots lovage, is confined mostly to rocky Scottish coasts, although it just gets into England on Lindisfarne, and is also found elsewhere in north-west Europe. A member of the carrot family, it has spreading heads of white flowers and glossy, bright-green leaves.

Although sea cliffs themselves are largely untouched by human influence, farms increasingly encroach to their very edge. Maritime heathland, which once formed the landward margin of many cliffs, survives extensively along the north coast and on Shetland and Orkney, but even there it has shown a marked decline in recent years.

This heathland is dominated by various heathers, including crowberry, which has shining green needle-like leaves and glossy black berries. More open areas amongst the heath often produce glorious displays of spring squill, like a miniature blue hyacinth, together with the yellow pea-flowers of bird's-foot trefoil and kidney vetch, and carpets of thyme. The Scots primrose (Box 6) is found in open grassy areas on the clifftops of Orkney and Caithness.

More sheltered clifftops, especially on the east coast, are often dominated by gorse (known as whin in Scotland), which shelters woodland species such as wild hyacinth, red campion and lesser celandine. In Shetland the campion has particularly deep-red flowers, a stronger stem and larger seeds – useful adaptations to the severe northern climate.

Salt-marshes usually form in sheltered estuaries where mud accumulates; their typical plants are specially adapted to cope with flooding by sea water at the highest tides. The outer edge of salt-marshes is often fringed with glasswort, whose spiky cactus-like form is adapted for storing water. Inland of this zone we find sea aster (a relative of garden Michaelmas daisies), sea lavender, sea plantain, sea purslane and sea arrow-

Silverweed has adapted to life on the shifting sands.

5. GIANT HOGWEED: AN ALIEN INVADER

Giant hogweed (*Heracleum mantegazzianum*) is one of the most impressive plants in the Scottish landscape, as its statistics show: it grows up to 12 ft (3.6 m) tall, with hollow stems 4 inches (10 cm) in diameter, and huge rhubarb-like leaves over 3 ft (1m) across. A member of the carrot family, it has tiny white flowers arranged in large umbrella-shaped heads.

Giant hogweed was introduced into British gardens from south-western Asia around 1893. From about 1930 it began to spread outside gardens and today it is common in most of Scotland.

Its typical habitats (the banks of rivers and railways) relate to its methods of dispersal. Its seeds are spread by the wind, and can travel 30 ft (9 m) in strong winds before they settle and germinate; the slipstream of trains therefore helps spread them along railway banks. The seeds can also float in water for up to three days, allowing them to colonise riverbanks up to 240 miles (380 km) away.

Giant hogweed has a bad reputation because its sap produces painful blisters on contact with the skin in bright sunshine. Merely brushing against the plant can cause blisters, by breaking the fine stem hairs and releasing the sap. Calamine lotion will soothe these uncomfortable symptoms but it is best not to touch the plant without gloves.

Perhaps even more harmful is the way in which giant hogweed swamps native vegetation, producing impenetrable jungles in some parts of Scotland. Efforts are being made to control its spread in most regions, but this can only be achieved by the repeated use of herbicides – a costly and time-consuming business.

grass, along with thrift, scurvy-grass and a variety of true grasses. Salt-marshes are highly susceptible to human disturbance. Many have been damaged by grazing sheep or cattle, while others have been 're-claimed' – planners still tend to see salt-marshes only as 'wasteland' that is ripe for development.

A remarkable plant found beyond the salt-marsh is eelgrass whose long leaves wave, snake-like, in the tide. It is the only truly marine flowering plant and forms extensive beds on muddy shores well below the low tide mark. Known as widgeon-grass in parts of Scotland, its seeds are food for widgeon and other duck. It declined dramatically in the late 1930s as a result of wartime pollution, combined perhaps with endemic disease. It now seems to be recovering, although it has yet to recolonise some former Scottish sites.

Scotland boasts some superb sand-dune systems, including Torrs Warren in Wigtownshire, Culbin in Moray, Tentsmuir in Fife, St Cyrus in Kincardineshire and the Sands of Forvie in Aberdeenshire, the last three of which are National Nature Reserves. These include few exclusively Scottish plants, although they are excellent examples of the succession by which a series of plants progressively stabilises the sand. St Cyrus is notable for several species which are adapted to milder climates and which reach their northern limit there, including clustered bellflower and wild liquorice.

Sand dunes, too, are often damaged by human activities. Recreational use often destroys their growing edge and opens up bare areas of sand which are then extended by wind action, while 'poaching' by grazing animals can have similar effects. In many parts of the east coast this erosion has been partly halted by planting sea buckthorn, a native of more southerly coasts, with some impact on the local vegetation.

Perhaps the truly unique Scottish habitat is the machair of the western shores of the Outer Hebrides (see also Chapter 9, Box 1). Machair consists of short grassland enriched by shell-sand blown in from the sea by the prevailing winds, and kept open by traditional crofting agriculture. Each year the crofter turns over patches of machair so that the surface vegetation adds humus to the thin sandy soil allowing barley or potatoes to be grown. The soil is further enriched by the spreading of seaweed, which fertilises it and adds 'body' in a way no chemical could. However, the harvesting of a single crop scours the nutrients from this tenuous soil so that it has to be left fallow for several years to be refertilised by the natural vegetation. These fallow areas produce vast swathes of colourful wildflowers which are of enormous conservation value; but their survival depends upon the maintenance of the traditional system of crofting agriculture.

The machair has no rare plants but produces some superb massed displays of flowers – an echo of the flowers that once brightened farm landscapes through-out Britain. Each piece of machair has its own charac-

Sea thrift at Elgol, Loch Scavaig, Isle of Skye.

6. SCOTS PRIMROSE: A SYMBOL IN DECLINE

The Scots primrose (*Primula scotica*) is a very special Scottish plant, found on the exposed cliff-top turf of Orkney, Caithness and Sutherland. Although closely related to the Norwegian *Primula scandinavica*, it is now accepted as a unique species found nowhere else in the world – a truly Scottish endemic.

Usually it is little more than one inch (2.5 cm) tall, although it can reach four times this size. Its leaves are yellow-green above and mealy-white underneath, and hug the ground in a tight rosette for protection against gales. Its rich pink flowers appear in May and June, often with a second limited flowering in July and August. The flowers are half an inch (1 cm) across, with five notched petals united into a short tube, and a bright yellow 'eye' at the mouth of the tube to guide pollinating insects to the nectar at its base.

In the last century the Scots primrose declined dramatically as a result of agricultural 'improve-ment' of its clifftop habitat; in Orkney, for exam-ple, half of the thirty sites known last century have been destroyed. Recent research suggests that climate may also be implicated in this decline, with plants only flourishing in years with mild winters and infrequent summer gales. With the current trend towards colder winters in the north, this steady decline seems likely to continue.

Practical conservation can help the Scots prim-rose, and several colonies are protected within nature reserves or Sites of Special Scientific In-terest. But the best safeguard for Scotland's only endemic flower would be for more people to appreciate the beauty of this gem of the cliff tops.

Scots primrose in Sutherland.

51

Bogbean is common among the lochans of the Western Isles.

Yellow Flag Iris survives on the croft lands.

ter, but the commonest colours are the yellows of lady's bedstraw, bird's-foot trefoil, kidney vetch, yellow rattle and lesser meadow-rue, the blue of Scots bluebell (harebell), the red of clover, the purple of tufted vetch and the whites of yarrow and ox-eye daisy or gowans.

Around the edges of machair fields, poppies, bugloss, fumitory, sun spurge and corn marigold add a further blaze of colour while, inland, the wet machair supports yellow flag iris, red bartsia, eyebright and masses of ragged robin. This wet machair is also the habitat for one of the few machair specialities: the Hebridean subspecies of early marsh-orchid, recognised by its more deeply blotched purple flowers. The resulting explosion of flowers produces one of the finest botanical displays in Britain and ensures the machair international recognition as a unique plant habitat.

THE FLORA OF THE FUTURE

With large areas of semi-natural vegetation still remaining in Scotland, the threat to individual species is far less severe than in England, although the damage to plant habitats and communities is just as great. Of fifty-eight rare Scottish species listed in *The British Red Data Book: Vascular Plants*, most are threatened by the destruction of their habitat rather than individual pressures, although there are exceptions.

One of the rarest species, alpine coltsfoot, is confined to a single ledge in the Grampian mountains where it was discovered in 1814. Although it is abundant in the Alps there are scarcely two dozen plants in Scotland, and its origins remain mysterious. But its rarity has attracted large numbers of visitors to the site, causing erosion and threatening a landslide that could destroy the entire colony.

The network of reserves established across Scotland has helped protect the best examples of vegetation types. The major problem of Highland conservation is undoubtedly the population explosion of the red deer (see Chapter 4), but few landowners want deer numbers to be reduced because of the income they get from deer stalking. The situation has arisen because many estates, while shooting stags in large numbers, have failed to cull sufficient hinds. As a result, red deer have increased from 155,000 in 1960 to an estimated 300,000 in 1989: a situation which the Red Deer Commission admits is 'jeopardising the credibility of the deer industry'. At least one plant, alpine sow-thistle, faces possible extinction as a result of increased grazing by deer and sheep.

Public attitudes in Scotland have changed with the 'green revolution' of the late 1980s, though more slowly than in England. The interest in creating 'wild gardens' and small-scale 'ecological parks' has fostered understanding of the practical difficulties of conservation, but the lessons are less easily applied to wider countryside problems. In many cases these point to the root issues of Scottish politics: the questions of land ownership and of

Flowers of the Machair on croft at Shader, Barvas, Isle of Lewis.

public versus private responsibilities.

Plants remain a potent symbol for the future. Many people enjoy the colours of a wild flower garden or a meadow in full bloom, and it is heartening to see families with rucksacks and field guides enjoying the countryside. The tourist potential of our wild flowers is still largely unexploited, although far more people go to the Highlands in summer to enjoy the natural environ-ment than go there in winter to ski.

If people can only be helped to understand the beauties of a wet meadow or the machair, the natural rock garden of a mountain cliff, the pattern of plants on a rocky shore or the intricate community of a native woodland, then the real value of these habitats will be recognised, and the future of Scotland's flora could be truly secure.

Mountain hare in winter camouflage.

The World of the Mammals

ANDREW KITCHENER

In this chapter, Dr Andrew Kitchener, Curator of Birds and Mammals at the Royal Museum of Scotland, tells the story of how Scotland's wildlife has changed radically over the last 10,000 years.

More than 12,000 years ago, the eternal winter of the last Ice Age finally began to end. Revealed for the first time was a scarred and desolate landscape of mountains smoothed by moving ice, and valleys chiselled out by glaciers.

Only the south was free from the ice cap at any time during the last Ice Age, and even here on the permanently frozen tundra few mammals could have survived except possibly the polar bear, arctic fox, musk ox and reindeer – the kind of mammals we find in the Arctic today.

For a brief 1,500 years a warmer climate prevailed, and it was during this period that sedges, grasses and willows and, later, birch scrub began to green the landscape, encouraging the arrival of land animals such as lemmings, mountain hares and giant deer (Box 1), and birds such as snowy owls and ptarmigan.

But the Ice Age had not quite relaxed its icy grasp. Suddenly the whole of northern Europe was once again plunged into a new winter that lasted for more than a thousand years. This final freeze saw the extinction of the giant deer ('Irish elk') in the British Isles, and drove the rest of the fauna south into what is now England and across the dry North Sea to continental Europe. An ice cap spread over the western Highlands as far south as Loch Lomond, thereby earning it the name of the 'Lomond Readvance' (see Chapter 1).

With the final end of the Ice Age the climate warmed rapidly and the sea level rose as the melting ice drained to the coastal waters. The last Ice Age had caused a drop in sea level of about 80 metres (260 ft) leaving much of the English Channel and North Sea as dry land, so that the British Isles were an extension of the European continent. Now that the sea level was rising once more, those animals which migrate overland had limited time to recolonise Britain. Many animals from southern Europe simply did not reach Britain before it became an island again. Consequently, although Britain's animal wildlife is sometimes described as being impoverished or 'depauperate', it should really be called 'incomplete'.

The new warm phase heralded the first in a series of changing climax vegetations which in turn led to subtle changes in the animals that depended on them. The return of the birch saw the re-arrival of the reindeer (Box 2) and the mountain hare; but as the climate warmed further and the vegetation changed, conditions became unsuitable for the reindeer and it became extinct in Scotland more than 8,000 years ago.

The mountain hare, which turns white in winter, became restricted to the Highlands; it is still relatively common on heather moorland, particularly in north-east Scotland, but is also found on many of the Western Isles and in the Borders, where it was deliberately introduced in the nineteenth century. The warming of the weather must have been the main reason for its retreat into the higher mountain areas. The birch forests were being gradually replaced by Scots pine and hazels as temperatures continued to rise.

Another factor in the retreat of the mountain hare may have been competition from a new arrival, the brown hare, which probably became established naturally in Britain at the beginning of the warm phase when there was more open ground. However, if the brown hare did reach Britain then, it may have died out as the forests thickened and spread; it is thought to have been re-established by the Romans, some 7,000 years later, and is now widespread in southern Scotland as well as in the eastern half of the country.

Another animal whose distribution was clearly upset by the intervention of the last Ice Age is the weasel, a predator which is found nearly everywhere on mainland Scotland but on very few of the islands. In the north of Europe and in Asia the weasel changes its coat to white in winter; but, oddly enough, British weasels very rarely change colour, even in the colder climate of Scotland where they might be expected to do so. This is because our weasels are descended from animals from farther south in Europe where weasels never undergo a seasonal change of colour. The weasels from eastern Europe, which do change colour, could not recolonise Britain because of the barrier of the North Sea.

By 9,000 years ago, Britain's present-day mammals were all established: foxes, badgers, otters, stoats, weasels, wildcats, roe deer, red deer, hedgehogs,

The Mongolian (Przewalski's) Wild Horse at the Highland Wildlife Park, Kingussie.

The northern lynx disappeared as the forests were cleared.

the fate of Scotland's wildlife lay in the hands of our own species.

People's earliest impact on the environment was the clearance of forests for farmland to grow crops and provide grazing for livestock. The destruction of forests, combined with an increase in hunting, led to the early extinction of animals which depended most on woodland habitat; these included the lynx, the wild horse and the moose. The wild ox, an enormous creature that stood up to 6 ft(1.8 m) at the shoulder, survived to the Iron Age, just before the Romans arrived; the last few animals in Scotland may have disappeared through inter-breeding with their domestic cousins from southern Europe. The wild horse may have suffered a similar fate, but much earlier.

THE FIRST STOWAWAYS

The Neolithic farmers did not just bring their livestock; they also accidentally added to the British fauna. The first of these stowaways were the ancestors of the common vole (not to be confused with the field vole) and the wood mouse on Orkney. In their isolation, Orkney voles had already evolved much larger bodies than the common voles of Europe by about 4,500 years ago. But why did they grow so much larger? One possible explanation is that, in the absence of ground-living predators, the right conditions were created for the natural selection of bigger voles that did not have to escape from anything by bolting into small cracks or holes in the ground. A further reason may simply be that, in order to survive in the open windswept islands of Orkney, voles need to be of a more robust build, and larger voles have evolved as a result.

But voles were by no means the only stowaways to reach our shores. Another Neolithic stowaway was the house mouse which, far from being isolated on an island, spread throughout the length and breadth of the land with human help.

shrews, wood mice and voles were spreading through Britain's forests and moving northwards to Scotland. But there were also larger mammals which do not survive in Scotland today, including the lynx, the wild horse, the reindeer, the moose (elk), the wild ox (known as the aurochs or urus), the brown bear, the beaver, the wild boar and the wolf.

Humans also recolonised this virgin land after being driven out by the great freeze. Middle Stone Age (Mesolithic) hunters brought their dogs with them as they exploited the rich animal and plant life. They began to colonise Scotland from southern Britain about 8,000 years ago. Less than a thousand years later the New Stone Age (Neolithic) farmers and their domestic livestock had at last reached Scotland from southern Europe (see Chapter 7). Until this period the animals and plants of Britain had been influenced almost entirely by natural events; but as soon as people arrived,

1. THE GIANT DEER

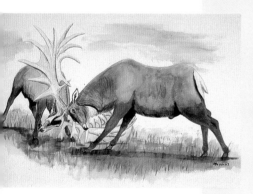

Artist's Impression of Giant Deer fighting.

Popularly known as the Irish elk, the giant deer (*Megaloceros giganteus*) was neither exclusively Irish nor related to the elk or moose of mainland Europe. Ranging from Ireland to Siberia it was dependent on a unique and vanished wildlife habitat known as the 'mammoth steppe'. Changes in climate at the end of the last Ice Age led to the disappearance of the mammoth steppe, and with it went one of the largest deer the world has ever seen.

The giant deer is famous for its huge, spade-like antlers, which are similar in shape to those of the fallow deer, its closest probable relative. Until recently these enormous bony structures were thought to be have been used only for display purposes, designed to intimidate rival stags and attract females during the breeding season or the 'rut', as it is known; but a mechanical analysis of the antlers has shown that they are superbly designed for actual fighting: the giant deer was indeed a fighter, just like other deer.

Other rodents which are common on the mainland occur apparently at random throughout Shetland, Orkney and the Hebrides. For example, the common vole (i.e. the Orkney vole) is found only on Orkney, but the bank vole occurs only on Raasay, Mull and Bute. Another vole, the field vole, is found on the Uists, Eigg, Muck, Mull, Bute, Skye, Islay, Jura, Gigha and Arran, but not on Raasay, Shetland, St Kilda, Lewis and Barra. The odd distributions that we see today are now known to have been caused by a combination of natural events and human introductions.

The wood mouse seems to have made it to most of the islands. However, those that invaded Shetland, St Kilda, Fair Isle and most of the Hebrides are more closely related to Norwegian wood mice than to the animals of the Scottish mainland, whereas the wood mice on Mull and Colonsay are of Scottish descent. The clear implication is that the wood mouse first reached many of the Scottish islands with the Vikings and has travelled with the human population ever since.

The story of the St Kilda house mouse is a sad one. Its ancestors were introduced to St Kilda by the Vikings, along with wood mice, and they evolved into a unique island race that remained dependent on the human population. However, when the people of St Kilda were evacuated in the 1930s, they left the house mouse open to competition with the more independent wood mouse, and within a few years house mice became extinct. In less than a thousand years the St Kilda house mouse had evolved into a unique race, flourished, and disappeared into extinction.

The black rat, or ship rat, was originally an invader from Asia and was probably brought to our shores by the Romans. It would later earn itself eternal infamy as the carrier of the fleas that introduced the Black Death, or bubonic plague, to Britain in the fourteenth century. Today the black rat is faring badly. Competition from the more adaptable brown rat has left it hanging on in only a few ports and docklands, where constant re-

invasions from overseas probably bolster the population against ever more efficient poisons and keen competitors.

The brown rat arrived in Britain from Asia in the early eighteenth century, but it was not recorded in Scotland until the second half of that century, and it did not reach the Highlands until the beginning of the nineteenth century. It quickly displaced its longer-tailed cousin, the black rat, from many of the areas it occupied. Today the brown rat is found everywhere, from the sewers of our cities to the farms of our countryside. As the ultimate survivor it can live off human waste and garbage and anything else that comes to hand, making it one of the world's most formidably successful mammals.

The St.Kilda wood mouse.

The black rat brought bubonic plague to Britain in the fourteenth century.

2. THE REINDEER

There has been much argument about when the reindeer became extinct as a wild animal in Scotland. In the thirteenth-century Icelandic *Orkneyinga Saga*, an account of the Norse earls of Orkney, there is a reference to reindeer-hunting on the mainland of Scotland in the eleventh century; but it is now believed that the author confused reindeer with the native red deer. Recently, reindeer bones found in the Inchnadamph caves of Sutherland have been radiocarbon-dated; the results suggest that Scotland's last-known reindeer died more than 8,300 years ago.

There were some unsuccessful attempts to reintroduce reindeer in the eighteenth century, at Dunkeld and on Orkney. Two centuries later, in the early 1950s, a small herd of domesticated reindeer from Swedish Lapland was successfully established at Rothiemurchus in the Cairngorms. The semi-domesticated herd now numbers about a hundred and is maintained as an attraction for the tourists; although they could survive in the wild without much difficulty, they can hardly be classified as part of Scotland's wildlife as yet.

LARGER MAMMALS

There were other comings and goings among our Scottish wildlife, mostly of larger mammals. The Romans admired the great Caledonian brown bears they found in Scotland and shipped many of them home to amuse the citizens of Rome in bear pits and the gladiatorial contests of the Coliseum. Eventually the brown bear in Scotland was killed off by human hunters and by the destruction of its forest habitat in the tenth century.

The fallow deer with its palmate antlers was probably introduced by the Romans, but it was only widely established following 1066 when William the Conqueror used it to stock many deer parks. Several parks were later established in Scotland; there have been many escapes into the wild, but it is much less common than the red deer or roe deer and is still considered a 'park animal'.

The Normans also brought the rabbit, which they kept in warrens where it was bred for meat and fur. It soon escaped and, although far removed from the sunnier climes of southern Europe, it spread and prospered. At first rabbits were considered a luxury, jealously guarded for the rich. The rabbits in the Royal Warrens of King Alexander II of Scotland were protected from poachers by statute during the thirteenth century; and the Earl of Orkney's rent book records 1,200 rabbit skins as part of his annual rent at the end of the fifteenth century.

Rabbits on Scottish islands are often black or of other colour varieties because they are descended from domestic breeds that have escaped. However, despite their abundance in the Lowlands of Scotland, rabbits were not successfully established in the Highlands until the eighteenth century.

Their destructive effect on the regeneration of scrub and forest became clear in the 1950s and 1960s when the introduction of the myxomatosis virus decimated Britain's rabbit population. Areas that had been bare of woodland soon became covered with scrub and young trees. However, the rabbit population later became largely immune to myxomatosis and their numbers have increased again.

The beaver was prized for its luxurious fur and was also hunted for a glandular musk-like secretion called castoreum with alleged medicinal properties. This secretion actually contained salicylic acid, the active ingredient of aspirin (derived, no doubt, from the beaver's diet of willow bark), so its value as a medical panacea may have had some foundation in fact. We do not know when the beaver became extinct in Scotland, but the last beavers in Britain were recorded in Wales in the twelfth century. It has been suggested that the beaver could well be re-introduced to Scotland today, but foresters might not take too kindly to their tree-felling activities nor to their voracious appetite for tree bark.

The red squirrel continues to decline along with its forest habitat.

58

3. THE RED SQUIRREL

Scotland is now regarded as the last stronghold of the red squirrel in Britain, but this has not always been the case. With the clearing of the ancient pine forests of the Highlands during the eighteenth century the red squirrel became virtually extinct in Scotland; it had already disappeared from the Lowlands by the early 1700s. Perhaps a few lingered on in Speyside, but to all intents and purposes the red squirrel had disappeared.

As extinction proceeded in the Highlands, re-introductions began in the Lowlands, starting at Dalkeith in 1772 and Dunkeld in 1793, using animals from England and Europe; by the end of the nineteenth century they were extremely common once again – so much so that they achieved the status of 'vermin'. The gradual spread of the re-introduced red squirrel coincided with the restoration of the forests, particularly in the Highlands, where the new plantations provided the habitat which the squirrels needed. At the beginning of this century, however, the red squirrel population crashed, probably due to disease.

Meanwhile the American grey squirrel, introduced into Britain from 1876 onwards purely because it looked nice, began to make inroads into red squirrel habitat and territory in England as the red squirrel died out. The commonly held view that the grey squirrel forced the red squirrel out of its territories is wrong; the evidence is that the grey only moved into areas after the red squirrel had disappeared.

Introductions also took place in Scotland early in this century, starting at Edinburgh Zoo in 1912; the grey squirrel is now found throughout central Scotland, but it is still isolated from the rest of the British population.

Today, by an irony of history, the red squirrel is extinct in most of southern and central England and only survives in any numbers in Scotland. It is one of our most attractive and elegant creatures and Scotland may become even more important as its last stronghold. Large areas of coniferous forest may have to be specially managed to exclude the alien grey squirrel. Yet, by another irony, the current drive to encourage the planting of deciduous trees such as the oak may actually promote the spread of the grey squirrel into the Highlands, and assist its invasion into the remaining habitat of the shyer and less competitive red squirrel.

4. THE RED DEER

The red deer is Britain's largest surviving land mammal and its population has probably never been higher in Scotland than it is today, with at least 300,000 now roaming the Scottish hills. Originally a woodland animal, the red deer had to adapt to Scotland's increasingly treeless hills and glens; even today very few red deer are to be found in the new conifer plantations. Its enormous population increase has been due entirely to the management of deer as a game species to the point where there are now serious problems of over-population that need to be addressed urgently.

To the visitor the red deer epitomises all the grandeur and wildness of Scotland's mountain areas. Yet as a result of having to live on the over-grazed pastures of Scotland's deforested mountains for so long, the Scottish red deer has become one of the smallest and most malnourished in the world. When Scottish red deer were introduced to New Zealand in the nineteenth century, the rich food supply there produced a massive increase in body size in subsequent generations, until today New Zealand red deer are as large as their mainland European cousins.

Like Scotland's native wildcat (Box 5), the red deer also faces a threat from hybridisation – in this case from its close relative the sika deer, introduced from Japan and eastern Asia. These were first imported to Scotland as decorative and exotic parkland animals in the 1870s; later they were also brought in for sporting purposes. The population and distribution of sika deer increased considerably in the 1970s, and during the 1980s some cases of hybridisation between sika deer stags and red deer hinds were noted. It is not yet known how much of a threat this might represent to the survival of the pure-bred native red deer – but in south-west Scotland it is already very difficult to distinguish between the two species.

The wild boar was another common woodland animal in Scotland until as late as the seventeenth century. It was an important food source and was greatly prized for hunting by the nobility. Hunting and destruction of its forest habitat eventually caused the wild boar's extinction. When it finally went, Britain lost one of the most important contributors to the natural regeneration of woodlands since, through its selective feeding habits, the boar assists forest growth. Today wild boar are kept for sport on a farm at Ben Wyvis and there have been various attempts to re-introduce them elsewhere, but without much success.

The wolf, which for centuries was the main predator of the forests, was hunted to extinction in Scotland sometime in the eighteenth century. It was not really a threat to people but became a very real threat to livestock whenever its natural prey, the red deer, became scarce. Several Acts of Parliament were passed to exterminate the wolf. The remote Highlands were its last refuge, and the Highland forests were often destroyed in order to drive the wolf out. According to tradition the last wolf in Britain was killed in 1743, in Moray, by a stalker with his bare hands.

THE RISE OF THE GAMEKEEPER

During the nineteenth century much of Scotland was turned into a sort of 'outdoor leisure centre' for the landed gentry (see Chapter 17). The red deer (Box 4), which had been taken for food in the past, was now carefully conserved for wealthy sportsmen to hunt. Heath and moorland were opened up by tree clearance and managed for red grouse by burning the heather. Mountain hares also benefited from this management of open moorland, and they were deliberately introduced to the Borders and some Scottish islands. The capercaillie (see Chapter 5) was re-introduced and protected from predators for the guns of the sportsmen. Trout and salmon fishing were also promoted on Scotland's rivers and streams by killing all fish-eating predators, including herons, ospreys and otters. The development of Scotland as a rich man's hunting ground resulted in a tragic change of fortune for many animals which suddenly became the gamekeeper's enemies.

With the rise of the gamekeeper no carnivore was safe. The belief that game could be best encouraged by destroying all predators was flawed, but it continues to this day. Polecats and wildcats suffered most because they were large and easily trapped or poisoned. However the smaller stoats and weasels, as well as badgers, foxes, pine martens and otters, also suffered.

Birds of prey such as eagles, ospreys and peregrines also fared badly; as soon as they took to the wing they were blasted out of the skies. By the beginning of the twentieth century the carnage had been so relentless and efficient that the pattern of Scotland's wildlife had been profoundly altered.

Overgrazing by 300,000 red deer poses one of the most serious threats to the remaining native woodlands of Scotland.

The pine marten is gradually recovering from former persecution.

The elusive wildcat with its distinctive banded black-tipped tail (Box 5) only just survived in the western Highlands; it is a legally protected species now, but is still threatened.

The polecat was totally exterminated (see Chapter 15, Box 1); an attempt was made to re-establish it in western Scotland in the 1970s, but such attempts are probably doomed since it has now interbred with domestic ferrets that have gone wild.

The pine marten suffered severely from a combination of persecution, habitat loss and the near extinction of one of its favourite foods, the red squirrel (Box 3). The loss of its woodland habitat drove the pine marten out of the dwindling forests and up on to the rocky hillsides, particularly in Sutherland where it may have filled the niche left by the eradication of the polecat. Persecution by gamekeepers became intense in the latter half of the nineteenth century and it is something of a miracle that the pine marten survived at all. Now a protected species, it has extended its range very considerably and has recolonised woodlands even around the towns and cities of central Scotland, where the occasional animal has been spotted crouching observantly high in the tree tops.

The delightful otter, a larger member of the weasel family, suffered because it became fashionable to hunt it. Packs of otter hounds were specifically bred to hunt down this beautiful carnivore. This was not just good sport; gamekeepers believed that killing otters saved large numbers of trout and salmon for the game fisherman. In fact poaching by local people probably had far greater impact on fish populations. Apart from persecution by gamekeepers the otter is notoriously accident prone, and many otters are killed by drowning in lobster pots and fishermen's nets, or fall victim to cars. The otter has also been affected by pesticides and chemical poisons leaching into waterways and contaminating the fish stocks.

The otter is now a protected species. Its survival in many parts of southern Britain in still in the balance but, although it has declined in some areas of Scotland, it is happily still thriving in the western Highlands and Islands.

For many decades the gamekeeper's gibbet was heavy with the corpses of all these carnivores, slaughtered in order to demonstrate to estate owners that he was doing his job preserving game birds and deer. Cruel traps were supplemented with even crueller poisons in an attempt to eradicate all wild creatures that were of no value for sport.

The First World War brought much of this carnage to an end. After the human butchery on the battlefields of Europe, less than a quarter of the gamekeepers returned to Scotland's shooting estates and grouse moors. Much of the land was turned over to forestry. It was too late to save the polecat, but it helped to save the wildcat which has prospered and recolonised many of its former Scottish haunts despite continuing persecution.

SOME NEWCOMERS

There have been accidental introductions in this century, often of commercial species like the musk rat and the American mink which at first were confined to fur farms; unfortunately they escaped and became established in the wild in the 1930s.

In Scotland the musk rat became established for a time in the valley of the River Earn, from where it could have spread to have disastrous effects on our waterways. Fortunately a change in the fashion for its fur led to a vigorous extermination campaign which saw its demise by 1937.

The mink, on the other hand, has continued to spread and is now common in much of Britain. Its adaptability as a water-loving and ground-living predator means that it has often been regarded as a formidable enemy and destroyer of wildlife, particularly of ground-nesting birds such as terns and moorhens. Islands are no longer safe sanctuaries. Certainly in some areas the mink has devastated waterfowl and water voles, but in other areas wildlife populations seem unaffected by its presence. It is now official policy to ban the establishment of fur farms in sensitive areas and to do everything to keep mink off hitherto uninfested islands. Whether or not the mink is bad for Scotland's native wildlife, it is probably here to stay.

So far this chapter has concentrated largely upon land mammals, because birds are dealt with separately in the next chapter. But there have been two natural bird colonisations this century that demonstrate their advantage of flight as contrasted with the ground-living mammals.

One is the fulmar, which was once considered a very rare bird in Britain when it was confined to the extreme west and north on St Kilda and Shetland. However, it

5. THE WILDCAT

The Scottish wildcat lived throughout Britain long before the domestic cat even existed; but its range has gradually contracted under the impact of the destruction of Britain's forests and persecution by gamekeepers, until it now survives only in a few Scottish strongholds. Even in Scotland it became virtually extinct, except in the western Highlands; but the wildcat is now a strictly protected species under the Wildlife and Countryside Act 1981, and a relaxation in the ceaseless persecution, combined with extensive reafforestation, has allowed the wildcat to extend its range.

Yet it is still far from safe. Although now found in many of its former Scottish haunts, the native wildcat faces a new and insidious threat from its domestic cousin. Domestic cats are descended from the African race of the wildcat and as such are closely related to Scotland's wildcats. First domesticated by the Ancient Egyptians 4,000 years ago, they were brought here by the Romans and have spread ever since. Beneath the benign disguise of your home-loving moggie is a ruthless predator quite capable of surviving in the wild as a feral animal.

The close relationship between wild and domestic cats, coupled with the recovery of the wildcat population, resulted in hybridisation between these two species. In common with many mammals, males recolonise areas first. Finding no wildcat females with which to mate, these males probably mated with local domestic females. The resulting hybrids have continued to mate with wild, domestic and other hybrid cats to produce a whole array of different shapes and sizes of cat belonging to the hybrid population.

One commonly occurring colour variety is the black Kellas cat, named after the Moray village where the first specimen was recorded. This handsome-looking animal is often thought of as a new species of cat in the popular press. Now that we have several specimens to study scientifically the situation is clear – they are no more than one of the complex hybrids between wild and domestic cats.

At this stage the threat of hybridisation to the pure-bred wildcat population is uncertain. It is to be hoped that current research can discover the extent of this threat and formulate a plan to preserve the Scottish wildcat for future generations.

has spread southwards, starting from Shetland in 1910, until by 1970 it had spread throughout Britain. With a present population of 300,000 it is one of the most successful seabirds around our coasts, resilient and adaptable; there is even a unique inland colony of fulmars now nesting on the cliffs of Salisbury Crags on the slopes of Edinburgh's volcano, Arthur's Seat.

The collared dove, in contrast, came to Britain from south-west Asia in 1952. The first recorded nest was discovered in Norfolk in 1955. Within two years it had reached the north of Scotland, with a pair nesting in Moray in 1957. Within ten years the British population had soared to 10,000 birds, and it is now classified as an extremely common resident.

We are now entering a new stage of conservation, where bodies such as the Nature Conservancy Council for Scotland and the Royal Society for the Protection of Birds are attempting to restore Scotland's wildlife through selective re-introductions. Although the peregrine falcon, osprey and golden eagle have largely recovered from former persecution, others such as the sea eagle and the red kite have not. It will be extremely interesting to see how well the policy of re-introductions succeeds.

LOOKING TO THE FUTURE

Although its wildlife has been irrevocably altered by humans and natural events in the last 10,000 years, Scotland is still fortunate in being relatively sparsely populated; so there are large areas where wild plants and animals have been able to survive with little or no conflict with humans. However, we cannot be complacent; there are new threats facing the remaining fauna and flora.

Large areas of Scotland are still managed primarily for the benefit of game, which means that in some areas predatory birds and mammals still fall illegally to the

The clean rivers and sea lochs of Scotland are the last stronghold of the otter in Britain.

The Scottish wildcat is threatened by interbreeding with feral cats.

Grey seal

gamekeeper's guns, traps and poisons. A better under-standing of the relationship between wild carnivores and game animals would help us to develop new management techniques which avoid the recourse to wholesale slaughter: otherwise, despite legal protec-tion, golden eagles, wildcats and pine martens will continue to be killed by traps and poisoned baits allegedly set for vermin.

As regards the marine environment, Scotland's seal populations are important in international terms. The grey seal population, in particular, is substantial, with Britain being home to about half of the total world population, most of which are to be found in Scottish waters. But their voracious appetite for fish brings them into competition with human fishermen and salmon farmers. It is claimed that grey seals eat the equivalent of half the tonnage of fish landed from the Scottish fisheries, although the fish which seals eat are not necessarily commercial species. Finding a resolution of this perpetual conflict will not be easy. The grey seal is a legally protected animal, although fishermen are allowed to shoot seals in the vicinity of their nets and salmon cages. But any attempt to reduce the seal population, by the culling of cubs for instance, is met with public outrage. The problem, as is so often the case, is that we simply do not have enough information on the true picture.

In 1987 a deadly disease struck the North Sea common seal population, killing more than 18,000 animals during an epidemic of the newly-discovered phocine distemper virus. Mercifully the Scottish popu-lation of common seals, which is found largely along the west and north coasts, was much less severely affected than that in other countries. We do not know why Scotland's seals escaped so lightly; but Scottish animals may become an important source of stock to repopulate the North Sea when the pollution problems, which may have reduced the seals' ability to resist this disease, are resolved.

But seals face new threats from a new and expanding industry. Salmon farmed in cages in the sea lochs are a ready-made food source for all fish-eaters, and this has brought seals, in particular, into conflict with humans. Investment in better protection for the farmed salmon could help to solve this particular problem.

Whales, dolphins and porpoises are also common around Scottish coasts, especially in the west. Inshore species such as porpoises and bottle-nosed dolphins have suffered greatly in recent years from pollution, waterside developments and disturbance by speedboats and jet-skis. Even now the last inshore school of bottle-nosed dolphins which survives in the relatively unspoilt Cromarty Firth is threatened by industrial expansion and the construction of a raw sewage outfall. We must look very carefully to balance human needs and wildlife needs: if we carry on as we are doing, the dolphin problem will cease to be a problem as the last dolphins disappear.

On land the banning of chemical pesticides like DDT and dieldrin in the 1960s was successful in helping the

Bottlenose dolphins in the Moray Firth are threatened by pollution from sewage and industrial effluents.

peregrine falcon and other raptors to recover from disastrous breeding results caused by eggshell thinning, and adult deaths caused by direct poisoning (see Chapter 5). But new threats face our wildlife. The infamous PCBs (polychlorinated biphenyls) are known to concentrate in the predators at the top of food chains; this means that hawks, dolphins, whales, seals, otters and other predators are at risk. We do not know what effect PCBs will have on carnivores in the future, or whether we can rid the environment of them; but the only safe thing to do is to stop them being released into the environment and to continue to monitor their presence in animals.

Not all Scotland's wildlife is on the defensive, however. Some animals have responded very well to the new urban habitats created by humans. Foxes, and now badgers, have infiltrated cities to take advantage of our wasteful food habits: one human's rubbish is clearly another animal's food. Safe from persecution, and with an assured supply of food, foxes and badgers can survive at higher population densities than their country cousins.

Sparrowhawks have also invaded the suburbs, despite their normally shy nature. They have exchanged their traditional woodland homes for parks and gardens as new hunting grounds. No doubt bird tables and garden nest-boxes have helped to ensure a good food supply.

Scotland's wildlife is basically in good shape – but what might happen in the future? Some people have suggested that the wolf could be re-introduced to control Scotland's huge deer population. This usually receives a swift and negative reply from sheep farmers, who see their stock as fair game for the big bad wolf. But if we can overcome our primal fear and hatred of the wolf, would it be such a bad thing? In Italy the wolf has somehow managed to survive, and active conservation has seen its population rise to over 300. In Italy attacks on livestock have been minimised by re-establishing the natural prey of the wolf, and a compensation scheme for both real and alleged kills made by wolves has proved very popular with local farmers.

The lynx is another predator which could conceivably be re-introduced to Scotland, but only with local support. Again, fears of sheep-killing weigh against this at the present time. Attempts to re-establish the lynx elsewhere in Europe have had varied results. In successful cases the lynx has flourished almost unnoticed, for it is extremely shy of people; but elsewhere, notably in France, lynx have become sheep-killers, perhaps because they could not find sufficient natural prey.

Far more important than restoring lost species, though, will be to ensure that we keep what we already have, and we can only do this by protecting the habitat of the animals in question. It is up to us if future generations are to be able to appreciate, use and benefit from Scotland's unique wildlife heritage. Scotland's wildlife is very special; let us all do our best to keep it that way.

Puffins in Shetland have not bred successfully for some years due to the lack of sand eels.

The Birds and their Habitats

DAVID MINNS

David Minns, RSPB Senior Conservation Officer for Scotland, focuses on some of the problems facing Scotland's birdlife.

The Royal Society for the Protection of Birds (RSPB) has identified a list of 116 'priority species' of birds in Britain which are under threat for various reasons. More than half of these occur mainly or wholly in Scotland. But that does not make them solely a Scottish concern; many of them migrate to Scotland to breed or to spend the winter here, and thus we also have obligations to the world for them.

SEABIRDS

When we say seabirds we tend to think of gulls wheeling around our harbours and seaside towns or terns darting and swooping along summer beaches. But many groups of birds use the sea; some of them, like guillemots, razorbills and puffins use it all the year round; others only at certain times, like grebes and divers which winter on sheltered inshore waters but nest on inland freshwater lochs.

It is essentially for cliff-nesting seabirds that Scotland provides so many living places. Our towering cliffs may hold some six million birds in summer. Scotland is home to well over half of all the world's razorbills, more than half of the world's gannets and a high proportion of Europe's ground-nesting terns. The great skua, that splendid robber-baron of the northern seas, has its world headquarters in Shetland (where it is called the 'bonxie'); and Shetland is also home to many of Britain's arctic skuas and red-throated divers (Box 1).

All of these birds, and many human communities too, depend on fish, a resource which we have traditionally regarded as limitless. But as far as seabirds are concerned it is the smaller fish, hitherto not normally caught for human consumption, that have caused the most recent problems – in particular, the sand eel. The warning signs came in 1984, when the arctic terns on Shetland raised very few chicks. In 1985 and 1986 they failed again, almost totally: tern chicks were literally starving to death because their parents could not find any sand eels, their staple diet, to feed them with. The crisis has grown and the tern population has dropped by 60 per cent. Puffins and kittiwakes have also suffered badly, since they also feed on sand eels near the surface of the water.

Although there is no scientific proof yet as to why the sand eels have disappeared from their traditional areas round Shetland, it is reasonable to assume that the relatively recent commercial fishing of sand eels (for fish-meal for salmon farms!) must have had at least a contributory effect. Fortunately, after several years of campaigning by the RSPB, the Shetland Bird Club, the Scottish Wildlife Trust and other bodies, this fishery has been closed until stocks recover. How long this will take remains to be seen.

WADERS AND WILDFOWL

Waders are among the most attractive and popular groups of birds in the world: long-legged and gregarious creatures that add vivid life to their wetland haunts. They breed in marshy tundra, moorland and grassland. They winter on estuaries and muddy or sandy seashores and can be found at freshwater margins chiefly on migration in spring and autumn.

Scotland has two areas that are of special importance for breeding waders: the machair land of the Western Isles and the Flow Country in Caithness and Sutherland.

The first special place, the machair, is found mainly down the west coast of the Western Isles and in a few other places like Tiree and small areas of Orkney and Shetland. The low-intensity use of the land and the very low levels of pesticides have resulted in exceptionally high numbers of birds.

To walk on the machair in summer is an amazing experience: the birds are everywhere, together with carpets of wild flowers such as are seldom seen nowadays except on nature reserves. Dunlin, ringed plover, oyster-catcher and lapwing nest here at some of the highest densities found in Western Europe. For example, in 1988 on the 1600 acre (650 ha) RSPB reserve at Balranald on North Uist there were no fewer than 178 pairs of oystercatcher, 94 pairs of ringed plover, 288 pairs of lapwing, 93 pairs of dunlin, 60 pairs of snipe

The gannetries of Scotland are of international importance.

and 115 pairs of redshank nesting, as well as 125 pairs of ducks and eleven calling corncrakes! (Box 3).

The other area of enormous importance for breeding waders is the Flow Country of Caithness and Sutherland. Not many years ago this area near the top of mainland Scotland was virtually unknown, perhaps even to residents of these two districts who seldom had cause to go into it unless they were anglers.

'Flows' (from the Old Norse word *flói*, meaning 'marshy ground') are areas of blanket peatland for which Scotland is internationally important. From above they show a distinctive pattern of pools and vegetation in concentric arcs which appear to 'flow' across the landscape. The largest area, almost 1,500 square miles of east Sutherland and west Caithness, has been practically untouched by human hand for 7,000 years.

Until the end of the 1970s this land was largely grazed only by deer, together with some sheep, and was famed mainly for the high-quality fishing on its many lochs and rivers. It was also excellent for waders, with some 70 per cent of the European Community's breeding population of greenshank, as well as providing a home for 20 per cent of the Community's dwindling numbers of black-throated divers; but there had been few proper bird surveys. The Flow Country was not regarded as threatened in any way.

In the early 1980s, however, several huge estates were sold off to a private forestry company. Between 1980 and 1986 it bought up nearly 100,000 acres (40,000 ha) at the amazingly low average price of £15 an acre. By 1987 some 35,000 acres (14,200 ha) had been sold on to private investors, in parcels averaging 350 acres (142 ha). Tax relief was the main attraction because in those days people paying the top rate of 60 per cent income tax could, when the planting grant was included, have 70 per cent of their forest paid for by the taxpayer. This could amount to nearly £300 per acre which, over the average parcel of land mentioned, came to over £100,000. In addition, all timber sales would be tax free, making forestry the only industry subject to a 'double subsidy'.

By 1987 some 80,000 acres (32,000 ha) of prime flows had been ploughed up and drained. The ecological damage caused was incalculable, but sample surveys suggested that some 640 pairs of golden plover, over 300 pairs of dunlin and, rarest of all, over 120 pairs of greenshank had their unique habitat destroyed. Worse still in some people's eyes, a huge part of this pristine area of primeval country had been violated beyond redemption – and to no good purpose, because earlier experimental plantations by the Forestry Commission had indicated that the waterlogged windswept peat was totally unsuitable for forestry.

The RSPB, supported by the Nature Conservancy Council, launched a vigorous campaign against the whole project; the media responded with gusto, and in

Red Throated Diver

1. DIVERS

Britain has two resident species of divers, both of them confined to the north and west of Scotland – the red-throated and the black-throated. Of the two the black-throated is much the rarer, with only about 150 breeding pairs left in Britain; the red-throated bird is particularly a denizen of Shetland where its 700 breeding pairs make up 70 per cent of the British population.

Divers are always listed first in bird books because they are considered the most primitive of birds. Their legs are set at the rear of the body in order to maximise their paddle-power, which makes them extremely ungainly on land. They are water birds par excellence and as such are wonderfully elegant and attractive.

The main difference is that the red-throated diver nests on small lochans but seeks its food in the sea whereas the black-throated feeds in the freshwater loch where it nests. This makes it particularly vulnerable to the general deterioration in the upland environment – the removal of the natural vegetation of forest and scrub coupled with the problem of acid rain affecting the water of the lochs, and the plantations of conifers that acidify the watercourses.

Both divers are extremely shy birds and are easily disturbed from their nests, often by fishermen. These nests are sometimes on the shores of a loch, but more usually on an island where the birds feel more secure. Some organisations, notably the Forestry Commission, are now providing artificial islands for nesting divers in our northern lochs. These may not solve the problem of declining populations; but they are a welcome step in the direction of trying to keep for Scotland some of our most hauntingly lovely northern birds.

the 1988 Budget tax relief on forestry was abolished.

In the wake of the campaign The Scottish Office urged the Highland Regional Council to produce a 'land-use strategy' for Caithness and Sutherland, and the Nature Conservancy Council was set the task of designating large tracts of land as Sites of Special Scientific Interest (SSSIs). The Highland Regional Council's report eventually divided the whole of the two districts into four zones according to their availability for forestry, classified as Unsuitable, Undesirable, Possible and Preferable.

It was an uneasy compromise and the potential for conflict is still there; but at least the conservationists, having lost a lot of early ground because they were never consulted, were able to save what could be saved by their strong rearguard action.

GEESE

Huge flocks of geese spend the winter in Scotland – and their numbers are increasing. In September and October they migrate south from their breeding grounds in Iceland, Greenland and arctic Russia and stay in Scotland until March or April the following year (Box 4).

The geese which come to Scotland have nested on tundra during the short arctic summer. They nest in a hostile environment under precarious conditions; if the arctic summer is late starting, they may not rear any young at all. For geese, therefore, winter survival is much more critical for the species than it is for more prolific breeders such as our garden birds, some of which rear three broods a year.

The sight of skeins of these magnificent birds scything across the skies; the sound of their haunting voices as they call to each other for contact or in alarm; the view of a feeding flock seeming to form a rolling grey carpet as they move over the fields – there is no doubt that wild geese can, and do, stir the heart of even the most hardened city-dweller.

However, not everyone welcomes the return of the geese each winter, particularly in districts where the largest flocks gather. Traditionally geese wintered on stubble, rough pastures and unreclaimed salt-marshes; even then there was conflict as farmers needed the grass for their cattle and sheep. But farmers increasingly sow winter cereals which sprout from January to March, providing an unexpected feast for geese during their hardest months when food is in short supply. This new source of food in these critically cold months must have been an important factor in the increase in the numbers of geese now wintering in Scotland.

The island of Islay, in particular, has suffered a large increase in numbers, particularly of barnacle geese. Some 70 per cent of the Greenland stock now winters on the island, over 20,000 birds in all. The main goose areas, at Gruinart, Bridgend and Laggan, are now

Greenshank are threatened by the afforestation of their habitat in the Flow country.

2. THE GREAT AUK: SCOTLAND'S OWN DODO

The great auk (*Pinguinis impennis*) was once abundant and widespread throughout the North Atlantic, living in huge colonies on rocky islands. But it was flightless, like the penguin, and so became an easy source of food and feathers and fat for Man. By the end of the eighteenth century the number of great auks plummeted until they were close to extinction. The last Scottish great auk met its end on St Kilda in 1840 at the hands of people who did not know what it was and were actually afraid of it. The last two recorded birds anywhere were killed on a remote rock stack off south-west Iceland in 1844 in the cause of 'science', their bodies destined for the taxidermist. The great auk is now extinct throughout the world; it can never be brought back.

Nowadays the word 'dodo' is often used to signify someone who is stupid. But who was the more stupid – the flightless dodo in Mauritius or the men who, as with our own great auk, killed off a ready food supply and a charming species?

Reconstruction of the Great Auk, Scotland's own dodo, by the National Museums of Scotland.

67

The corncrake has disappeared from mainland Scotland and survives only in the traditional crofting areas of the Western Isles.

3. THE CORNCRAKE

The corncrake is more often heard than seen. It has a loud rasping call which can be imitated by drawing two notched bones across each other, which gave rise to its onomatopoeic scientific name, *crex crex*. The unmistakable voice of the corncrake sounding across the early summer meadows and hayfields at dusk evokes all the nostalgia of the countryside. And nostalgia it is, because the corncrake has declined greatly all over Western Europe throughout this century.

It is a summer visitor to Britain, arriving here to breed during late April or early May after spending the winter in south-east Africa. It is extremely shy and elusive, a solitary well-camouflaged creature that hides among long grass and other tall plants, betraying its presence only by that distinctive call in the evenings. When it takes flight the large bright chestnut areas on its wings catch the eye and mark it out from similar birds like the quail.

Today in the British Isles the corncrake is almost entirely confined to the Western Isles of Scotland, with a few surviving enclaves in Ireland. The reason for its catastrophic decline is that it has been unable to survive alongside intensive agriculture. The loss of hedgerows, hedgebanks and rough field margins has left the corncrake with ever fewer suitable areas for breeding; and earlier mowing of grass, especially for silage, has destroyed nests, thus preventing corncrakes from raising their young in hayfields.

Only where traditional methods of agriculture are still used, as in the crofting machair lands, does the corncrake have a chance. Its survival depends on how and when the farmer mows the hay. If mechanical mowers are used in May or June, working a field from the outer edge inwards, they will destroy the nest and the sitting bird, or drive any chicks towards the centre of the field where they are killed.

Sadly, the decline in corncrake numbers is still going on; but sympathetic and concerted action by the farmers involved, supported by compensation schemes, can save it from extinction in its last refuges.

designated as Sites of Special Scientific Interest (SSSIs) and farmers on such land can receive compensation for destruction of crops by grazing geese and for managing it in a particular way. Farmers may also receive government grants for licensed scaring of the geese off land which lies outside SSSIs. But not all farmers benefit from these schemes, which can lead to resentment.

The RSPB, for its part, purchased Aoradh farm at Gruinart and manages it as a nature reserve to provide winter pasture for the geese. The grass is grazed by cattle which keep it at the right length for the birds. The RSPB aims to create a sanctuary which will attract as many geese as possible, thus relieving grazing pressure on other farmers' land.

Are there too many geese now for the island farms to sustain? Do they still require the rigorous protection afforded by law to endangered species? Some licences are issued each year to farmers to shoot small numbers of marauding birds on their land; but there are those who now suggest that there should be controlled culling of the birds, particularly the barnacle geese. But however large the numbers may seem in any one year, the precarious conditions under which they breed mean that goose populations can fluctuate widely and are potentially under considerable stress. Deterioration or disturbance of their wintering grounds could add a further threat to their continued survival. There is still a lot of research to be done before we can decide how best to conserve these magnificent creatures – and at what population level.

BIRDS OF PREY

Scotland boasts a good selection of birds of prey, which enjoy varying fortunes. Some, like the golden eagle (Box 5) and the osprey (Box 6), are thriving; others, such as the dashing little merlin and the fierce hen harrier, are not.

For many decades Man regarded birds of prey as a threat to his activities. Sadly, in many areas, the attitude still persists that any bird with a hooked bill should be exterminated. Traditionally, birds of prey were shot or trapped – and that still happens; but nowadays many of them are poisoned.

It is all too easy. A rabbit carcass is laced with poison and slung out on to the hill, supposedly to be taken by foxes and crows. But poison is indiscriminate. Many a carcass is spotted by a sharp-eyed bird of prey which promptly swoops down for a feed. Often the poison kills so quickly that the bird is found dead beside the bait.

The number of birds killed in this way is unknown, but reported cases have been rising steeply in recent years: twenty-seven in 1986, thirty-eight in 1987, forty-five in 1988, seventy-three in 1989. However, these are only the tip of the iceberg; poisoning is usually carried out in remote and sparsely populated areas where many victims perish unnoticed. In the last five years alone the RSPB has recorded some forty-five buzzards, ten other birds of prey and 156 other wildlife species, all poisoned; in addition, twenty-three dogs were killed in this way. In 1983 a gamekeeper actually died after ingesting a small amount of a poison called Phosdrin which he had been diluting in a cup. That chemical has been withdrawn by the main manufacturer, Shell, but it still turns up: in 1989 seven out of forty cases handled by the Department of Agriculture's Wildlife Investigation Service involved Phosdrin.

This continuous flouting of the law is a grave affront to everyone who has the nature of Scotland at heart. It has been suggested that poisons could be chemically 'tagged' so that they can be traced to the individual purchaser as a way of bringing him to justice. But perhaps the most effective weapons for the future will be education and the power of publicity. Estate owners cannot afford to have their image constantly tarnished by the law-breakers; there is now unprecedented public interest in wildlife, and public opinion is not going to allow the present shameful situation to continue.

Some areas of Scotland are more badly affected than others by the use of poisoned bait. One of the worst affected is the Borders region. I have been travelling up and down in the Borders for over forty years, and I have never seen a single buzzard there, let alone a golden eagle, despite the fact that the buzzard is the commonest of Britain's larger birds of prey. There are one or two pairs of buzzards – but they should be common everywhere, as clearly visible to the casual visitor's eye as they are in parts of the Highlands. The habitat is perfect for them, with a good mixture of moors, woods and farmland. The only reason for their absence is deliberate persecution by Man. I love the Border country very much; it has beautiful towns and villages as well as handsome countryside. But it is a national disgrace that these splendid birds are not allowed to roam free for everyone's enjoyment.

But at least there is one success story to report in the movement to save our raptors from wanton destruction, and that concerns the peregrine falcon (Box 7). The peregrine is one of the most successful species in the world; but in the 1950s, numbers dropped disastrously and apparently without explanation. Eventually, after patient scientific detective work, it was found that the peregrine was being systematically, but accidentally, poisoned by the pesticides which man had been developing, specifically the persistent organo-chlorines such as DDT.

Chemicals like DDT had been used extensively during the Second World War against insects which transmitted diseases such as malaria, and had saved the lives of untold numbers of servicemen. After the war they were used against agricultural pests, and again were found to be extremely effective. But during the latter half of the 1950s reports began to come in of large numbers of seed-eating birds found dead in farming districts; the cause of their deaths was traced to the birds having eaten grain treated with some of the new insecticides. It was now only a matter of time before birds of prey such as the peregrine, at the top of the food chain, became affected by eating poisoned birds. As

4. WINTERING GEESE

Scotland is of international importance as a wintering ground for several particular species of wild goose, all of which have remarkably restricted breeding ranges.

The most common is the pink-footed goose, which has its largest breeding colony in the central hinterlands of Iceland and smaller colonies in east Greenland and Spitsbergen. There are about 180,000 of them now and as many as a quarter of them descend each October on a small loch in Strathmore in Angus, on the east coast of Scotland. The elegant dark-headed pink-feet are cousins to the slightly larger greylag goose (the ancestor of our farmyard goose), whose numbers have also increased dramatically in the last thirty years, from 25,000 to 110,000.

The white-fronted goose (so named because of the white on the front of its head at the base of the bill) is the smallest of the 'grey geese' that come to Scotland – and the rarest. It nests in Greenland and Siberia; the Scottish birds all come from Greenland, a race known as the Greenland white-fronted goose distinguished from other white-fronts by having an orange bill. There may be only 10,000 of the Greenland race in the world and some 8,000 of them winter in Scotland, where they concentrate on the green jewel of the Hebridean crown, the island of Islay; the rest winter in southern Ireland.

The smaller grey-black-and-white barred barnacle goose is the third of Scotland's important wintering geese; it was so named because people thought that they emerged from barnacles every year! Barnacle geese breed in the Arctic, where they form three distinct populations: the largest, from Siberia, winters in Holland; another breeds in Spitsbergen and winters on the Solway coast; a third nests in east Greenland but spends the winter on Islay and a few other west coast islands. By the end of October there may be as many as 30,000 barnacle geese on Islay, feeding in tightly-packed congregations at a few choice locations. Under the protection of the law the world population of barnacle geese has risen from some 30,000 birds to 70,000 today; and many people now consider them an agricultural pest.

Barnacle geese on the Isle of Islay.

5. THE GOLDEN EAGLE

Ask most people which bird they think of when Scotland is mentioned and as often as not the golden eagle will be their first choice. It is a majestic bird, and few sights can be more thrilling than an eagle soaring and spiralling over its mountain territory.

It is also Scotland's bird par excellence. There are some 400–450 breeding pairs in Britain, and all but one or two live in Scotland – the largest population in Europe apart from Spain and north-ern Scandinavia. But it is still extremely vulnerable. Eagles are long-lived birds which are slow to mature – they do not normally breed until five years old, and they normally rear only one young per year. Their habitat has been seriously reduced in modern times by forestry plantations and on top of all that they are still heavily persecuted by gamekeepers. It is something of a miracle that any survive at all!

well as killing adult birds the pesticides also caused the thinning of eggshells, which broke when the birds tried to incubate them. The poisons also caused adults to exhibit grossly abnormal behaviour such as eating their own eggs.

The scientific evidence presented by the RSPB and the British Trust for Ornithology was so strong that several chemicals for treating seed, including dieldrin, were placed under voluntary ban in the spring of 1962. The restrictions were extended in 1964 and, although DDT itself was not officially banned until 1984, its use declined sharply, probably because of the adverse publicity which had been incurred.

By 1967 the peregrine population began to pull out of its plummeting decline. By 1981 some 90 per cent of pre-war eyries were being occupied again. The saving of the peregrine, one of our most magnificent wild crea-tures, was part of the coming of age of the modern science-based conservation movement, and an object lesson that wildlife can act as a vital indicator of the health of our environment.

RE-INTRODUCTIONS

Even with the peregrine restored to its former eminence, and the golden eagle quartering most of the available territory in Scotland, there is still so much open space and open sky in Scotland that there is ample room for the other birds of prey which once flourished here. And there are two exciting enterprises under way to restore Scotland's portfolio of raptors to something like its former glory: one is a project to re-introduce the sea eagle, the other is an attempt to bring back the red kite.

The sea eagle (Box 8), or white-tailed eagle as it is sometimes called, used to nest round the rocky coasts of northern and western Britain and originally as far south as Cornwall; however its main stronghold was always Scotland, with more than a hundred pairs nesting around the north and west coasts, although a few nested inland in places such as Rannoch. After a century of almost continuous persecution by shepherds and gamekeepers, when the Highlands were 'cleared' for sheep and red deer, the sea eagle finally became extinct in Britain early this century. The last known breeding attempt in Scotland was on Skye in 1916, and the very last bird, an albino (white) female believed to have been about thirty years old, was shot in Shetland two years later.

Fortunately the sea eagle breeds over a wide range across the northern hemisphere and, despite major declines in other European countries, it held on in Scandinavia. People waited in vain for it to recolonise Britain naturally, as the osprey has done: but our islands seem to be beyond wandering range of other sea eagles, which are less far-ranging than ospreys. There were two early attempts to re-introduce the birds, to Glen Etive in Argyll in 1959 and to Fair Isle (by the RSPB) in 1968 involving seven birds in all, but both projects came to nothing.

Eventually, in 1975, a more thorough programme was launched on the island of Rhum, which is owned and managed by the Nature Conservancy Council for Scotland as a National Nature Reserve. Over the next ten years, eighty-two young sea eagles from northern Norway were flown over to Scotland (courtesy of RAF Kinloss) and released on Rhum. This was a joint enterprise involving the old NCC, the RSPB and a generous sponsor, Eagle Star Insurance.

The birds were kept tethered and provided with food for a while to accustom them to their new surroundings, and then released to fly free. The first nest was built in 1982, and in 1983 two pairs laid eggs but failed to hatch them. In 1984 there were at least four nests, two of them with eggs, but still no successful hatching. At last, in 1985, came the breakthrough, when a Scottish-born sea eaglet took to the Scottish skies for the first time in almost seventy years. Since then there has been slow but steady progress: in 1989 eight pairs laid eggs, from which five young birds hatched. This brought the total up to thirteen young successfully reared in Scotland.

However, it is all too certain that the sea eagle's lot will not be any easier than that of its cousin, the golden

6. THE OSPREY

The osprey, or fish-eagle as it is sometimes called, has been a spectacular success story for determined conservationists. Once upon a time the osprey bred freely, although not commonly, throughout the Scottish Highlands as well as in other parts of Britain. But throughout the nineteenth century it was severely persecuted by gamekeepers, along with the red kite and the sea eagle. It was also the victim of Victorian collectors and trophy hunters who sought its beautiful skin and boldly-blotched eggs. By the turn of the century it was practically extinct as a breeding bird in Britain.

After an absence of some fifty years, single birds began to return to the lochs and pine forests of the Highlands in the breeding season; and soon attempts at breeding occurred. The news leaked out, and some early nests were robbed of their eggs by fanatical collectors. So in 1959, to enlist public support, the RSPB 'went public' over the successful hatching of three osprey chicks at Loch Garten – and invited the public to come and see them from a special observation hide at a safe distance from the eyrie. Within the next six weeks, while the birds were still at the nest, no fewer than 14,000 visitors came to see the osprey family.

Since then the nest has been guarded night and day. Hundreds of volunteers and RSPB staff have kept watch over the Loch Garten birds in 'Operation Osprey', and well over a million members of the public, who might otherwise never have seen these spectacular birds, have visited the osprey centre. Closed circuit television now brings the nest and its occupants even closer.

The focus of attention on the Loch Garten site has allowed a growing number of ospreys to nest undisturbed; there are now well over fifty pairs in Scotland, producing a total of about seventy-five young each year. With prospects of recolonising England, ospreys can now be said to be out of danger in this country.

eagle: already at least two sea eagles have been found poisoned by illegal baits, one in Caithness and one in Skye. It remains to be seen whether the sea eagle will now be able to recolonise permanently or whether further re-introduction may be necessary in order to reinforce the tiny 'native' population.

The red kite is a beautiful, swallow-tailed, agile bird

7. THE PEREGRINE FALCON

The peregrine is the prince of all falcons, the consummate master of the air. Down the centuries it has been prized by falconers above all other birds for its speed and rapacity. The hunting peregrine is one of the fastest birds alive, reaching 50 miles per hour (80 km/h) in level flight with rapid shallow beats of its long pointed wings and stooping on its quarry with its deadly talons at speeds of up to 180 mph (290 km/h). It is also a great wanderer, or peregrinator as its name implies, and occurs throughout the world. It is everyone's favourite falcon.

Yet there was a time in the 1960s and 1970s when the Scottish Highlands held probably the only remaining healthy population of peregrines in the world. It was the time of the great population crash caused by chemical pesticides. But Scotland's birds survived. Because of our temperate climate there is less pressure on Scottish peregrines in the Highlands to migrate south in the winter; they simply move from the higher country down to farmland or to the coast. When the pesticide crisis struck, Scotland's birds were less affected than the populations of other countries, although their numbers did show a decline. They are now comfortably back to pre-war levels.

The main threat to the peregrine is no longer pesticides but the robbing of nests by egg collectors.

The snowy owl occasionally ventures as far south as Shetland to breed.

The sea eagle was exterminated by game keepers during the 19th century but has been reintroduced to Scotland during the 1980s.

were brought across to Scotland from Sweden, where numbers are high, and released in a suitable part of the Highlands after the necessary period of quarantine and acclimatisation. They were fitted with lightweight radio transmitters which enabled RSPB researchers to track their movements for the first six months.

Tragically, after only five months of freedom in Scotland, one of the six was found poisoned. If nothing else, it shows how widespread the illegal use of poison must be for one of only six such birds in the whole of Scotland to fall victim within such a short time.

PINEWOOD BIRDS

Our last group of special birds are denizens of one of the most threatened habitats in Scotland – the ancient Caledonian pineforest, the fragmentary remnant of the great 'wildwood' that carpeted much of Scotland after the last Ice Age (see Chapter 3). Today there are fewer than 30,000 acres (12,000 ha) left: in the past 500 years we have destroyed over 99 per cent of our equivalent of the rain forests. Thirty years ago we were left with a mere one per cent; since then we have destroyed a quarter of even that meagre one per cent.

A whole community of birds lives in and around the remnants of the pinewoods, which provide a rich and diverse habitat for a marvellous assemblage of fauna and flora; but we shall concentrate on three very special birds.

The first is our largest grouse, the capercaillie. It is yet another of the birds of Scotland that was driven to extinction by a combination of habitat loss through deforestation and through over-hunting: the last two cock capercaillie were shot in Aberdeenshire in 1785. Fifty years later the capercaillie was successfully re-introduced when a collection of thirty-two birds from Sweden was brought to the Breadalbane estates in Perthshire in 1837, and quickly became widespread

which was once very common but is now one of Britain's rarest birds of prey. Throughout the nineteenth century it was persecuted almost to extermination until, by the start of this century, only a few pairs were left hanging on in the remote valleys of central Wales. Kite protection schemes were started as early as 1904; but by 1989 there were still only fifty-three breeding pairs in Wales.

The hope has always been that they would spread out, but this has never happened, partly because of poor breeding success in Wales and partly because of the inevitable poisoning and illegal shooting. So in 1989 another ambitious re-introduction project was launched jointly by the NCC and RSPB: six young red kites

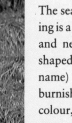

8. THE SEA EAGLE

The sea eagle is a magnificent creature. Its colouring is a light brownish grey, the feathers of the head and neck a lichen white, with a short, wedge-shaped tail of pure white (hence its alternative name) and a massive hooked bill of brilliant burnished yellow. The eyes are a pale honey colour, which has earned the bird the poetic Gaelic name of *Iolaire suil na greina*, 'the eagle with the sunlit eye'.

It is a huge bulky bird, with very broad wings and a wingspan of well over six feet (1.8 m), the largest of any British bird. It has a heavy flapping flight as it hunts low over land and water, feeding

on fish, seabirds and small mammals, and it announces its presence with a variety of barking calls.

Like the golden eagle the sea eagle does not mature for breeding until it is about five years old, but the courtship display is well worth waiting for. The birds grapple their talons in mid air and plummet cartwheeling earthwards in a spectacular frenzy. They nest on sea-cliff ledges, or sometimes in trees; these nests are guarded by the NCC for Scotland and the RSPB as if they were the crown jewels themselves.

again in many parts of Scotland. But there was a major problem, arising from a historical anomaly; although the capercaillie was clearly a game bird it was never classified as such because it had become extinct by the time the first game laws were drawn up; and its winter diet of conifer shoots and buds and young cones made it so unpopular with foresters that it was treated as a pest. It was only when it did become treated as a game bird by sportsmen that it began to thrive again.

For the last fifteen years, however, the population has been in decline again, and for the same old reasons – habitat loss as the pinewoods were destroyed and over-shooting. This time, however, there is a general desire to ensure its survival. Several estate owners (including the Forestry Commission) have stopped all shooting on their land and official and voluntary bodies alike are working on woodland management policies with the capercaillie specifically in mind.

Our second special bird of the pinewoods is the delightful crested tit. This charming little black and white bird with a distinctive crest on the back of its head is so shy and elusive that it can often be detected only by its trilling call. It is widespread on the continent, but in Britain is only found in the Scottish pinewoods, and even there it is confined to just a few areas. Its main territories are found in the woods along the valley of the River Spey and those to the north in the catchment of the Beauly river; for some unknown reason it is not found on Deeside, to the east of the Cairngorms, even though there are some beautiful pinewood remnants there. But it is our hope that the bird will find its own way there one day, unaided.

Our third bird is the most special of all, because it is Scotland's only unique species: the Scottish crossbill. Originally it was regarded as a race of the common crossbill, which occurs much more widely throughout Britain and Europe but recently it has been classified as a full species, *Loxia scotica*.

Whereas the common crossbill feeds mainly on soft spruce cones our endemic native bird depends largely on Scots pine, particularly mature trees. It has evolved a powerful cross-over bill to deal with the much tougher cones of the Caledonian forest; it holds the cone down on a branch with one foot while it prises the cone open in order to extract the seed with its tongue.

The male is a striking crimson red, while the female is a subdued olive green. They nest early in the year, often in March or even February while the snow is still lying deep, when the food supply is coming up to its peak.

There may be as few as 300–400 pairs of Scottish crossbill in existence now, although numbers are difficult to estimate because it is hard to distinguish them from common crossbills in the field. But there is considerable hope for the future: the indications are that our native pinewoods have at last reached the nadir of their fortunes and are now on the way up again. Increasingly, more and more people recognise the

aesthetic and wildlife value of balanced forests of regenerating native pinewoods and associated broadleaves like birch and rowan.

The Scottish crossbill is the only bird that is unique to Scotland.

THE FUTURE

The challenge as we approach the 21st century is whether we can finally discard the outdated idea that nature is only there to be conquered or tamed: to be exploited to the limit in order to meet our immediate short-term needs. Perhaps, instead, we can genuinely accept the idea that it is not only beneficial but essential to safeguard as many of our natural resources as possible.

There are three valid reasons for this.

First, for ecological reasons: as we destroy one part of the matrix of life, we inevitably affect other parts. Sometimes this may not matter too much; but if it is done on a large enough scale, as we have done with our pinewoods and our fish stocks, then we progressively impoverish the resources which sustain our own lives. Remember, too, that birds like the peregrine are valuable indicators of the general health of our environment because they are at the top of the food chain (like humans). They are also relatively easy to observe and monitor.

Second, for genetic purposes: we do not know if or when genetic material in plant and animal species, which at present have no apparent use, may prove to be of vital importance. Who would ever have predicted that penicillin would be discovered by studying mould?

The third reason for conserving and cherishing our wildlife is essentially spiritual or aesthetic: birds give so many people so much pleasure. Who has not been charmed by the song of a blackbird or the sight of a robin? There are no urgent conservation reasons for giving full legal protection to such common birds: they are in no way endangered. But we do protect them, simply because we like them. It is up to us to demonstrate with our actions that we care for our world, our own habitat, much more than we have done in the past.

9. THE BIRDWATCHER

I found myself facing a steel dawn. Sharp stinging raindrops whiplashed into my face on a northerly wind as I turned up my tweed collar and I was pleased to climb into the Land Rover and slam the door.

I was out in the grey dawn to watch capercaillie, the giant grouse of the Caledonian pineforest, strutting defiantly on the lek, wattles gorged, fan tail spread and great secateur bill thrust arrogantly upward. I tiptoed closer on cushions of sphagnum moss beneath a wood of ancient gnarled pines, through which the great birds planed in, twisting and turning on down-curving pinions to parade and affect like popinjays.

I lingered on long after the show was over, head back against the orange jigsaw bark of an old pine as I craned my neck to glimpse the flash and trill of tiny goldcrests weaving amongst the highest cones. As I did so a troop of Scottish crossbills swung in. Suddenly my early morning silence was strident with the gaudy shrieks of green and scarlet courtiers haggling over cones, snapping, clicking, cracking with forceps bills to extract the feathery seed and tumble the ravaged cone earthwards. For

a few minutes the forest rained pine cones and the trees were alive with riotous destruction – and then they were gone, their shrieks fading with each undulation as they swung away to a distant glade. I was alone with a single crestie, the tit which belongs to the pinewood, which trilled and fluttered around me in delicate contrast to the departed jesters.

For me the great prize of the Highlands is the golden eagle (Box 5) and its recently introduced cousin the sea eagle (Box 8). To witness these great birds spiralling upwards on huge open-fingered wings, or perched haughtily on a lonely crag, is to experience the very essence of wildness. Wildlife is there to be sought out in every season. In spring there are squelchy, muddy, bog-hopping days, tramping mountains of burnt-cork hue with red deer stags in brochure silhouette on the skyline and ptarmigan scuttling over lichen-patterned scree a few yards in front of you and, forced into flight, belching like drunks as they peel across the corrie in a snow flurry of silver and white.

There are delicate dotterel on the high tops, absurdly tame and a sexual paradox as the drab male incubates the eggs while the stripey eye-shadowed female stands and watches.

Thin piping laments of greenshank and golden plover waft across these hills on wind which sings like surf, and snow buntings, the pied sparrows of the Arctic, lurk and flit among the great jumble of glacier-strewn rocks.

Far below in the glens lie the glinting cloud-filled lochs and burns. Here among the gurgling peaty runnels are dippers and grey wagtails, ring ouzels and pipits. A glance upward to the piebald hills will often reveal the crossbow shape of the darting merlin, our smallest falcon; or suddenly and unexpectedly, invisible at first against the blue of the sky and the distant hill, your ear is tantalised by strains of blood-tingling music. Slowly eye and ear converge on a broad chevron of whooper swans, whiter than the April snow with bills thrust ever forward to their arctic breeding grounds and their haunting calls echoing round the corries below.

On the loch you will find goldeneye ducks, now breeding successfully in Speyside, bright and buoyant as they dive and bob back to the surface in twos and threes. The osprey (Box 6), wild-eyed and hunch-backed, grips the bleached branch of a dead pine, its red-indian headdress a rattle of feathers all defiant and spiky as it picks at the fist-clenched

Capercaillie displaying on the 'lek'.

trout. Once more it crashes into the loch in a shower of silver spray and grabs air on elbowy wings to fly over the pinewood to a family of five jammed into a foul-smelling nest.

Or yet again, on a smaller lonely loch, you can find one of Britain's rarest and most spectacular waterbirds, the Slavonian grebe, with outrageous marmalade eyebrows and glossy black satin jacket. These birds seem to have little fear of humans and sail breath-catchingly close if you sit quietly on the loch-side. When two meet they greet each other with elaborate sign language and display, eyebrows erect, ruby eyes sparkling, and the immaculately rehearsed grebe dance, upright, treading water to a high-pitched and penetrating trilling call.

On a few lonely northerly lochs you can find the most exquisite example of divine engineering and virtuoso art: the black-throated diver (Box 1), the pearl-diver whose eerie call echoes back and forth through the sad, beautiful upland it inhabits. It is as close to design perfection as one could ever hope to find. From the tip of its aqua-dynamic lancet bill over its streamlined black velvet head and pyjama-striped neck, it seems that droplets of shining water, like a handful of pearls, have been sprinkled across its coal-glossy back. Below the water-line even its shin bones are moulded into knife blades for cutting water on the forward stroke, and maximum thrust when the powerful webbed paddles push back.

On the coast, Scotland offers great oceans crashing in slow thunder against some of the oldest cliffs in the world; towering high-rise slums where hundreds of thousands of guillemots and gannets crowd together in a haggling squalid tangle of bills, wings and jarring wailing calls. Or again great expanses of shimmering shell-sand, white and shining to the fluttering waves. Here waders stand about one-legged and drowsy, killing time while the tide turns: curlew, dunlin, lapwing, oyster-catcher, godwit, ruff and reeve, and many more. Here one can witness scenes of great drama and thrill as a peregrine screams by, shattering the idyll and scattering frightened waders like chaff.

And, at the day's end, turning for home, from far out on the tidal mud come the calls of a thousand pink-footed and greylag geese to set the blood tingling and fix the unforgettable memory. They, too, head north to Iceland and beyond to far-off breeding grounds, up and away over the clouded

hills. They will be back before the year is out; and so, for certain, will I.

Sir John Lister Kaye, Chairman, North West region of the Nature Conservancy Council for Scotland.

The rare black-throated diver nests by a remote lochan.

75

The Peacock

The Beauty of Butterflies

RICHARD SUTCLIFFE

Richard Sutcliffe is the Assistant Keeper of Zoology at Kelvingrove Museum, Glasgow. He is chairman of the Glasgow and South-West Scotland branch of the British Butterfly Conservation Society (BBCS).

Scotland has only twenty-eight resident species of butterfly today in contrast with the sixty resident species found in Britain as a whole. The reasons for this are partly to do with the nature of Scotland itself in terms of climate and geology; but they are also closely connected with the great changes in farming practices over the past decades which have badly affected butterflies throughout Britain.

Climate has always been the major factor affecting the distribution of species, together with geology which determines the kind of food plants that grow in any area. The physical geography has sometimes isolated populations and has occasionally given rise to distinct subspecies, like the Meadow Brown in the east and the west of Scotland.

Butterflies have probably been present in Scotland for millions of years, apart from the gaps caused by the Ice Ages; there is no proof of this however, because no fossilised remains of butterflies have yet been found in Scotland. In fact we have no evidence of which species were present before recording started in the eighteenth century (Box 1); however we can to some extent hazard a guess as to which species have been present since the end of the last Ice Age.

Pollen records indicate that almost all of the food plants required by the caterpillars of today's Scottish butterflies had probably reached Scotland soon after the ice retreated. Such pollen records cannot of course prove that today's butterflies were actually present at that time, but it is likely that many species quickly recolonised Scotland as the climate improved.

Since Britain was still connected to mainland Europe by a land bridge until about 7,500 years ago, it was relatively easy for continental butterflies to move into Britain, following the spread of their food plants as they moved northwards. As temperatures rose, the first butterflies to arrive would have been migratory species like the Red Admiral and the Painted Lady, although they would not have been able to become resident here owing to the cold winters. However other species such as the Large and Small Whites may have become resident at that time.

These would have been rapidly followed by arctic and alpine species which could tolerate the cold conditions. Species from northern Europe would have moved in next, followed by the rest of the butterflies which we enjoy today. The last species to arrive would have been those whose caterpillars were dependent on trees for their food, such as the Purple Hairstreak which feeds exclusively on oak.

As the climate warmed, the arctic and alpine species probably died out or, like the Small Mountain Ringlet (Box 2), adapted to higher and cooler habitats. About 7,200 years ago there were probably twice as many species established in Scotland as there are today; indeed some continental species such as the Large Ringlet, Northern Wall Brown, Pearly Heath, Sooty Copper and Heath Fritillary may once have been quite common.

Apart from climate changes, Man has had a major effect on our butterflies – but only in recent times. At first the coming of early people to Scotland may actually have benefited butterflies (see Chapter 7). Small-scale forest clearance by Neolithic farmers would have diversified the available habitats, allowing some species to expand into new areas. As the clearance of forests continued through the centuries it was the large-scale felling of trees to produce charcoal for the iron smelting industry during the eighteenth century which probably affected butterflies most. Today there are very few areas of truly natural countryside in Scotland and most butterflies are found only in modified or man-made habitats.

The growth of towns and factories during the Industrial Revolution, together with the accompanying pollution, resulted in the further fragmentation and destruction of many former butterfly habitats; their decline has been most marked in the Central Belt of Scotland during the nineteenth and twentieth centuries.

Most of Scotland is farmland and changes in farming practice have drastically affected many butterfly sites. Many fields have been 'improved' by drainage schemes; thousands of miles of hedgerows have been grubbed out; much of our native broadleaved woodland has been destroyed and nearly all of our wildflower meadows and flower-rich hay meadows have been impoverished by herbicides. The massive increase in the use of fertilisers, herbicides and insecticides may have been healthy for farmers but it was extremely unhealthy for butterflies and other creatures which depend on natural habitats for their survival; chemical pesticides had the most damaging effect because they killed butterflies and other useful insects as well as the insect species for which they were intended.

As sites become smaller it becomes harder for some species to survive and local extinctions may result. The remaining sites become more isolated, making it increasingly difficult for butterflies to recolonise from surrounding areas as would have happened naturally in the past.

Butterfly collecting, which like egg-collecting was once a popular a pastime for vicars and schoolboys, probably did not have a great effect on butterfly populations, except where colonies had been reduced to critical levels by changes in climate or habitat. Today, however, there is very little justification for collecting Scottish butterflies, even though they are not protected by law as rigorously as are wild birds and their eggs. We can learn much more about butterflies by simply watching them, and taking photographs is far more rewarding than killing butterflies for display in a glass case.

SCOTLAND'S BUTTERFLIES TODAY

Although many of our butterflies are widely distributed

they are often not commonly seen. Most people are only familiar with three or four different butterflies: the 'Cabbage White' (actually two species, the Large and Small Whites, which some regard as pests), the Small Tortoiseshell and the Red Admiral, which are often seen visiting flowers in town gardens. It comes as a surprise to be told of the considerable variety of butterflies to be found in Scotland.

Most of them have quite different food and habitat requirements which account for their distribution. The Dingy Skipper, for example, must have bird's-foot trefoil for its caterpillars to feed on; nothing else is acceptable and if the plant does not grow in the area the butterfly will not be found. But the presence of the correct food plant does not always guarantee that the butterfly, too, will be present. The main food plant for the larvae of the Small Pearl Bordered Fritillary is the marsh violet, a common plant found throughout much of Scotland; but the butterfly has a much more limited distribution than the plant.

Not only must the plant be present but it must be at the right stage of growth and in a position which receives the right amount of sunshine and at the right temperature for the eggs and larvae to develop. This means that only a small proportion of all the available marsh violets is actually suitable for the insects to lay their eggs upon.

Some species such as the Marsh Fritillary (Box 4) and the Speckled Wood prefer a damp oceanic climate and tend to be found on the west coast. Other species, like the Small Heath and Meadow Brown, are much less

Johan Fabricius made the first recorded observations of butterflies in Scotland

Qvi Vetera illuſtri novitatis luce reſpergit
Atq vetuſtatis madat honore Nova.
FABRICIVS, Veterum quæriſimus atq Novorum.
Nonne inter doctos paginam utramq facit.
Jo Candorph. Wolfius.
Pa. E adS. Cathar Hamburg.

1. EARLY RECORDS

The earliest surviving records of Scottish butterflies date from the 1760s and come from Dr John Walker (1731–1804). He recorded the Peacock from Dumfriesshire and Iona in 1766; the Scotch Argus (Box 3) in Drysdale, Dumfriesshire and what was almost certainly the Large Skipper from Bute in 1769. The first published description of a Scottish species came in 1793 when Johan C. Fabricius (1745–1808) described *Hesparia artaxerxes* (the Northern Brown Argus (Box 7)). The nineteenth century saw a large number of naturalists collecting Scottish butterflies, so that the distribution of many species was quite well documented by the end of the century. Remarkably, however, it was only in 1939 that the Chequered Skipper (Box 6) was first collected in Scotland.

From these old records it appears that some species recorded in the past are now extinct in Scotland. The Small Skipper was recorded from Edinburgh in 1811 and Alloa in 1845. The Grizzled Skipper was recorded from southern Scotland: Glasgow in 1857 and Cairnryan in 1896. There are records of the White-Letter Hairstreak in Dumfries in 1859 and near Dunoon in 1884; similarly the Duke of Burgundy Fritillary in Dumfriesshire and Roxburghshire in the 1860s. The Comma and the Silver-Washed Fritillary certainly both occurred in Scotland in the last century but then suffered major declines. Many other species that have been recorded in Scotland were probably just vagrants and never became firmly established.

78

particular and are found throughout Scotland.

Different butterflies pass the bitter winter months at different stages of their life cycle: the Purple Hairstreak overwinters as an egg, the Common Blue as a larva and the Green Veined White as a pupa (chrysalis) while the Small Tortoiseshell and the Peacock both survive the winter by hibernating as adults. As a result each species is on the wing at different times of the year, usually between April and October. In addition a few species are able to complete their entire life cycle in a relatively short space of time. The Wall, the Speckled Wood and the Large, Small and Green Veined Whites are able to produce two and occasionally three broods of young each year. June is definitely the best month of the year to see butterflies and in a good year it is possible to see nearly all the Scottish species within that month if you are prepared to travel around a little.

A few species of butterfly migrate to Scotland regularly. The most common of these are the Red Admiral and the Painted Lady. In good years large numbers of these two species may appear anywhere in Scotland and often reach Shetland, the Western Isles and even St Kilda. Many of these butterflies may have travelled thousands of miles from north Africa and southern Europe, reaching Scotland as early as April. They may breed here, resulting in large numbers of 'home bred' individuals later in the year. However very few manage to survive the cold Scottish winters and thus they cannot establish themselves permanently here. There is often a noticeable southerly migration of these species in autumn as they seek warmer areas. The Clouded Yellow and the Camberwell Beauty also turn up from time to time, usually in very small numbers; however they cannot be relied on as regular visitors.

Very occasionally other species from the north of England may stray over the border into southern Scotland. The Holly Blue, for example, has turned up near Dumfries and there are reports of the Gatekeeper

2. THE SMALL MOUNTAIN RINGLET

At first glance this species is very similar to the Scotch Argus but it is in fact much smaller in size and lacks the white-pupilled eye spots. As its name suggests, the Small Mountain Ringlet is a species which prefers the mountains and is found at altitudes of up to 3,000 ft (1,000 m); it is mainly found in Inverness-shire, Argyll and Perthshire; an isolated population is also to be found on Ben Lomond. The only other localities where it is found in Britain are in the Lake District. Colonies tend to be quite small and are often confined to small gullies which tend to be more sheltered than the open hillsides. The butterflies emerge earlier at lower altitudes; the males fly in criss-cross patterns in search of the females which usually sit in the grass and fly much less.

One of the best places to see this butterfly is on the National Trust for Scotland's Ben Lawers Reserve on the northern side of Loch Tay, where it is usually common in early July.

3. THE SCOTCH ARGUS

As its name implies, the Scotch Argus is restricted to Scotland apart from a couple of sites in northern England. In Scotland, however, it is widely distributed, especially on moorland over 300 ft (90 m) above sea level; the only exception seems to be central Scotland where it has not been found.

The Scotch Argus can often be found close to established woodland or young forestry plantations, or in sheltered boggy areas where there is an abundance of its larval food plant, purple moor grass.

When the butterfly is found, there are often very large numbers. It tends to hide in long grass in dull weather but sunshine will quickly bring it out to take flight. It is unmistakable with its bright red (male) or orange (female) eye-spotted bands on each very dark brown wing. It is the latest of all the Scottish butterflies to appear, emerging only in July, and can be found until September.

The Common Blue

4. THE MARSH FRITILLARY

The Marsh Fritillary is in serious decline through-out Europe, and Scotland is probably one of its last great strongholds. It is a very sedentary species and even small barriers, such as hedges, arable land and woodlands, will often deter it from expanding into other areas. For this reason it tends to be restricted to very distinct colonies, usually in damp meadows, rough pasture or moorland, where it can find devil's bit scabious, the food plant on which the larvae feed. It is therefore particularly vulnerable to damage to its habitat and can quickly be exterminated from a given area. It is also prone to parasitism by an *Apanteles* wasp which occurs naturally in Marsh Fritillary colonies where it takes its toll of many larvae each year.

It is now almost confined to Argyll, apart from some of the Inner Hebrides, parts of Inverness-shire and Dunbartonshire. It was once found in other areas of Scotland but had disappeared from the Borders by the end of the nineteenth century, and from Perthshire and Dumfriesshire by 1950. This decline was probably due to the development of a more oceanic climate which began in the mid nineteenth century.

This very attractive butterfly is on the wing from the first week in June and can normally be found for about four weeks. It flies low over the ground, usually only in sunshine.

being seen close to the Solway Firth. It is possible that other species may turn up from time to time.

THE FUTURE

The Orange Tip is one of the few real butterfly success stories of recent years (Box 5). In the 1850s it was probably found throughout much of mainland Scotland but it suffered a major decline in the second half of the nineteenth century. For many years the species was confined to two areas in the Borders and the north-east. In the 1950s it began to expand its range outwards from these centres, probably as a result of gradual climatic changes with reduced spring rainfall and more sunshine which appeared to suit it. By the early 1980s it was clear that this expansion was gaining pace and it was turning up in many areas where it had never been recorded before. It is now widespread in the Lothians in the east and along the River Clyde and its tributaries in the west; it is also spreading southwards from Perthshire and is probably commoner in Scotland today than it has ever been since records began.

Other Scottish butterflies will undoubtedly benefit from climatic changes in the future. If global warming happens it would probably lead to an increase in those species for which southern Scotland is the northerly limit at present, such as the Wall and the Large Skipper. Unfortunately species like the Small Mountain Ringlet might find a warmer Scotland too warm and disappear. Much would depend on whether the climate became more oceanic or more continental, since subtle differences in the climate would affect different species in different ways.

The continuing loss and fragmentation of habitats are the main threats to Scotland's butterflies in the future. Misguided attempts to 'tidy up' areas of parkland or urban wasteland often destroy good breeding areas for many species of butterfly. This is particularly so for species such as the Small Heath and the Meadow Brown whose larvae feed on grasses. Long grass and other vegetation in parks is often cut routinely, destroying food plants while caterpillars are still feeding on them. If parks departments could be persuaded to cut only at times calculated to fit in with the butterflies' life cycles it would greatly reduce damage to colonies in those areas.

We need far more studies of Scottish butterflies in order to assess their needs and promote their conservation. Most work on British butterflies has been carried out in England where there are more species to study and more people to study them. Comparatively little work has been done on Scottish species, apart from some detailed work on the delightful Chequered Skipper (Box 6) and to a lesser extent on the Northern Brown Argus (Box 7).

For example the Ringlet's requirements in the cold wet acidic areas of central Scotland are probably very

5. THE ORANGE TIP

The male Orange Tip is unmistakable. The forewings have a bright orange patch, tipped with black on the otherwise white upper surface. The female is more difficult to distinguish at a distance, resembling a Large or Small White at first glance. Both sexes are easily recognised when the undersides are seen, as the hind wings exhibit what appear to be distinctive green marbled patterns. This is in fact an illusion: the green colour is produced by the combination of black and yellow scales on the wings.

The Orange Tip lays its eggs singly on a variety of plants but prefers lady's smock and to a lesser extent garlic mustard and dame's violet. The resulting larvae are cannibalistic so that only one will survive on each plant – a strategy which should ensure that there is enough food to satisfy the survivor rather than have several individuals starve. The caterpillar stage lasts about six weeks, after which it finds a suitable place to pupate. The pupa or chrysalis resembles a large thorn on the stems of the plant and the insect passes the winter in this state. The adults will emerge in May or June and will be on the wing for several weeks.

different from the needs of the same species on the warm dry alkaline chalk downlands of southern England, but nobody knows for certain since the research has not been done.

Scotland is such a huge and diverse country with so

6. THE CHEQUERED SKIPPER

The discovery of the Chequered Skipper in Scotland can be regarded as one of the great butterfly discoveries of the twentieth century. It was well known in the Midlands but its range extended only as far north as Lincolnshire and Rutland. The first definite Scottish sighting seems to have been made by Miss C. Ethel Evans near Loch Lochy in June 1939 but this fact was not announced until ten years later. In the meantime the butterfly had been independently discovered in western Inverness-shire in 1942 by Lt Col D. W. Mackworth Praed.

By the 1970s the Chequered Skipper was rapidly declining in its English haunts and it was decided to try to identify other sites where it might occur in Scotland. An SWT-sponsored survey turned up many new sites where it occurred in Inverness-shire and Argyll, showing that it was in fact far more widely distributed than had been previously thought. It is now known to exist on at least forty sites in Scotland.

The species is now extinct in England, the last individual having been seen in 1976. Plans are being made to re-introduce it into some of its former English habitats in the near future, but in the meantime English enthusiasts must come up to Scotland in search of this attractive species. The Chequered Skipper prefers sheltered sunny sites, close to deciduous woodland containing the plants which it needs; these include purple moorgrass for the caterpillars and suitable nectar-giving plants for the adults, such as bugle. Many of its preferred sites are quite inaccessible which is why it went unrecorded for so long; however it is well established along the shores of Loch Arkaig, to the north west of Spean Bridge, where it can often be seen within a few metres of the road. It flies from early May to late June, the exact dates varying from year to year.

The Chequered Skipper was given full protection under the Wildlife and Countryside Act 1981, mainly in order to protect the English populations. Ironically these were already extinct before the Act came into force. It became clear in the early 1980s that the Scottish populations were under no immediate threat and so the species was removed from Schedule 5 of the Act in 1987.

many remote areas that it is not surprising that butterflies tend to be under-recorded. A species such as the Green Hairstreak is particularly elusive, since it blends in so well with the green leaves on which it rests. Similarly the Purple Hairstreak usually flies around the tops of oak trees and can often be seen only through binoculars; thus both species tend to be overlooked, even in areas where they may be quite common. It is vital that the changing status of butterflies is known and this can only be achieved through the regular monitoring of sites; this enables the results to be compared from year to year and from place to place so that any trends can be recognised before it is too late.

Such monitoring is carried out in various parts of Scotland by means of a 'butterfly transect': a surveyor walks a standard route once a week throughout the butterfly season and records the numbers of each kind of butterfly found along the route. The results can be used to help plan conservation strategies for particular species.

CONSERVATION

Several organisations are involved in encouraging the conservation of butterflies and other insects. The Nature Conservancy Council for Scotland looks after a great many National Nature Reserves and Sites of Special Scientific Interest which contain important butterfly habitats. At Taynish National Nature Reserve in Argyll, for example, nineteen species have been recorded, including Marsh Fritillary, Speckled Wood and many more. All butterflies on such a reserve are protected since collecting is not allowed, and a butterfly transect is monitored by the reserve's warden. The Forestry Commission is also more enlightened today regarding the needs of wildlife in its forests, and in some areas it takes butterflies into account when planning for the future. At Mabie Forest near Dumfries an area has been set aside as a Forest Nature Reserve as a direct result of survey work which found at least seventeen species of butterfly in the area.

The Scottish Wildlife Trust (SWT) encourages butterflies on its reserves and in one case has actually purchased a reserve (Linn Dean in Midlothian) specifically because of the presence of the Northern Brown Argus. Almost all the Scottish species are found on SWT reserves and in many cases areas are set aside and managed with butterflies in mind. For example, another SWT reserve in Tayside consists of an old railway line where the Small Blue is found; the area requires regular scrub clearance to prevent kidney vetch, the food plant of the butterfly's caterpillars, from becoming smothered by other plants.

Careful attention is also paid to the amount of grazing by sheep and cattle which is allowed on some reserves. A certain amount of grazing is often beneficial since it prevents coarse grasses from taking over a site.

Too much grazing, however, may result in the complete loss of essential food plants for the butterflies. Careful management of this kind is vital nowadays to conserve many of our endangered species.

One society specialises in butterfly conservation, namely the British Butterfly Conservation Society (BBCS) whose aim is to encourage interest and awareness of butterflies and their conservation. The society has a network of nearly thirty branches throughout Britain. The first Scottish branch (Glasgow and South-West Scotland) was formed in 1985 and it is hoped that other branches may follow. Members do much useful recording work as well as active conservation work, including scrub clearance, planting and, where appropriate, re-introductions – usually in conjunction with other conservation bodies. Above all they help to publicise the plight of our rapidly disappearing butterflies.

Some people would like to re-establish populations in areas where butterflies have become extinct. There is no doubt that properly planned and monitored butterfly releases can safeguard the future for some of our rarest butterflies. However random releases, such as freeing surplus breeding stock, are to be deplored and in fact it is illegal to release non-native species. The BBCS has produced a policy and code of practice on butterfly releases, with criteria which must be satisfied before re-introductions are attempted. The serious problems facing butterfly populations cannot be solved just by artificial introduction however, since the process of re-introduction is long and difficult and may not succeed.

WHAT CAN YOU DO?

One way that you personally can help butterflies is by growing suitable plants in your garden to attract them, but you don't have to fill your garden with nettles and thistles! The butterflies that may be attracted to a garden will very much depend on where you live in Scotland. However if you plant aubretia, candytuft, lavender, scabious and of course buddleia (the butterfly bush), which are all good nectar sources, you may attract a good variety of butterflies to feed on them.

If you can also supply food plants for the caterpillars, such as stinging nettles, coarse grasses, bird's-foot trefoil and nasturtiums, or if you are prepared even to sacrifice a few cabbages in your vegetable plot, you may be lucky enough to have a few butterflies breeding in your garden as well. Of course many other plants are also suitable and the greater variety you have, the more butterflies you may attract.

It is hoped that several Scottish butterflies will achieve greater legal protection in the future, but it is no good protecting the butterflies if the habitats and the environment on which they totally depend are being destroyed around them.

Apart from being beautiful in their own right, butterflies are very sensitive to changes in the environment and as such are very good indicators of the general health of the countryside.

If an area has a good variety of butterflies it is very likely that it has a generally rich flora and fauna. It is to be hoped that Scotland's butterflies will continue to thrive in the future; but much will depend on what we as individuals and as a nation are prepared to do about it.

7. THE NORTHERN BROWN ARGUS

Also known as the Scotch Brown Argus or Scotch White Spot, this delightful species was first discovered on Arthur's Seat in Edinburgh. It was described in 1793 by Johan C. Fabricius (Box 1) and so became the first Scottish butterfly to be recorded in the literature. In the early nineteenth century Arthur's Seat was the only known site and dealers employed local people to catch large numbers of specimens for sale to collectors. It was later found in much of southern, central and eastern Scotland in the mid to late nineteenth century. The butterfly finally became extinct on Arthur's Seat about 1870, probably as a result of over-collecting.

The larvae feed mainly on rockrose and the butterfly is mainly to be found in areas where this plant grows, often on south-facing grassy slopes below sea cliffs. The adult butterfly, which is usually found from June to July, is very active in sunshine; males often return to settle on the same flower heads time after time as they patrol their territories. The upper surfaces of the wings are very dark brown, almost black, have an iridescent sheen and are fringed with white. There are bright orange patches along the hind margin of the wings and there is a single white spot on each forewing.

8. BUTTERFLY FARMS

There is no better way to learn about the life history of a butterfly than to see it at first hand on a butterfly farm. There are currently five butterfly farms in Scotland: Lasswade near Edinburgh, Giffnock in Glasgow, Kinross, Drumpelier near Coatbridge, and Aviemore. They are usually open from Easter until October, but Aviemore Butterfly Farm is open all the year round.

Butterfly farms are essentially large greenhouses maintaining hot and humid conditions similar to a tropical jungle environment. Paths wind their way among tropical plants, pools, waterfalls and mudflats, giving visitors the experience of being inside a jungle.

Many varieties of butterflies and moths from all over the world fly free within these enclosures. One can see iridescent blue Morphos from South America, Swallowtails from Africa and Asia, Monarchs from the USA, Common Crows from Australia, moths such as the Indian Moon Moth and even some British species such as the Red Admiral and the Comma.

Native Scottish species are encouraged in the areas around the farms by planting large numbers of suitable food plants and nectar sources for the adult butterflies. You are free to walk around and to approach the live butterflies as close as they will allow before flying off. Special areas are set aside to show the butterflies egg-laying, to show caterpillars feeding and pupating, as well as adults emerging from the chrysalis and drying their wings. However if you look carefully in the main flying areas you can see these activities taking place there as well.

A very popular feature is the 'Butterfly Pub'; many butterflies are strongly attracted to rotting fruit, so an area is set aside where they can feed on bananas, oranges, apples and other over-ripe fruits. Butterflies feeding on the fermented fruit actually become drunk and incapable of flying!

In addition to butterflies the farms exhibit moths, scorpions, Tarantula spiders and giant millipedes. Most of the livestock comes from the Far East, Central America and Africa; however this does not mean that all the stock is taken from the wild. On the contrary, many countries now breed butterflies in captivity to sell to European butterfly farms. Thus it is in the interest of local people to conserve their butterfly habitats; as a

direct result of this a few endangered species, such as Bird Wing butterflies from Papua New Guinea, have been brought back from the verge of extinction.

The Edinburgh Butterfly and Insect World at Lasswade has helped directly with butterfly conservation abroad. Members of staff have visited parts of Africa, funded by the World Wide Fund for Nature, to record what species are present in the ancient Korup rain forest of Cameroon. They have played a part in establishing breeding farms for butterflies there, which help to conserve butterflies and also create local employment, thus giving conservation a practical value in the local community.

The educational potential of butterfly farms is very great and school parties are always encouraged. Many children and adults get a terrific thrill when an exotic butterfly settles on their arm, allowing them to see such an exquisitely beautiful insect at really close range.

Edinburgh Butterfly World

Pierced standing stone at
Onich, West of Scotland.

The Coming of Man

ANNA and GRAHAM RITCHIE

Dr Anna Ritchie and Dr Graham Ritchie are a distinguished husband-and-wife team who have excavated many significant sites in Scotland. Anna Ritchie is a freelance archaeologist; Graham Ritchie is an investigator with the Royal Commission on the Ancient and Historical Monuments of Scotland.

THE HUNTER-GATHERERS

Archaeology has been unkindly described as the study of other people's rubbish, and there is more than a ring of truth to the saying. Our knowledge of the first folk to make their way into what is now Scotland is based almost entirely on the things they discarded. Such people made their way along the eastern and western seaboards as bands of hunters, at first making the journey north at certain seasons of the year before returning to a southern base-camp. In order to study the way of life of these people, archaeologists examine the scatterings of tiny flint flakes, the debris of a working place or refuse heaps of shellfish, the remains of gargantuan but monotonous limpet stews. These domestic middens can reveal more about the nature and culture of a people than the most sumptuous hoard of buried treasure.

The date at which people began to arrive in Scotland has been the subject of debate in recent years, with new evidence coming to light and objects found long ago being re-examined with more precise scientific methods. There is circumstantial evidence for the activity of hunting groups in late glacial times about 13,000 years ago, and there was probably a permanent population from at least 9,000 years ago. The bands of hunters may have had distinct territories and they probably had seasonal cycles of activity centred on fishing, gathering berries, digging up roots and hunting woodland animals.

An awareness of nature's seasonal bounty would give orderliness to a lifestyle we find hard to envisage. In addition the seas might occasionally provide an unexpected harvest, such as a small whale stranded on a tidal beach. Today such an event is just a mild curiosity; but to the hunters of early times the carcass would offer a wealth of food, oil and bone. For people who lived in tents or made temporary bivouacs in caves, the bones might have been used as weights around the sides of a tent made from animal hides.

An astonishing range of animals, birds and fish could be exploited: red deer, roe deer, boars, otters, bears and wolves, while the birds may have included guillemots and cormorants. But such hunting had only a limited effect on the natural landscape and its wildlife.

Excavations in Denmark have revealed what is so far lacking in Scotland: carefully deposited burials and elaborately decorated wooden objects show that early people may have had beliefs and interests beyond day-to-day survival, as modern hunter-gatherer societies demonstrate. In Denmark, adult males at this time were about 5ft 7in (1.7 m) tall and women averaged 4ft 11in (1.5 m) in height; their facial features seem to have been coarser than today. A life expectancy of between forty and sixty years bears testimony to a healthy way of life in Denmark as contrasted with the earliest farming communities in Scotland, where people seem to have died on average much younger. But then one American anthropologist has described hunting and gathering communities as the original affluent societies!

House interior at the ancient village of Skara Brae, Orkney.

THE FIRST FARMING COMMUNITIES

Around 4000 BC Scotland experienced one of the most significant episodes in her entire history – the introduction of farming. The idea of a settled life with permanent homes, cultivating plants and breeding animals, was a new and important development introduced into the British Isles by colonists from western Europe. This enterprising lifestyle spread quickly: using scientific dating, archaeologists have discovered that farming spread as far north as Shetland soon after its introduction into the southern parts of the British Isles.

Just why these early pioneers felt such compulsion to press on ever further is one of the unsolved puzzles of prehistory. It is as if every visible shore had to be explored. Shetland proved to be the northern limit of their island-hopping, for the next island group to the north, the Faroes, is well out of sight and would have

Interior of the tomb at Maes Howe, Orkney.

Skulls from 'The Tomb of the Eagles' at Isbister were found mingled with the bones of sea eagles.

presented an inhospitable prospect to any accidental visitors.

It is difficult to estimate the numbers of new farming settlers. But there is no doubt that there was a movement of people into Scotland rather than simply the spread of ideas, although in time the new way of life was also adopted by the existing population.

The farming pioneers brought with them seeds for cereal crops and young animals that were to be the start of their domestic herds, for these were resources that did not exist in Scotland. The incomers grew wheat and barley and bred cattle, sheep and goats, which were the most vital possessions that they brought with them from Europe. Other innovations could be carried in the head as knowledge and experience; in this way they brought knowledge of farming methods, how to build permanent houses, how to construct tombs of timber and stone, and how to make pottery.

The burial tombs were built to last and many have survived the intervening 5,000 years or more, some virtually intact. Their design varies from place to place, as do pottery styles, according to the tastes of the communities that created them, and this evidence shows the links between those communities. It is clear that the farmers who settled in Scotland came up the east coast from Yorkshire to colonise the fertile coastal plains and river valleys as far north as the Moray Firth and probably beyond. Others used the western seaways to settle Argyll and the Outer Isles, as well as northern Scotland, Orkney and Shetland.

Their transport for sea and river travel was probably by skin-covered canoe or the log-boat, made from a hollowed tree trunk, and possibly rafts for the livestock. The climate of those times was a little warmer than today and helped to ensure good harvests, allowing them to grow wheat and barley as far north as Orkney and Shetland. The good weather also made for calmer seas making journeys easier. The bones of red sea bream and corkwing wrasse have been found in Orcadian tombs, implying a slightly warmer sea temperature than

today when both fish are rarely encountered so far north.

In the words of Stuart Piggott, 'Throughout Scottish prehistory echoes the sound of the woodman's axe'. Indeed the theme of forest clearance runs through every stage of social development in Scotland, from the earliest farmers to the charcoal-burners supplying the eighteenth century iron furnaces of Argyll. The prime concern of the early settlers was to clear land for agriculture, and by felling woodland they created the first dramatic man-made impact on the Scottish landscape. The timber itself had many uses, from boats, houses and stock-enclosures to platters for the family meal.

The axe was perhaps the farmer's single most important tool. In Scotland axe heads were usually made of hard volcanic rock, ground to a sharp cutting edge and set in a wooden haft. Many were of local stone, such as Shetland felsite, or the greenstone outcropping at Killin in Perthshire, but others were imported, such as those made of porcellanite from County Antrim in Northern Ireland.

A good axe was a prestigious gift. The role of the axe was so important that it was used as a status symbol; some axes are of exceptional beauty, meticulously crafted from rare stone, and were clearly only used for ceremonial purposes.

Once a suitable area had been cleared of trees the farm could begin to take shape. The house would be oblong or square with rounded corners, built of timber or a combination of stone and timber, and it could be of spacious proportions: the post-holes of a timber house excavated beside the River Dee in Grampian mark out a great hall fully 80ft (24 m) long and 40ft (12 m) wide. The house would be surrounded by a working yard, animal enclosures and small cultivated fields with open pasture beyond.

By 3000 BC the process of forest clearance and farming had even created sufficient grassland to allow the occasional stripping of large areas of turf and topsoil in order to build imposing burial mounds. The mounds were often built on top of old farmland, thus preserving traces of the agricultural methods used. Both the spade and a very simple form of plough were common.

The forests remained a major source of food as well as timber. Wild game was hunted but the native pigs were soon domesticated. Berries, crab apples, nuts, roots and fungi would have been gathered to enrich the diet (Box 1).

THE NEW TECHNOLOGY OF METALWORKING

The early farmers began the long process of changing land-use, and their basic economy and lifestyle persisted throughout prehistory with the addition now and again of new technical developments.

They also embellished the landscape in a less practical way with public buildings. They altered skylines with the tombs of ancestors set beneath pale stone cairns; great slabs of stone were set up in circles, rows or pairs or as single mighty sentinels. Many of these monuments were central to the life of the community for a thousand years or more; some became the focus around which later ceremonial building took place and they remained sacred for many centuries more.

The first major technical innovation in Scotland was metalworking, again introduced into Britain from Europe. Unlike farming, however, the basic ingredients of copper, gold and tin were already available in the British Isles (iron-working was to be discovered later). Surface deposits of copper occur widely in Scotland though gold is less common. The knowledge of how to work copper and gold reached Scotland around 2500 BC, probably arriving with traders and craftsmen looking for new supplies of raw metal. Gold was fashioned into jewellery and copper into axe-heads; ownership of either would have been equally prestigious.

Few copper objects have survived, because people soon discovered that the addition of tin to the copper produced a harder and more useful metal, bronze. Tin could only be obtained from Cornwall or Europe, pointing to the far-reaching trade networks existing between communities. Later still, some time after 1000 BC, lead was added to improve the casting qualities of bronze.

Around the time that knowledge of metalworking reached Scotland a new wave of incomers appeared in the population; there may have been a link between the two developments but it does not seem to have been a simple matter of migrants bringing new technology. A type of pottery known to archaeologists as 'beaker pottery' made its first appearance in Britain around 2500 BC. Comparing the earliest Scottish beakers with those in Europe, it is clear that the new settlers came in small numbers to eastern Scotland across the North Sea from the Netherlands.

They buried their dead in single graves rather than communally as in earlier tombs, and they seem to have had broader skulls than the native farmers. They were buried with their personal belongings, often including bows and arrows and a beaker which, at least sometimes, contained a mead-like drink. These new people with their novel pottery and burial rites were soon absorbed into the existing population.

Cremation became increasingly popular from about this time, and the large amounts of timber required both for cremating the dead and for metalworking led to more forest clearance. Peat was not a significant fuel until the major growth of blanket peat was under way around 1000 BC.

Peat formation was caused by a worsening climate, and the colder and wetter weather affected farming. Bad weather led to more frequent crop failures and it is also possible that the early farmers had exhausted the soil in some places. All these factors led to growing social pressures: there was less farmland to support a growing population and competition for land would have increased. The social effect can be seen in an increased production of swords and shields by the bronze industry and in the building of fortifications.

CELTIC SOCIETY

Few words evoke as many different reactions as the word 'Celtic'. It may suggest a style of modern jewellery

1. THE PEOPLE

Fortunately for the archaeologist, ancestors seem to have been important to early people since they put considerable effort into building tombs to house the bones of their dead and modern excavations have yielded a reasonable sample of bones for analysis. On average, adults were only a little shorter in height than today's norm but their lives were considerably shorter. Of those who survived their childhood few lived beyond their twenties – and those few must have been vital to their communities in passing on knowledge, technical skills and traditions. From about 3000 BC some of those traditions were concerned with circles and alignments of standing stones, and there has been much discussion in recent years over the possible geometric skills and astronomical purposes behind the construction and use of such settings. The plain fact is that the observable level of technical expertise among the early farming communities is such that sophisticated knowledge of geometry and the universe is most unlikely.

Despite the overall youth of the population a very common health problem was spinal disease, usually osteo-arthritis, detectable as malformation of the bones. This was probably caused by the hard physical work of daily life, carrying very heavy loads and manhandling large timbers and slabs of stone.

Their clothes appear to have been made entirely from animal skins, for no spinning or weaving equipment survives from this period and the sheep probably did not produce wool suitable for textiles. The skins could be used either as furs or, with the hair removed, as leather. Virtually every part of the animal would be used, especially the bones for tools, beads, pendants and toggles. Furs were also essential as bedding, laid on top of straw or springy heather; furniture was made of wood or stone or even from the massive ribs and vertebrae of stranded whales.

Mr Simison, the farmer who discovered the Tomb of the Eagles at Isbister, Orkney.

The stone circle at Callanish on the Isle of Lewis, Western Isles.

The Ring of Brodgar, Orkney.

with interlace and spirals; it may describe the family of languages that include Gaelic and Breton; for many Scots it conjures up a green and white football scarf. In prehistoric terms it is used to describe a series of tribes active in central Europe and France from the sixth century BC who spoke a language that was ancestral to modern Gaelic and who did indeed have a distinctive art style, although they did not use interlace. Celtic society was composed of tribes with leaders, warriors, farmers and craftsmen in metalwork, pottery and wood. The Celts have recently been introduced to a far wider audience through the adventures of Asterix the Gaul and the village life of Vitalstatistix, Obelix and their friends.

The names of Celtic gods are known and their worship may have involved the ritual casting of objects into sacred pools and lakes. The introduction of certain aspects of this way of life into Britain, along with the adoption of the Celtic language, was once thought to be the result of a series of waves of invaders and settlers from the continent. In recent years, however, archaeologists believe that large-scale immigration was not the cause of the changes evident in the archaeological record of later centuries BC. Perhaps the arrival of small groups of people who gained a measure of political ascendancy was responsible for the introduction of the Celtic language, but trade and other contacts may also have made the new ideas fashionable.

As we have seen, the farming communities of many parts of Scotland seem to have been subjected to social pressures which resulted in the building of defensive enclosures formed by stout palisades of timber.

Palisaded stockades and fortifications of stone with wooden frameworks required large quantities of straight timber beams for their construction and hastened the deforestation of upland Scotland. The building of one palisaded settlement in the Borders is estimated to have required at least 2,600 upright posts. Hilltop fortifications also needed large quantities of timber for their construction, as a criss-cross framework often stabilised the rubble walls. A stout timber gateway would have led into a bustling community living in timber houses, some set against the fort wall. One of the main industries, iron-working, would have required large areas of coppiced woodland in order to have a ready supply of charcoal.

Many hill forts caught fire either accidentally, as a result of attack, or most plausibly as a result of deliberate burning after a successful campaign. The wall cores fused into 'vitrified' lumps because of the great heat, but it should be stressed that this was not a deliberate constructional technique.

The many fortifications found all over Scotland imply a way of life that involved raiding neighbouring tribes; in some cases such refuges are no more than a defended farmstead, in others the equivalent of small fortified towns. Security could be obtained by building a stout stone wall round the top of a small rocky knoll, but in many parts of Scotland people sought safety by building their homes on an artificial island or 'crannog' of stone and timber a little way offshore in a loch or perhaps in an area of marshy shallows. The timber and thatch

The Broch of Mousa in Shetland.

The interior of the Broch of Mousa.

houses built on these islands could only have been reached by boats or by causeways, making them easier to defend.

Many rural settlements can be detected as 'crop markings' on aerial photographs, the holes in which upright timbers were set appearing as darker marks in growing crops. The economic basis of society appears to have involved both grazing animals and mixed farming, the balance depending largely on climate and topography, much as today.

Broch towers, epitomised by the Broch of Mousa in Shetland, have captured the imagination of archaeologists and tourists for over a century. These drystone constructions, described as 'the only really advanced architectural innovation invented entirely within Britain', have in the past been seen as indicating that the west and north of Scotland were subjected to invasion, probably from the south-west of England following Roman occupation of that area.

Nowadays the architectural innovations of broch construction are seen to have an acceptable local ancestry, and large-scale folk movements were not involved. On the other hand the building of such powerful symbols of authority and prestige underlines the uncertainties of the times. It is perhaps not surprising that the name of the first north Briton to be recorded is Calgacus, or 'Swordsman'.

THE ROMAN ARMY IN SCOTLAND

With the march of two columns of Roman soldiers into southern Scotland in AD 79 we take that faltering step from prehistory to history. We know some dates, we know the names of two of the players on the stage – Agricola (the Roman general) and Calgacus (the leader of the Celtic army at the fateful battle of Mons Graupius) – but the bulk of our information, particularly about the environment, comes from archaeology.

The Roman period in Scotland has an unusual fascination for archaeologists and historians. Roman influence in Scotland was brief and only affected parts of the country, but the surviving remains are among the best preserved in the northern Empire.

In fact Roman troops were stationed in Scotland for only two periods, each of about twenty years' duration; the first at the end of the first century AD and the second in the mid second century AD. A further period of intense military campaigning took place between AD 208–11, when the Emperor Septimus Severus led a massive army into Scotland. Thereafter some measure of political authority was exercised in southern Scotland until AD 367. The economic impact on the native population is likely to have been considerable. The Roman army obtained supplies locally, and demands for grain and other foods as well as leather and wool for uniforms and clothing must have radically altered the former economic patterns of local exchange.

The frontier earthwork known as the Antonine Wall, built around the year AD 142 for the emperor Antoninus Pius, ran for almost 37 miles (60 km) from Bridgeness on the Firth of Forth to Old Kilpatrick on the Firth of Clyde. It was designed to control travel and trade rather

The Bridgeness Slab from the Antonine Wall in West Lothian depicts a Roman legionary defeating barbarians.

than as a defensive work. The wall was in fact a turf rampart at least 10 ft (3 m) high and on average some 15 ft (4.5 m) wide at the base, and the stripping of such a large quantity of turf is itself testimony to the extensive areas of grassland available. A recent estimate has suggested that some 800–950 acres of land were stripped, and that to complete any breast work along the top about one million cubic feet of timber were needed.

The diet of the Roman soldier included bread as well as meat from cattle, sheep, pigs, red deer and chicken. Examination of plant debris in a cesspit at the fort of Bearsden has revealed some exotic additions to the diet, including figs, coriander, wild celery and opium poppy. Roman soldiers clearly also enjoyed the variety offered by local raspberries, brambles, strawberries and bilberries!

BRITONS, PICTS, ANGLES AND SCOTS

Life in Scotland altered little after the departure of the Roman army in the middle of the second century. On the domestic front rectangular houses became more popular, although circular designs (which had been the norm) continued to be built virtually throughout the first thousand years AD. In southern Scotland it is likely that the native British population received some new blood through intermarriage with Roman soldiers; but that blood was not truly Roman or even Italian but German, as a result of local recruitment into army units stationed in Germany before being sent to Britain. The most important effect of the Roman presence in north Britain was political: opposition to Rome seems to have fostered a degree of unity among the tribes beyond the frontier zone. The original small Celtic tribes appear to have gradually merged until, in the fourth century AD, the entire population north of the Forth–Clyde line was known by one name, the Picts.

This process of political amalgamation led, by the sixth century, to the emergence of distinct kingdoms in Scotland as elsewhere. There were three British kingdoms in southern Scotland: Gododdin with its major stronghold at Edinburgh; Strathclyde with a stronghold on Dumbarton Rock; and Rheged based on the Solway Firth. In the meantime German migrants known as Angles (or English) had been settling along the coastal plains of Yorkshire and Northumberland, creating the Anglian kingdoms of Deira based on York and Bernicia based on Bamburgh.

The Britons of Gododdin and Rheged were the first to suffer from Anglian territorial ambitions in southern Scotland; Bernicia and Deira had been fused into a single powerful kingdom, Northumbria, in AD 605 and Anglian war-bands penetrated north and west, occupying British lands. Edinburgh was captured in AD 638 and much of Rheged was conquered during the rest of the seventh century. From this time on, the population of southern Scotland was to be of mixed British and Anglian stock until Lothian was taken over by the Scots during the late tenth century.

The Scots had come originally from Ireland and there was already strong Irish settlement in the Rhinns of Galloway by the sixth century, not mentioned in historical sources but detectable through place-names and archaeology. The documented settlement of Argyll by the Scots was on a grander scale. The 'Scotti' were an Irish tribe in County Antrim for whom the visible shores of Kintyre had long beckoned with the lure of new land; sporadic migration seems to have taken place over perhaps a century or more, until around AD 500 the ruling dynasty of the tribe transferred itself to a new kingdom of Dalriada in Argyll. In so doing, the Scots displaced Pictish political influence in the area but not the bulk of the population.

By the seventh century, Dalriada stretched from Kintyre northwards to Ardnamurchan, with major strongholds at Dunaverty at the south end of Kintyre, Tarbert, Dunollie at Oban, and Dunadd near Kilmartin (Box 2). Years of uneasy relations with the kingdom of the Picts led finally to a Scottish takeover of Pictland around AD 843.

None of these political developments had any long-term effects on land-use in Scotland. The various peoples shared a basic economy of mixed farming and a common settlement-pattern of princely strongholds and farms. Political takeover was normally accompanied by the physical takeover of existing power-centres in order to demonstrate the new authority. We know from historical, place-name and archaeological evidence that the British fort at Dunbar was taken over by Angles, and similarly the Pictish royal centre at Forteviot in Perthshire became the palace of the Scottish king.

The various kingdoms were also linked through the Church. Key figures in the spread of Christianity were St Ninian, based at Whithorn in the fifth century, and St Columba, founder of the monastery on Iona in AD 563; and by the end of the seventh century the Church was a strong influence among Britons, Scots, Picts and Angles alike.

Monasteries were self-sufficient farming units. Secular power and ecclesiastical power were closely linked, with the same noble families providing the leaders in both spheres and craftsmen enjoying the patronage of both.

Pictish stone-carvers were renowned for their skill, and their repertoire of distinctive symbols was greatly increased by the addition of Christian motifs and iconography. The creation of elaborately decorated cross-slabs was a challenge to which Pictish sculptors responded to magnificent effect. It is thought that the eighth century high crosses of Iona were commissioned from Pictish master-sculptors and, after the union with the Scots, Pictish workshops continued to produce sculpture for their new masters (though without the symbols that had identified the old Pictish kingdom).

Carved stones must have become a familiar component of the man-made landscape from about AD 600 onwards; several hundred survive today, intact or in fragments, and more must once have existed. Some marked graves, some stood in the grounds of monasteries, some marked land boundaries, some were wayside prayer crosses; all were part of everyday life.

A favourite theme on these stones is the hunt, and this too was part of everyday life, though perhaps enjoyed only by a privileged few. We see horse-riders and their hounds in pursuit of fleeing hinds and archers crouched to take aim at charging boars. Horses are particularly well portrayed, with a real understanding of the animal and more than a hint of sophisticated training of a fine breed. Carvings of salmon perhaps indicate another preoccupation.

Unlike the Picts, the Angles had no tradition of stone-carving before their conversion to Christianity, with the result that Anglian sculpture in southern Scotland is purely church art, from high crosses to shrines carved to hold the bones of saints. The Church developed a network of contacts throughout western Europe, and Scotland was thus part not just of what was happening in Britain and Ireland but of early medieval Europe. Ships laden with jars of wine, mass-produced pottery from France and all kinds of exotic goods from further afield plied their trade all round the Irish Sea. People themselves travelled, especially missionaries and the craftsmen who created fine metalwork.

The influence of the Church could involve mundane matters as well as spiritual affairs. Among the innovations that Irish monks brought to Scotland seems to have been the horizontal corn-mill, a water-powered and larger version of the old hand-quern in which the paddles of the mill-wheel were set horizontally rather than vertically as became normal later. Such horizontal mills date from as early as the seventh century in Ireland and there is evidence on Iona for the use of similar mills there before the eighth century. Mechanised grinding machinery would have made an immense difference to the hard labour of producing flour from grain. Excavation of only part of the contemporary Scottish fort of Dunadd has yielded the remains of some fifty hand-querns, eloquent witnesses to the 'daily grind' in a place lacking the water-courses suitable for mechanised mills.

THE IMPACT OF THE VIKINGS

Contacts across the Irish Sea were disrupted in the final decades of the eighth century by Viking activities. Monasteries kept brief records or annals of important events and Viking raids are mentioned from AD 793 onwards: 'Devastation of all the islands of Britain by the gentiles', wrote an Irish monk in AD 794, and the following year saw the pillage of Skye, Iona and several

Irish monasteries. This pattern of swift and terrifying raids along the western seaway continued throughout the ninth century and it was one of the factors that encouraged the kings of Dalriada to look eastwards into Pictland for their political future.

The raiding Vikings came from Norway and it is likely that they had bases in the Northern Isles for their seasonal campaigns. The prevailing winds in the North Sea favoured a spring voyage westwards and an autumn return to Norwegian fiords. But the advantages of permanent settlement in the Northern and Western Isles were obvious; there was good land for the taking, close to the sources of rich pickings, and it was not long before Viking war-bands returned with their women-folk and belongings to build farms.

From the evidence of archaeology, place-names and documents, it is clear that Pictland and Dalriada rapidly lost their northern and western fringes to the Norsemen during the first few decades of the ninth century. At one time scholars assumed that this process involved extermination of the local people, or at best dispossession and enslavement, but excavations over the last twenty years have uncovered a more subtle picture of what happened. The majority of Norse settlements were built literally on top of the demolished ruins of earlier native homes, which in most cases had been abandoned some time previously.

At the Brough of Birsay in Orkney, a large settlement of special importance both in Pictish and Norse times, the Viking-age houses were placed so that they occupied the same individual plots of land as their Pictish predecessors. In other words, we see the Norsemen establishing their authority and overlordship by taking over existing estates and land-patterns and occupying existing power-centres. For the local population this

The incised footprint carved in this stone on the summit of Dunadd fortress may have been part of the initiation ceremonies of the kings of Dalriada.

93

Viking houses on the Brough of Birsay.

Norman motte at Bass of Inverurie, Gordon, Grampian.

Their chief contribution to the landscape was dramatic for they built huge earthen mounds, or mottes, as bases for their timber castles. In many cases the motte was surrounded by an outer bailey, enclosed by a great ditch and ramparts, in which domestic buildings could be protected, and the whole enterprise represented a massive earth-shifting operation. The castle and other buildings required large quantities of timber to be felled. The fashion for mottes caught on among the Scottish lords and the number built is reflected by the surviving remains of more than 300.

A marked characteristic of Scotland in early medieval times was the rural nature of its settlement-pattern. There were no urban centres to emulate Viking Dublin or York, and Scotland lacked any coinage of its own until the twelfth century. There was certainly trading and a degree of craft-specialisation, but the trade was based on barter and exchange, and the craftsmen were mostly itinerant metalworkers. A cargo of wine and fine glassware might be exchanged for slaves, furs or exquisite brooches, or in Norse times for silver bullion, carefully weighed on the folding scales found in pagan Viking-age graves.

Wine was for princes and warlords and most feasts were washed down with mead or ale, both mentioned in early documents. Diet could be quite varied, particularly for those living near the sea; excavations have yielded the bones of cattle, sheep, goats, pigs, deer and domestic fowl, along with a wide range of fish, shellfish, seabirds, seals and whales. Many of these provided more than meat of course, for they were sources of wool, skins and furs for clothing and bedding, and bones, antlers and horns for tools, as well as dairy products, eggs and oil. Crops such as barley, wheat and oats were processed into bread, porridge, bannocks and, in the case of barley, fermented brews.

Wild fruits and berries, nuts, roots and herbs were gathered. Peat had become an important fuel: Turf-Einar Rognvaldsson, a ninth-century Viking earl in Orkney, was so-called by his compatriots because 'he was the first man to dig peat for fuel, firewood being very scarce on the islands' – a wise man not slow to learn native ways!

In the north and west, stone remained the main building material, but both Picts and Norsemen used a wind-proof combination of stone and turf for the walls of their houses, with a good stone face on the inside and an outer cladding of turf. Turf on a timber framework was probably also used for roofs. South of the Moray Firth, timber was more widely used, and traces of early medieval houses are consequently more difficult to find.

Place-names incorporating the element *carden*, or copse, underline the prevalence of woodland in the landscape and its relationship to the Pictish settlement pattern between the firths of Moray and Forth. The crannog, familiar from earlier times, remained popular among the Scots and Britons of the west and south-west, who now built rectangular as well as round

meant new masters and little more – some enslavement, no doubt, but slavery was already a familiar part of life among all peoples at that time.

The Norsemen acquired native equipment such as bone combs and pins, and they were prepared within a few generations to adopt the local religion, Christianity – there are few pagan graves after the end of the ninth century.

Norse farms were similar to those of the existing population, but at least one new and important crop was introduced: flax. Fine linen tunics were essential to the affluent Viking wardrobe and special glass linen-smoothers were used to produce a good finish to the cloth. Fibres from the stem of the flax plant were spun into linen, and flax seeds have been found at Norse settlements in Orkney.

The Norsemen also breathed new life into the soapstone carving industry in Shetland; Norway has its own sources of soapstone (also known as steatite) and the Norse settlers in Scotland were accustomed to using bowls and lamps and other items carved from this relatively soft stone. In Shetland there was intensive exploitation of steatite outcrops in Norse times, on Unst and at Cunningsburgh, south of Lerwick.

The Scandinavian settlement of Scotland, from the ninth-century land-grabs of the far north and west to the tenth- and eleventh-century penetration of the south-west, was the last major influx of migrant people in early medieval times. Another new element was added to the population during the twelfth century, but it was considerably smaller in numbers and more peaceful in intent: these were the Anglo-Norman and Flemish families to whom David I and his successors gave grants of land in southern Scotland, Fife and Moray.

houses on their island-platforms. Crannogs used the surrounding water as a natural defence, and forts were similarly located on naturally defensive land sites such as isolated hills or coastal promontories. Both crannogs and forts made extensive use of timber, for the ramparts of early medieval forts were reinforced internally by wooden beams, as had been the forts of earlier times.

AN ARCHAEOLOGICAL HERITAGE

The people who made Scotland their home from the earliest agricultural communities of prehistoric times to the Anglo-Norman families of the twelfth century have left enduring monuments in the form of burial mounds or fortifications. Only a tiny fraction of such sites have been examined in detail by excavation and our knowledge about the dates or social contexts of the remainder is limited. The archaeological landscape of Scotland is known in detail only in a few selected areas, Orkney and Argyll for example, and many other parts of the country are as yet unsurveyed in any depth. The impact of modern development on the countryside from afforestation, opencast mining or land improvement places a burden on the sparse archaeological profession in Scotland to ensure that as little information as possible is lost.

The wealth of archaeological information in lowland Scotland which has been discovered as a result of a concentrated programme of aerial photography shows that many sites may potentially be at risk as a result of deeper ploughing methods or farm woodlands. No archaeologist would seek to halt inevitable changes in land management; indeed our study is one of constant change brought about by the demands of agriculture and timber exploitation. But by surveying and excavating sites in advance of change, and conserving sample areas of landscape illustrating a range of sites – cairns, field systems, houses (perhaps with some reconstructions) – the archaeological heritage of Scotland could be better understood and presented to Scots of today.

2. THE KILMARTIN VALLEY

An exploration of the Kilmartin valley in mid-Argyll allows the visitor to appreciate the monuments of prehistoric and early historic times even though the setting has been much altered with the passing centuries. There is an impressive cairn at Nether Largie and you can still drop into the long stone-capped chamber and try to imagine the shrouded burials of members of early farming communities with pottery vessels laid reverently alongside. The stone circle at Temple Wood was used for rituals and burials over many centuries and was finally sealed with a cairn of stones; but look out for the double spiral decoration on one of the uprights.

Burial cairns laid out along a straight line give the impression of a cemetery of a local dynasty; several of the individual stone coffins or 'cists' (the Scottish word for a chest) can still be seen, some with carved decoration on the slabs in the form of axes – surely a symbol of status. Several groups of standing stones dot the valley, some decorated with cup-and-ring markings – mute testimony to forgotten rites. The great rock expanses at Achnabreck and Cairnbaan a little to the south are carved profusely with cup-and-ring markings and have puzzled antiquaries for years.

Shortly after 2000 BC peat began to form across the valley floor and covered several sites, including Temple Wood, until drainage and peat-clearance in the ninth century when the neat present-day fields were laid out. There are several forts and duns built on rocky knolls on the margins of the valley from the first few centuries BC onwards.

The climax of any visit to Kilmartin should be the rocky stronghold of Dunadd, one of the citadels of the Scots in the seventh and eighth centuries AD; it is however quite an imaginative feat to recreate the bustling fort with timber buildings set within the walls, blacksmiths and bronze-workers, and the feasting halls and domestic quarters of a chief.

On a rock surface just below the summit two carved footprints and a basin may betoken royal inauguration ceremonies, while an incised boar in a very Pictish style may even commemorate contact with their eastern neighbours in the seventh or eighth century.

The location of the present village on a little terraced apron set above the valley floor has, like the gravel terraces opposite, probably been a focus for settlements from earliest times. A carved cross, now in the church, shows that there was a Christian community here from about the tenth century; there is another fine cross of sixth-century date. Many fine grave slabs in the distinctive West Highland style show that Kilmartin remained a focus for burials in the later fourth and fifth centuries AD – as it had become so many millennia earlier.

Interior of the south cairn chambered tomb at Nether Largie, Kilmartin valley, mid-Argyll.

Pictish carved stone with cup and ring markings at High Banks, Kircudbright, Dumfries and Galloway.

95

Highland cattle are much hardier beasts than modern breeds and can survive the harsh northern winters and poor grazing.

The Farming of
the Land

ALEXANDER FENTON

Dr Alexander Fenton is Professor of Scottish Ethnology at Edinburgh University and Director of the School of Scottish Studies and of the European Ethnological Research Centre.

In April 1990 in north-east Scotland the air was filled with the cacophonic racket of a new phenomenon – the 'de-stoner', Reekie's 'Stone and Clod Separator'. Drawn behind tractors that dwarfed their drivers, these travelling riddles were at work on several farms, sifting and refining the soil and burying the stones they gathered, preparing seed beds that had the quality of garden ground. The drill-sown crops that followed would be potatoes, carrots and turnips; not the 'yellows' and swedes that had foddered the cattle in the winter byres for over 200 years, but smaller turnip varieties grown to suit the tastes of urban housewives who like the 0.5 to 0.7 kilogramme (1 to 1.5 lb) size, which growers then wax to make them keep until they reach the shops.

The coming of the 'de-stoner' may have been promoted by farmers moving to Scotland from England, attracted by currently cheaper land prices in Scotland. More certainly it marks one of the responses to central government, which is currently pressing for alternative forms of farming. In this case we see the emergence of a kind of 'supermarket gardening' to satisfy the food demands of a population increasingly distanced from the land.

From the viewpoint of the nation's heritage, the de-stoner sadly obliterates all traces of the archaeological record lying beneath the plough-soils of the last 300 years. Near the fields where I saw the de-stoner at work I have picked up flint arrowheads and a flint core from which flakes had been struck in Neolithic times (see Chapter 7); the plough has also taken the lid off a Bronze Age cist-burial which contained the remains of a bronze dagger, a pot, and the bones of a human being who could not have envisaged de-stoners in his wildest dreams. Change can damage the past as well as the future.

The de-stoner is a modern example of change and of the possible effects of change, not all of which can be foreseen and planned for unless we take a very broad view. The most obvious historical change has been demographic: the increasing concentration of people in the towns and industrial areas of the Central Belt of Scotland. In 1974 about 3.8 per cent of Scotland's total work-force was engaged in agriculture; today it is less than 1.5 per cent (see Chapter 10). Scotland's people are no longer based mainly in the countryside, as they were for most of the preceding centuries.

Also, in modern times, a real distinction has emerged between farming as a self-sufficient way of life (encouraged by governments during and after the two world wars) and agriculture as a food industry. The industrialisation of farming was characterised by mechanisation, a move away from tenancy to ownership and the subsidised production of crops. It has also created close relationships with the food-processing trades, and drawn support from interested groups like the National Farmers Union, co-operative societies and marketing boards. There is now a European drive to reform the structure of farming because of the pressure of too many on the land, the proliferations of holdings too small to be viable, and the waste involved in excessive fragmentation under certain kinds of landholding.

Until the 1700s the countryside of Scotland was more like the rest of Europe in having a settlement pattern with farming villages, or 'ferm-touns' as they were called, predominating; these were farms worked jointly by the families living on them (Box 1). But around 1700, when most of Scotland's people still lived on and depended on the land, there was no real way to improve crop yields or intensify the system of land-use except here and there through spreading lime on the land; and even that was not enough in itself without the support of good drainage. The pressure to produce more food from the land had become irresistible. The need for change had become vital, though it came much sooner for the Lowlands than for the Highlands. What were the factors that brought about, and financed, such change?

AGENTS OF CHANGE

A main agent of change was the pressure from the towns – and the demand of their markets, particularly in the growth of the grain and cattle trades.

Lothian and Moray grain was being exported to the

Reekie's de-stoner at work in the fields of East Lothian.

Netherlands, the Baltic, Norway and western Sweden in exchange for timber, and was also exported to England after the Union of 1707. The coastal trade in grain from the north of Scotland to Edinburgh increased substantially after about 1660 in response to demands from the capital's mills and breweries. Merchants offered landowners contracts for their annual crops, and annual rents were paid in the form of grain. The government put its finger in the national liquidity pie by controlling grain imports and putting a bounty on exports. There were strong pressures to increase the arable acreage of grain-growing areas, and the enabling Enclosure Acts of 1661, 1685 and 1695, as well as the Division of Commonties Act of 1695, can be seen as a government response under first James VII and II and then William and Mary.

Another factor in the growth of income was the role played by the celebrated 'black cattle' of the Highlands. From the early 1600s the pastoral Highlands had been supplying the Lowlands with cheese (some of which may have come from sheep's milk) in years of cereal scarcity; but the major economic resource, in national terms, lay in cattle. Before the Union of 1707, Scotland was already considered 'a mere grazing field to England', and Scottish beef helped to feed the city of London as well as the British army and navy. Scotland's unique banking system financed the growth in the cattle trade by facilitating cattle deals through loans to dealers from the south and elsewhere.

The droving trade had a marked physical effect on the landscape. The droving tracks became the progenitors of the road system (see Chapter 11) and by the 1580s grazing parks enclosed within stone walls or 'dykes' were appearing, for example near Edinburgh and in Galloway. Moreover, in the cattle-rearing hinterland of the Highlands, change was also becoming apparent in the traditional shieling or summer pasture system (Box 2).

The grain trade in the Lowlands and the cattle trade in the Highlands were not, of course, sufficiently profitable to fund the 'agricultural revolution' by themselves. Other factors, like the tobacco trade of Glasgow and the movement of capital (some of it from England) through the banks, have to be taken into account. By 1707, however, there seems to have been sufficient progress in agriculture to avoid the famine conditions of earlier years. But Scottish agriculture could not yet support a growing urban population or provide enough stocks of essential raw material. Since agriculture was the dominant sector of the economy, change was vital to strengthen the nation's weak exchange position if opportunities opened up by the Union of 1707 were not to be lost. Scotland's unimproved agriculture seriously handicapped the nation's opportunity to take part in a widening world economy.

THE NEW MONEY

At the time of the Union with England the landed interests had an infusion of new blood by recruiting merchants, bankers and lawyers to their ranks. They were willing and even eager to promote agricultural improvement and had a strong concern for the industrial aspects of economic opportunity, as shown by the industrial enterprises in most of the planned villages they established in the eighteenth century.

There had already been some investment, as evidenced by the rebuilding of some tower houses in the sixteenth and seventeenth centuries and the erection of new mansion houses, such as Kinross House (1686–91) and Hopetoun House (1696–1701), around which extensive areas of parkland developed after the 1760s. Foreign writers have remarked that England was a country of parks, and by the eighteenth century Scotland was catching up on this tradition. Formally laid out parks were created as part of estate improvements and these became elements in regularising the face of the countryside, with farmhouses and farms included. And part of the change they represented lay in the exotic trees and plants their owners introduced.

An enormous amount of our knowledge about the countryside comes from the estate plans which surveyors drew up to record the existing state of, and proposals for the improvement of, estates in most parts of the country. Something like 50,000 plans were made in the eighteenth century alone – a striking demonstration of intent concerning land management by aristocratic owners, lairds and bonnet-lairds (landowners who farmed their own land) alike, who in the 1770s controlled about 50, 40 and five per cent respectively of the agrarian wealth of Scotland.

Linked to such plans, three phases of eighteenth century improvement can be seen: a first generation thrust (1720–40s) by landowners and lairds who had capital to develop; a more businesslike set of team efforts (1750–70s) between owners, surveyors, factors and tenants; and from the 1770s, input from large capitalistic tenants with the tenantry doing most of the improving.

THE CHANGING LANDSCAPE

Running through these phases, and affecting them, we see the new agricultural technology that was to alter the face of the ancient farming landscape almost beyond recognition.

The ploughing technique in most areas had consisted of turning the soil into a series of long raised 'rigs', or ridges, with drainage furrows in between. The ridges varied in width, the older ones being up to 36 ft (11 m) wide while more recent ones were between 10 ft (3 m) and 18 ft (5 m) wide. This system of ridge and furrow was necessary for surface drainage. Traditionally, the farmers ploughed along the length of the ridge; sowers walked along one half of the ridge, then back along the other as they spread their seed with one arm from a sowing-sheet knotted around the shoulder; at harvest time, reapers with sickles also worked along the ridges.

Remains of the old ridge and furrow can still be seen today. They show up well in slanting sun over light snow and can be found beneath woods planted in the early nineteenth century, on the lower slopes of hills and on golf courses created from farmland in Victorian times.

The new agricultural technology which emerged in the eighteenth century affected not only husbandry but cropping and crop-processing. It appeared first in the

Run-rig cultivation beds are still evident on Duddingston golf course

Lime kilns at Esperton, Midlothian: lime was vital for improving the fertility of the land in the 18th century.

1. THE FERM-TOUN

The early ferm-touns contained up to a dozen households clustered in homes and steadings on the edge of their arable land, which was worked jointly by all the inhabitants. They were mainly organised on the runrig system whereby each family had several detached rigs (lengths of raised ploughed land) originally allocated by rotating lot each year, so that everyone would have a fair share of the more fertile land.

The arable land lay in strips and patches scattered amongst the heather and moor, the bog and waste ground, with rough grazing and moorland areas beyond. As the ferm-toun expanded (for instance by woodland clearance), single tenancy units came into being.

The use of the arable land was by 'infield' and 'outfield'.

The infield was the best land nearest the houses. It was manured regularly from every possible source available, including preying on the poorer land around. Dung from the byre and stable, household refuse, and turf from many sources (including composted earthen middens made from turf cut for the purpose) all went into the infield soil. The two staple crops were bere (a form of barley) and oats. In the best farming areas wheat was important since it produced cash from the sale of its white flour for the bread of the better off. Extensive parts of the surrounding land were continually being depleted to maintain the productivity of the relatively limited infield areas.

The outfield, or poorer quality land, usually lay a little further off. It was an essential complement to the infield, dedicated primarily to stock grazing and only secondarily to crops. It was a source of

grassy turfs for many uses. Shifting cultivation was practised on the outfield with stock being folded on different parts in turn with those parts being used for crops for a few years, without further manuring, until their ability to produce crops was exhausted. It was on the outfield that new forms of manuring were first tried, such as salt (from the late 1500s) and lime (from the 1620s), sporadically at first but later with increasing frequency. By spreading lime the outfield could be brought up to infield quality. In lime-bearing areas such as the Lothians and Ayrshire this led to a great increase in land under the plough in the late 1600s and early 1700s.

The surrounding rough grazing and moorland, the peat bogs and the wet scrub-covered land were necessary service areas. They provided peat for fuel as well as turf for building and for making earthen middens. They were also grazed by sheep and cattle, watched over by the young folk of the farms, and sometimes provided famine food like dry sprigs of heather.

From the infield, the outfield and the moorland there developed a kind of ecological energy cycle. In good times this economy fed men and animals, provided seed for next year's harvest and created a surplus to cover the rent and the cost of smithy work for plough and cart. It might also provide a mart (an animal fattened for winter slaughter and pickling, so that a meat feast might be possible at the New Year and at celebrations like weddings). But if the weather was bad and the crops poor the system, already stretched to its limits with the increase of population, could not readily cope and had no built-in flexibility in the less-favoured areas.

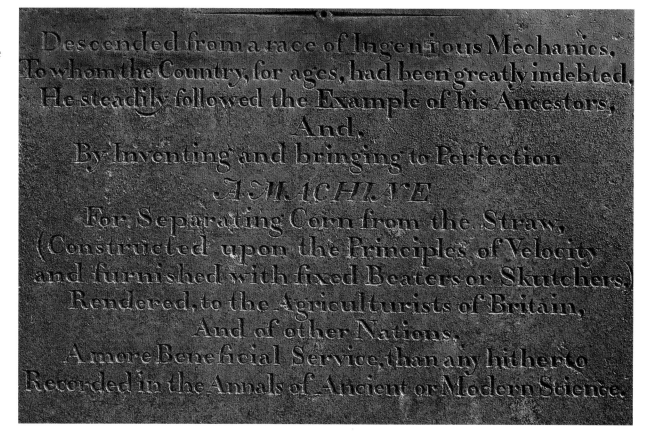

Gravestone of Andrew Meikle, inventor of the threshing machine, at East Linton churchyard, East Lothian.

Descended from a race of Ingenious Mechanics,
To whom the Country, for ages, had been greatly indebted,
He steadily followed the Example of his Ancestors,
And,
By Inventing and bringing to Perfection
A MACHINE
For Separating Corn from the Straw,
(Constructed upon the Principles of Velocity
and furnished with fixed Beaters or Skutchers,)
Rendered, to the Agriculturists of Britain,
And of other Nations,
A more Beneficial Service, than any hitherto
Recorded in the Annals of Ancient or Modern Science.

most basic of all agricultural implements: the plough. The early improvers looked to England for ploughs they thought better than the local type: they were men like Barclay of Urie in Kincardineshire, Grant of Monymusk in Aberdeenshire, and the Earl of Galloway, who had English plough types on his Orkney estates by 1747.

The Earl of Stair imported a Dutch plough in 1730 and sent a man to England to learn to make implements. But the real advance came with the plough developed in 1767 by the Berwickshire ploughwright, James Small. This combined the features of the northern English Rotherham plough and the native 'old Scotch' plough, and use of the new hybrid plough spread rapidly.

A second major innovation was the threshing machine. Experiments to replace the centuries-old hand-threshing flails with mechanical beaters had been going on from at least 1732. By 1758 water-driven horizontally turning scutchers were tried, modelled on

the flax mill. However the real breakthrough came with Andrew Meikle who produced the first successful threshing mill by feeding sheaves of grain through rollers into a revolving drum. Meikle's mill was developed in 1786 and spread rapidly, at first to the larger farms and then to the smaller holdings throughout the country. Four decades later, technology revolutionised the back-breaking labour of hand reaping in the fields. In 1827 Patrick Bell invented the first practical mechanical reaper which quickly began to replace the sickle and scythe.

But the development which most radically altered the farming landscape was the spread of systematic underground tile drainage, along with the enclosing of fields, from the 1840s. Since ridges were no longer needed for drainage they were gradually levelled. It was then possible to work the flat land across the vanished ridges which no longer hindered the worker with the scythe, nor the horse-operated machine-reaper, nor the horse-drawn sowing-machines and rollers or any of the machines that soon became commonplace. It took only half a century to erase the shape of the old farming world by creating fields with level surfaces which have been familiar to us now for nearly 150 years.

Although it did not happen overnight the change was irrevocable. Ferm-touns were replaced by consolidated individual holdings standing within their own enclosed fields on which crop rotation was practised, including sowing grass seed and allowing land to lie fallow in summer. Common grazing areas that had been allotted to owners were reclaimed and improved where possible

The mechanical reaper invented by Patrick Bell in 1827 revolutionised harvesting.

as part of the spread of the new agriculture. Such former grazing areas were sometimes cultivated by using the lazy-bed technique for potatoes, a crop that spread from big house gardens to tenants' fields in the 1700s. The lazy-bed system involved planting on undug strips of soil using manure and soil from adjacent trenches as a covering and was good for cleaning the ground. With such enormous changes the whole appearance of Lowland Scotland, or at least the farming parts, altered dramatically.

In the Highlands a different kind of agricultural revolution was taking place, involving not mechanical innovation but a new form of land-use: sheep husbandry on a massive scale. The coming of the sheep produced the most spectacular change of all – the trauma of human displacement known to history as 'The Highland Clearances' (Box 3).

At the same time planned villages with their rural industries were appearing, turnpike roads and other smaller linking tracks were spreading and two-wheeled carts drawn by solidly-built horses proliferated. These changes made the transport of goods easier. The countryside was becoming more market-oriented by supplying food for the expanding villages, towns and cities to which increasing numbers of people were moving. Food production for a wider market was the key to the new economy as people moved inexorably away from the self-sufficiency of the old and isolated farming communities whose resources had done little more than allow them to survive.

The feeding of people and the foddering of animals were interrelated. By about 1740 turnips, which like potatoes had originated in the gardens of the rich, had become a field crop in the Lothians and the Merse and eventually elsewhere. Turnips enabled farmers to over-winter stock and to fatten cattle for the market. The spread of potatoes also led directly to an increase in pig keeping, especially in dairy farming areas where whey was available for use as swill. Even the Highlanders, traditionally opposed to eating pork, were feeding small swine on potatoes by the 1790s. They sold thousands of such pigs at the Kinross and Cupar markets to Lowland farmers, millers and distillers who had *draff* (the dregs of malt after brewing) to fatten them. By the mid-nineteenth century married farm-workers living in cottar houses had begun to keep pigs in sties attached to their homes, as part of their allowances; or they might get a couple of stones (12 kg) of pork in lieu. For a long time pork was meat for servants, as beef was for their Lowland masters and mutton was to the Highlanders.

Cereal crops also changed in character. Extension of the outfield areas expanded the oats acreage and gradually new varieties of oats came in. The growing of wheat spread northwards from the Lothians and Merse, often at first to coastal areas where seaweed manure was plentiful. The baking of white-floured loaves in the towns and of flour-scones and the like on farm kitchen girdles spread with the availability of wheat. The old cereal 'bere', with its four to six rows of ears, was

Ploughing with oxen, from 18th century gravestone in Liberton kirkyard, Edinburgh.

2. THE SHIELING

The shielings were grazing areas to which stock were taken in the summer. For centuries the annual seasonal rhythm had been a movement in spring from the lower-lying village (the *wintertown*) to the higher-lying shieling areas with their clusters of huts of stone and turf or of wattle and turf (the *summertown*). Around the summertown the stock could enjoy the new hill grass while the new season's crop could grow to maturity in the wintertown. The stock was brought back to the lower levels after the autumn harvest when the village lands had been cleared of crops and were again thrown open to what amounted to common grazing.

But commercial pressures intervened to change the nature of the shieling system, both in the run up to the Act of Union of 1707 and afterwards. The use of the shieling areas was intensified as a result of the increasing commercial interest in cattle, particularly by lairds sending black cattle to the hills along with the stock of their tenants.

Such sharing, marking a period of co-existence under the conditions of cattle-trading, was rudely ended with the massive and widespread introduction of commercial breeds of sheep, Cheviot and Blackface, mainly in the nineteenth century. At this point the shieling areas were cleared and made into single farms for the use of sheep-farmers and sheep-men, many of whom came from the south of Scotland. Blue-slated farmhouses began to dot the lonely hills and, with the exception of Lewis in the Hebrides where shieling use ran on into the twentieth century, the 1800s saw the effective end, owing to economic pressures, of what had been a long-standing form of land-use in the more pastoral parts of the country.

The coming of the Blackface sheep hastened the end of the system of cattle grazing on the summer shielings.

replaced by the more productive two-eared barley. In fact oats had begun to replace bere in the Lowlands by the end of the seventeenth century and farm-workers bargained with their masters not to have bere-meal, but rather oatmeal, as part of the wages they received in kind.

Beef cattle like the Aberdeen Angus and the Shorthorn (a cross between native Scots and Midland English breeds) were fostered and became important items of trade. The Ayrshire, evolved in the second half of the eighteenth century, led to the establishment and spread from there of dairy farming, again in close support of the expanding urban populations. Plenty of winter fodder – turnips, hay and straw – and good summer grazings were needed to produce the quality of these animals and their produce, and the new farming was able to provide such fodder.

ALL CHANGE

Throughout the country, improvements to fields, tools and stock were matched, with regional variations, by improvements in housing. New mansion houses and their surrounding parks started off the process in the late seventeenth century. Farm houses and steadings followed, the estate mains farm usually acting as a prototype. The actual scale and layout of units varied according to the type of farming practised – for example, a hill sheep farm did not need a barn and cereal-processing space as much as a Lowland grain-growing farm – but the new arrangements had some common features.

Most noticeable, marking the changing status between master and workers, was the separation of the dwelling-house from the steading: the house having its own separate garden, with the cottar house a little way off. Bigger farms were already being arranged around a square by the 1690s and this form (usually with the midden in the centre) continued. For smaller-scale places buildings were arranged around three sides or could form a right angle. Smaller farms and crofts continued in the old linear form with house, barn and byre and possibly other elements arranged in a row. But as a stage in modernisation, internal access between people and cattle slowly came to an end, although this 'long-house' tradition survived into the twentieth cen-

3. THE CLEARANCES

Ruined croft house on Rhum.

Sheep husbandry developed apace in the Borders in the eighteenth century. Through the use of sheep enclosures, selective breeding was facilitated. Turnips were also one of the bases for winter feed for sheep in the Border area. From here the Cheviot and Blackface sheep moved in their thousands with southern shepherds into the Highland areas.

In the Highlands the numbers of sheep and cattle were about equal in the 1750s but by 1800 sheep were dominant. Increases in the prices of wool and mutton after 1815 led to a major thrust from the south when farmers from the Scottish and English borders rented from Highland lairds shieling areas for the summer grazing of sheep as well as arable stretches for wintering at lower levels.

In this way commercial interaction between Lowlands and Highlands, at the time of the so-called 'Clearances', brought two worlds into conflict. It led to massive disruption of the traditional forms of Highland life and substantial migrations of people from the sheltered straths down to windy coasts, infertile peat-bog and moorland edges. Great numbers of people emigrated to the New World.

The kind of estate surveying that had long been proceeding in the Lowlands now reached the Highlands too, as lairds looked for ways of increasing profits. Sheep farming may have been the first inspiration for this but a secondary opportunity came after the 1870s through the establishment of deer forests, sometimes through conversion of former sheep-farms north and south of the Great Glen. By 1912 deer forests covered 5,800 square miles (15,000 sq km) of the Highlands, though 40 per cent of this was above the 1,500 ft (460 m) level in areas marginal for sheep grazing. In this way lairds in the Highlands were able to tap into the wealth of Victorian industrialists, some of whose profits now went into sport and recreation.

Such activities, however, effectively altered much of the landscape of the Highlands; the crofting settlements were left as a kind of fringe, reshaped in the nineteenth century, often in linear streets with individual fields running below the house to the sea and above the house to the head-dyke on the hill, beyond which the crofters' sheep still graze in common. The individual enclosure of the arable land of the crofts is, on the one hand, similar to what occurred earlier on the Lowland farms; but the survival of common grazing points back to the days of communal or joint farming that have long vanished from Lowland Scotland.

tury in parts of the crofting counties. Probably the most remarkable of such survivals is the 'blackhouse' with its immensely thick walls and low-set thatched roof, well shaped to resist Atlantic gales; there is a celebrated survival, now a museum-piece, in the crofting township of Arnol in Skye. And the staple fuel was always peat (Box 4).

Such sequences of change, differing as they do in the Highlands and Lowlands, had a strong impact on the social structure of the countryside. In subsistence farming days a stake in the land, however minimal, was a form of social security. Improvements led to wage-labourers whose only link with the land was the work they did on it and the local produce they received in kind as part of their wages, whether they were single men in bothies or married men in cottar houses. A social gap came into being, marked among other things by the distancing of workers' quarters from the dwelling-house, the appearance of the farm grieve, overseer or steward as a buffer between men and masters, and a tendency to have food of different qualities. These changes were most common in bigger farming areas, although even the smaller farms were not without their symbolic status differentiations.

The nineteenth century north-east bothy ballad, *Auld Luckie of Brunties*, tells how the men supped their brose with spoons in the kitchen while 'ben the hoose' the knife and fork were wielded and breakfast included luxuries like tea and coffee, butter, eggs and cheese. In the crofting counties crofters and their families retained a land base, but because the 1886 Crofters Holdings (Scotland) Act froze their holdings at a level often too low to be fully viable in terms of producing a living, many had to supplement incomes by work not directly linked to the land.

THE HIGHLAND QUESTION

The cumulative effects of the immense changes in Scotland's land-use over the last 300 years have completely altered the appearance of the man-made landscape. Shared farms have become individual farms though some marginal survivals, like the farming township of Auchindrain in Argyll (now preserved as the Museum of Argyll Farming Life), remain as a pointer to earlier days. Tile drainage has levelled the corrugations of the old ridge-and-furrow system. Fences, hedges and stone dykes enclose Lowland fields within which grain, vegetable crops and grass grow in rotational sequences. Patches of arable farmland are no longer islands in great oceans of wilder moorland.

But the Highlands, which comprise one-sixth of Britain's land area, or 48 per cent of Scotland's (inclusive of the island of Bute), remain a problem area whose problems are only exacerbated by the pressures of European Community policies on Lowland farming as such. The real marginal periphery lies in the Western

Horses were used well into the 1950s on many farms.

Isles, the north-west coast and Shetland; a transitional zone covers Orkney and Caithness; and there is a favoured inner zone arcing from Kintyre, Islay and Lorn through Speyside to the Moray Firth coast where conditions approximate closely to those of Lowland farming. Neither the Highland nor the Lowland areas are homogeneous but the effects of crofting legislation on the Highlands, from the time of the Crofters Holdings (Scotland) Act of 1886 onwards and including the activities of the Highlands and Islands Development Board (now Highlands and Islands Enterprise), have had a marked effect on the landscape everywhere.

Since agricultural use of these areas, other than pasture improvement, is inhibited by the century-old crofting system there is less emphasis on land improvement than on forestry and on the development of alternatives linked to sport, recreation and the sea. Industrial possibilities have also been promoted including seaweed-drying, knitwear, a pulp mill, aluminium smelting and, more recently, the oil-inspired Moray Firth developments. The likelihood (or danger, as many see it, see Chapter 9) is that the human landscape of the crofting counties will become increasingly frozen into a kind of three-dimensional photograph of the agricultural past – a tourist theme park in which the making of lazy-beds, the building of head-dykes and so on will add a flavour of the history of human toil to the scenic beauty that attracts tourists in the first instance.

PEOPLE AND THEIR ENVIRONMENT

Amongst all these changes perhaps the hardest to describe is the way in which the attitudes of people to their environment and to the creatures around them have changed over the last three centuries.

There was, for instance, a continual broadening of personal horizons. An agricultural writer of 1797

Blacksmith at Fort William maintains a traditional craft.

whom the hourly and daily weather changes matter greatly.

The language of Scots also contains many echoes of pre-improvement conditions. Words like *rammel* and *rone* (brushwood), *scrogs* (stunted trees or shrubs), *etnach* (juniper) and *arnits* (pig-nuts) all point to untamed places and plants. Terms may survive locally long after peat clearance, drainage and the general processes of cultivation have completely destroyed the flora and fauna to which they refer. Words can become memorial stones to what has gone, and place-names act as pointers too. The farm name Bruntland (or *Brunties*) of north-east Scotland records places where mossy or peaty ground was regularly burned to fertilise the next crop. Natural features, all observed closely by country dwellers of the past, like *brae* (hillside), *cleugh* (crag), *drum* (knoll), *glack* (ravine), *heuch* (steep bank), *kip* (peak), *law* (hill) and so on have been immortalised in place-names.

Through words and place-names, Man's interaction with the natural world is held up as in a mirror. And the intimacy of such interaction is further highlighted by terms expressing character and physical attributes that liken people to creatures. Outcasts were symbolised as *bruits* (brutes), *cowts* (colts), *knappers* (ones who bite with their teeth, like animals, to drive off cats, etc.), or *tikes* (curs). Stupid folk were *anes* (asses), *gowks* (cuckoos), *hoolets* (owls), *mowdieworts* (moles), *nowts* or *stirks* (cattle) or *yowes* (sheep).

Time and again such words echo the reality of rural attitudes that contrast markedly with philosophical concepts of Man's superiority over the brute creation and of changing perceptions of scenery like those of Edward Burt in the 1720s. He saw Highland mountains as 'dismal brown', 'dirty purple, and most of all disagreeable when the heather is in bloom'; another unenthusiastic traveller, Dr Samuel Johnson, wrote in 1773 of 'this wide extent of hopeless sterility'. This contrasts vividly with the fashionable taste for romantic scenery largely initiated by Sir Walter Scott, whose *Lady of the Lake* (1809) 'sent visitors flocking to the Trossachs, and thus begat the tourist trade' (see Chapter 17).

Land-use is not just a matter of how farmers use the soil for arable and pastoral purposes. It is a reflection of a way of life that was that of most people until very recent times. In fact our landscape, buildings, language, attitudes and perceptions are still strongly conditioned or marked by the rural past to a degree of which most people are unaware.

The legacy of the countryside that lies both around the indwellers of Scotland and within their minds is at the same time the past in the present and a fundamental part of the present. Study of the details of this legacy can help us understand the path we have travelled from the past to the present. Such study provides us with a lens through which we can view the range and degree of

observed how in Berwickshire the farm servants had

> cast off the long clothing, tardy face and lethargic look of their forefathers, for the short doublet and linen trousers, the quick step and life of persons labouring for their own behoof, and work up to the spirit of their own cattle, and the rapid evolutions of the threshing mill.

Ministers of the church deplored the interest in expensive dress, including silk, among maidservants, the drinking of tea at breakfast, and the spread of whisky-drinking even among women of the lower class.

Such symbols of changing perceptions do not, however, affect the fundamental point that until well into the twentieth century the perceptions and attitudes of individuals still had a strongly rural basis. This is evident, for example, in the language of Lowland Scots, which reflects a picture of a relatively non-industrialised countryside whose inhabitants were on close terms with their environment and concerned with it in a way that is little known to the present-day majority.

Every detail of weather appears, sometimes as a prognostication. A halo or broch round the moon still means bad weather on the way: *a broch near is a storm far*. Such a halo was also called a *cock's eye, fauld* or *gow*, illustrating the tenet that a multiplicity of names indicates a topic of importance to rural communities for

Women in East Lothian planting potatoes; machines have now replaced people.

contemporary change as the clank of de-stoners echoes across a countryside that contains fewer and fewer people, sounding a drum roll for the end of a way of life that will never return.

4. THE FUEL OF LIFE

For centuries the main fuel for the fires that warmed the kitchens, cooked the food and boiled the water was peat. Untold quantities have been turned to smoke and ash. Those unfortunate enough to live in districts where it had been used up were badly off and had to cut it expensively from neighbouring areas, or resort to using earthy turf (the cutting of which spoiled the grazing areas) or dried cow-dung (which meant loss of manure). Estates always tried to conserve their precious peat resource by regulating the use of turbaries. And no wonder: no fewer than fifty or sixty cart-loads were needed to keep just one fire going for a year, and this figure was repeated for every house, every year, for centuries.

Peat cutting has led to immense changes in the landscape, including settlement patterns and the associated forms of land-use and flora. Most of the Lowland Scottish peat has been exhausted, although former bogs can be traced by the extreme flatness of fields on their sites. Yet so much remains, especially in the Highlands and Islands, that ten per cent of Scotland's surface is still under peat.

Underneath that peat lies widespread evidence of earlier land-use by prehistoric farmers from the period before the climatic deterioration that led to peat growth; while on the peat surface a rich variety of plants and animals survives in a habitat that conservationists regard as unique. Herein are the roots of the present-day clash of interests between those who seek to preserve the heritage of the past and those who seek to exploit the peatlands by large-scale commercial extraction or by alien afforestation.

Crofter cutting peat on the Ardnamurchan peninsula.

105

Crofting area near Elgol,
Isle of Skye.

The Way of Crofting

FRANK RENNIE

Dr Frank W. Rennie is a geologist by training who now lives and works as a crofter in Galson in the Isle of Lewis. He worked there as a scientific officer for the Nature Conservancy Council for four years and was the founding president of the 4,000–strong Scottish Crofters' Union. He is now a consultant in rural development and adult education.

The stereotypes of the confident self-sufficient farmer on the one hand and the work-shy state-supported crofter on the other are just as nonsensical as the idea that every conservationist sports woollies and green welly boots on excursions from the city every weekend. But the mythology dies hard.

Crofting is more than a mere remnant of traditional peasant agriculture. It is neither a primitive nor an impoverished form of farming; rather it is a unique social system in which small-scale agriculture plays a unifying role.

The word 'croft' does not refer to a house but to a smallholding, the tenant of which (the crofter) pays rent to the landowner and shares the common grazing with other crofters in a village known as a crofting 'township'. An individual croft may be less than a tenth of a hectare (quarter of an acre) in size, more commonly two hectares (five acres) or so, but sometimes it can be the size of a small farm.

The crofting system grew out of the semi-feudal Highland land system in the eighteenth century under which the chiefs rented land to tenants known as tacksmen; these in turn rented smaller plots to sub-tenants, usually on poorer soils requiring reclamation. In effect the sub-tenant was required to create his own croft; but he had no security of tenure and could be summarily evicted at the whim of the estate factor.

The Highland Clearances of the eighteenth and nineteenth centuries (see Chapter 8) caused the eviction of huge numbers of crofters to make room for large-scale sheep ranching and led to mass emigration to Australia and the Americas as well as to the industrial cities of Scotland. However, despite all the emigration, the Highland population kept rising, reaching a peak in the middle of the nineteenth century. This coincided with widespread poverty and destitution caused by disastrous harvests and the great potato blight. The poverty and despair of those cruel decades left a deep sense of historical grievance that has been slow to fade.

In 1886 Parliament passed the first Crofter Holdings (Scotland) Act, giving official recognition and legal protection to crofting as a system of land tenure. But crofts were not created as an act of generosity by landowners and politicians; the legislation was seen as a last attempt to stem the growing tide of civil disturbance that was spreading through the Highlands and Islands. The people in the rural areas were hungry, poor, landless and desperate. They had nothing else to lose and their obvious unrest was felt to be a subversive threat to the very existence of the nation.

The struggle for land at the end of the nineteenth and early in the twentieth century, one of the most radical periods of Highland history, has become popularly known as the 'crofters' war'. Indeed it is less than three generations since many peaceful crofters were fighting against the British army and the police force for their right to live and work on their native land. This link between the historical and the modern crofter is the key to understanding the motivations of the crofting community as a whole.

The history of my own village of Galson in the Isle of Lewis is a microcosm of the history of crofting. The existing crofting village and our two neighbouring villages were destroyed by the landlord in 1863 and the people were cleared off the land. The villages were turned into one large farm with a single tenant farmer firmly installed in the only house. This situation continued until 1921 when ex-servicemen returning from the First World War began, not surprisingly, to look for the land they had been promised ('a home fit for heroes'), for which they had been persuaded to fight overseas.

The owner of the whole of Lewis and Harris at that time was Lord Leverhulme, founding father of the multinational giant Unilever. He had many grandiose plans for industrial development on the island but the idea of land resettlement was anathema to him. The pressures to redistribute land, however, became intense. Several farms were peacefully raided and occupied by landless families and eventually the government

Blackhouse at The Skye Cottage Museum, Kilmuir.

directed the Department of Agriculture to purchase a number of farms and divide them into crofting units. Today Galson has fifty-five crofts, several with second houses built by the second or third generation of the original settlers, and a thriving population of 146.

THE PATCHWORK LANDSCAPE

Under the original crofting legislation, crofting in Scotland is limited to the seven former counties of Shetland, Orkney, Caithness, Sutherland, Ross and Cromarty, Inverness-shire and Argyll. The entire region is now classified under a European Community directive as a Less Favoured Area (LFA) (see Chapter 10). It is 'less favoured' because in the crofting areas the soils are generally shallow and mineral-deficient, suitable at best only for marginal upland farming. It is no coincidence that these are some of the most sparsely populated and scenically beautiful places in Britain.

Within this area there are around 17,700 registered crofts, of which over 85 per cent are tenanted rather than owned, for although they have the option to buy, most crofters choose to remain tenants with very strong rights guaranteed in Acts of Parliament. Within the total land area of the Highlands and Islands only 20 per cent is croftland, mostly in the Western Isles, Orkney, Shetland and the north and west coasts of the mainland. These individual crofts are generally small discrete units with some arable cultivation, mainly producing sheep and some cattle which are then sold to mainland farmers to 'finish' for the market. Most crofters also have access to larger areas of rough grazing near their townships; some of this grazing has been improved by fencing and re-seeding with grass but mostly this is undeveloped moor and hill land. Many of them are sited on coastal machair land (Box 1).

On the arable and 'inbye' land of the crofting villages there is considerable variation in the use of the croft according to the quality of land, the size of the holding and the circumstances of the crofter. A common example would be a croft with some permanent grassland and some hay as fodder for a score or two of sheep. Potatoes, turnips and perhaps rape or kale may also be grown as additional fodder. So with such a variety on each croft, and with each village a patchwork of crofts, there is a much greater variety of habitat available for the wildlife. This is in total contrast to the agri-business of intensive farms which may have individual fields of cereal or oilseed rape as large as a whole crofting township.

Most crofts provide only spare-time or part-time employment and fewer than five per cent are able to

1. THE MACHAIR

Shell sands at Smirisary, Glenuig. It is the calcium from these wind blown shell-sands that enriches the soil of the machair and produces the explosion of flowers, insect and bird life.

One of the most striking features of the crofting landscape is the so-called 'machair', a Gaelic word for the stretches of low-lying meadow land near the sands of the seashore. The lime-rich machair grasslands occur on the west coast mainland and in the Western Isles, where they provide a habitat for a wonderful variety of wading birds and other species such as the increasingly rare corncrake (see Chapter 5). The machair lands are studded with millions of wild flowers and are a prime example of low-intensity farming methods that have produced a wealth of flowers, animals and birds as well as sustaining a rich human culture. The diversity of wildlife that makes the crofting lands so attractive to nature lovers stems directly from the nature of crofting land-use itself.

On the lime-rich machair grasslands of the Western Isles and west coast mainland cattle have helped preserve the wide range of wild flowers and plants; cattle are more selective than sheep in their grazing, tearing off only the tops of the grasses and plants while sheep graze right down to the roots. On the hillsides the spread of bracken has been attributed to the decline of cattle; on the machair, cattle have also helped to keep out invading plants

like butterbur (*Petasites hybridus*) by crushing the large leaves underfoot. It is evident that the spread of this plant is most rapid where cattle have been taken off the land. In addition to the beneficial effects of cattle on plants, their deep hoof-prints on the wet areas of the machair are often used for shelter by delicate wader chicks before they can fly.

support a household on the produce of the croft alone; these are usually the larger crofts on the relatively better-quality land of the east coast mainland.

It is the full-time crofter who is often the most disadvantaged; his croft is not big enough to compete on an equal footing with the larger farmers but the croft leaves him too little time to permit a regular (non-croft) job to supplement the croft income. The small level of croft income is neither derisory nor insignificant, however; the additional income gained from the croft is often important in enabling families to stay in the rural areas of their choice despite the difficulty of finding alternative and/or adequately paid employment.

It would be a mistake to think that crofting has not changed in any way over the last century, but in comparison to the enormous changes in farming practice throughout southern Britain crofting is still very much a traditional system. One cannot really compare modern farming and traditional crofting, but to me there is no doubt whatsoever that the farming methods of crofting are very much more friendly to the natural environment than large-scale chemical-intensive agriculture.

The rich and varied patchwork landscape created by individual crofts ensures that a wide variety of wildlife habitats exists in a very small area. Croft land given over to permanent grass, turnips, potatoes, hay/silage and heather moorland all support subtly different communities of plants, insects and animals which in turn provide food and shelter for larger birds and animals. Many crofts have fields which are too small, or too rough, for tractors with spraying booms to be used; consequently crops are relatively free of the pesticides and herbicides used on more intensive farms, making croft products healthier both for humans and for wildlife. Where weed-killers and fertilisers are used they are usually applied using knapsack sprayers and in such small quantities that there is no comparison with industrial farming techniques.

PROTECTION AND PROTECTIONISM

It has long been apparent that the policies and grant incentives offered by different government departments concerned with land-use are often incompatible. Agriculture, forestry, nature conservation and other economic developments obviously compete with each other for land and resources.

People who live in towns demand greater access to the countryside for walking, climbing, and many other recreational pursuits. This growth in countryside recreation and tourism has applied greater pressure on rural amenities and highlights the need to protect scenic and environmental attractions. The benefits to country people may be only marginal, for tourism tends to be seasonal, dependent on weather and the economic

situation, and to provide generally low-paid jobs. Many people are concerned that tourist pressure is eroding the cultural identity of regional communities and destroying those cultural variations which attract tourists to the area. The choice is whether the countryside should serve simply as a weekend playground for townsfolk or whether it should be a place for the people who live in the countryside to earn a decent living for themselves.

The major cause of friction between conservationists and people who live in the countryside has long been the designation of Sites of Special Scientific Interest (SSSIs) by the old Nature Conservancy Council (NCC) (see Chapter 10). These SSSIs are designed to ensure the protection of areas which are of national importance because of the wild plants, animals, birds and geological features found there, and they can vary in size from a fraction of a hectare to over a thousand hectares.

Traditional methods of hay making, as at Barvas on Lewis, enable the corncrake to survive in the Western Isles.

Crofter hoeing potatoes at Shader, Barvas, Lewis.

Hand shearing of sheep is still common in the crofting areas.

What usually causes the friction is not the principle but the manner of the protection of the site. The crofter or landowner will be notified of a list of 'Potentially Damaging Operations' (PDOs) which the NCC thinks would have an adverse effect on the site (see Chapter 16).

That is where the problem starts, for number one on the list of 'potentially damaging operations' sent to those with an interest in the site is 'cultivation, including ploughing, harrowing, and reseeding', followed closely by 'changes in the grazing regime', the 'introduction of stock', and 'the application of fertilisers and lime'. To most people who make their living from agricultural operations the effect of this letter arriving on the doormat is enough to raise their blood pressure to danger point.

Of course the list only refers to activities which are potentially damaging and need to be cleared by the NCC before any work is started, and in many situations there is in fact no real cause for concern; but it is the perceived lack of adequate information and prior consultation and of an independent appeals procedure which is the root cause of the farmer's discontent.

The system has created SSSIs as isolated islands of nature conservation dotted around the Highland countryside, and it is felt that this system is unduly restrictive and inappropriate for the protection of these areas. Much of the land surrounding these SSSIs is also environmentally sensitive and scenically beautiful, but the system seems to imply that while the SSSIs need to be protected the other parts of the Highlands and Islands do not.

The conflict and confusion surrounding the identification and designation of SSSIs may be resolved by

paying greater attention to public information and encouraging greater consultation; however, the problem of the management of SSSIs is more pervasive.

Take for example an area of wet bog land; the high rainfall and shallow acid soils may mean that this area represents a loss of production to a crofter who wants to graze animals on it. The area may be quite small but in relation to the croft land available it may still be important to the crofter, who may even occasionally lose an animal in it. Consequently he may want to drain the land and improve it.

The bog, however, may be a very good site for wildlife – waterfowl and wading birds, for example – and conservationists may object to the crofter's plan to drain the area. Unless the bog is within a National Nature Reserve (NNR) or an SSSI there is apparently very little that the conservationists can do about it. Within an SSSI however, if the scientific value of the site would be damaged, and if no compromise plan can be worked out, the NCC can prevent the crofter from starting the draining operations. In such cases the law states that the farmer or crofter should be compensated for the loss of income which has resulted from the cancellation of the grazing improvement scheme (see Chapter 10).

The idea of getting payment for 'doing nothing', however, is alien to most crofters and upland farmers and does not rest easy with traditional notions of working the land. But there is another more serious complication, in that the management payment will be calculated according to an agricultural value, which is at best 'marginal', rather than for conservation value, which may be exceedingly high.

It is rather like offering £6.50 for a Van Gogh masterpiece on the basis that all you are paying for is a frame of wood, a square of canvas, and a couple of tubes of oil paint! Clearly this is absurd. In the same way no businessman would expect to pay only a few pounds for a piece of wasteland in the centre of London on account of its dilapidated condition. What he would be paying for is the development potential of the site, and whether it is the potential for erecting a building or for maintaining a valuable ecological system the same standards should apply.

In reality crofters are not wanting to hold the nation to ransom by threatening the destruction of a valuable nature conservation site unless hefty compensation is paid to them.

This is no begging bowl mentality, nor is it a form of conservation blackmail, for most crofters have no thought of deliberately destroying the natural environment which surrounds them. For a number of years, crofters and the Scottish Crofters' Union (SCU) have suggested that, if the maintenance and protection of the natural environment are to be given a higher priority by the public, the public purse must be prepared to help pay for it.

A SUSTAINABLE SUPPORT SYSTEM

It is ironic that while recent changes of emphasis in European agricultural policies are pushing farmers away from intensive over-production and towards land management systems which are 'environmentally beneficent', the crofting communities have come full circle. The crofting communities have never contributed to the agricultural surpluses, but now those crofters and upland farmers (who by their very methods of working, operate in a manner which is friendly to the natural environment) are being directed and controlled by the policy makers who wholeheartedly advocated industrial production methods that devastated the natural environment. Yet what these 'progressive' thinkers called 'uneconomic' systems or 'primitive' agriculture or 'unworkable' practices are the very systems which have safeguarded so much of the natural environment which was being lost elsewhere.

Many country people, including crofters, strongly resent the implication made by outsiders that 'development' (agricultural or otherwise) is a dirty word and that the land should be preserved in aspic as a large open-air museum in which country people themselves are among the living exhibits.

The people who live in the crofting areas may enjoy a wonderful landscape full of wildlife and scenic beauty but they cannot live off views and fresh air alone. The seasonal and low-paid nature of much of the available work often means that they suffer a lower standard of living. This makes it ethically difficult for conservationists to oppose appropriate local economic development on the grounds of minor environmental criteria unless they can offer other conservation-based ways of earning a living.

Obviously much depends on the definition of 'appropriate' development; for what may seem 'appropriate' to a crofter or hill farmer trying to maintain a decent living may be considered 'inappropriate' by an ecologist sitting at his desk in Edinburgh or London. Conversely the wholesale conservation of wild spaces, undrained wetlands and particular species of birds, animals and trees may seem to be an ill-affordable luxury to the crofter struggling for economic survival.

In the longer term we need to provide annual 'conservation management incentives' to all those land-users who engage in environmentally friendly farming, not just to those who have little islands of SSSIs within their land. The idea that environmental conservation must be actively managed rather than simply left to itself is not new and neither is the idea of conservation as a cash crop in itself. Unlike turnips or potatoes, however, the 'conservation crop' of a piece of land cannot be picked up and sold to consumers in a city marketplace. Some things simply cannot be bought.

Country people could be encouraged by direct tax incentives or by special payments to farm in ways which

are agreed to be environmentally beneficial but which may not be considered 'economically feasible' from a purely financial aspect. The introduction of the voluntary Environmentally Sensitive Area (ESA) scheme in the crofting lands of Uist in the Western Isles was a welcome step in this direction (see Chapter 16).

Both crofters and conservationists have also been concerned about the rapid decline of cattle numbers in the croft lands. If a cash subsidy were introduced to encourage crofters to keep more cattle a better cow-to-sheep grazing ratio could be created. This would maintain the grazing in better condition than would be the case under sheep alone. A good grazing mix of one cow for every four or five sheep promotes a greater diversity of herbs and flowering plants in the pastures – a nice example of how nature can be enriched and sustained through man's creative exploitation.

In some parts of the country it is barely a generation since almost every crofting household had a 'house cow' which would provide the family with milk, butter, cheese and a calf to sell annually. Cattle are much more demanding of the crofter's time whereas shepherding fits more easily into the part-time nature of crofting. This is one reason, along with changing work patterns and standards of living, why cattle numbers have declined. There is general agreement that there is a need to get more cattle back on to the land, not in large herds but through hundreds of crofters owning two or three cows with calves. Such a change would require a shift in our priorities, and if the commercial market for cattle could not support such a socially desirable policy then social funding should be made available to encourage land-users to adopt such schemes of environmentally friendly land management.

The crofting system, with its more relaxed and

Crofter and tractor in South Galson; crofters may be engineers, journalists, fishermen or civil servants as well as farmers.

Fishing for lobsters off Pladda.

balanced approach to agriculture and development, could set the trend for the future of sustainable farming in Britain.

DIVERSIFICATION AND INTEGRATED MANAGEMENT

One of the main benefits of the crofting system is that it maintains a healthy level of population in the crofting areas of the countryside. The crofting communities of the Western Isles, Skye, or Shetland offer a stark contrast to the vast unpopulated areas of north-west Sutherland and the west coast mainland whence the people have long since vanished. Scarcely a house remains standing in these empty glens. This is not true wilderness but a devastated landscape cleared of its native people and emptied by human greed. Those of us who remain do not do so out of romanticism, nor purely for economic gain, but from a deep conviction that the quality of life here is better than that we would have in a city.

The linch-pins of this social system are the rights of access to the land and security of tenure. Traditionally many crofts ran lengthwise from the sea, inland to the moor, in small clusters of scattered townships. The crofts were often further subdivided into narrower full-length strips among the surviving members of a family so as to give each descendant a piece of the moor, a piece of the good blackland, a piece of the machair and so on. This practice is no longer legal but it has left a patchwork of independent small family units, able to contribute to the family food supplies and, by selling the

surplus, to the family income. Such crofts were never intended to support the household without additional employment, but this handicap has now changed from a curse into a blessing.

The reliance upon employment other than agriculture but with the security of land on which to put down roots, to build a family home and grow crops for income and food has become one of the pillars of the crofting community. It has allowed crofters to remain where they want to live and has enabled the development of a very wide range of skills.

Here in my own village of Galson with its fifty-five crofts its population of 146 includes people who earn their living in catering, Harris Tweed weaving, civil engineering, publishing, the building trade, clerical work and a variety of other activities. All of these people are also involved in crofting.

One way in which the conservation movement could further help to reinforce the crofting system which has created and maintained this unique environment would be through the creation of conservation-related jobs for local people in rural communities. In this way the land-users (not simply landowners) would be able to act more effectively as custodians of the agricultural and conservation value of their own land.

This is well illustrated if we look at the IDP (Integrated Development Programme) for the Western Isles, which was launched a few years ago. The relative success of this development initiative has fostered several other development schemes in the Highlands and Islands. These have included an Agricultural Development Programme (ADP) for the Northern Isles,

Crofts above Loch Ness at Drumnadrochit, Great Glen.

Skye and the Argyll Islands; an HIDB development scheme for the north-west Sutherland area; and an HIDB backed Township Development Scheme for the Western Isles. None of these new projects has caused the same degree of local tension nor the sensationalist headlines which greeted the start of the original IDP. The media exaggerations at the time included such gems as 'Imminent Destruction Plan' (in the RSPB magazine *Birds*), and 'a poisonous little plan' (in the *New Scientist*)!

Those fears were largely born out of ignorance of the economic and social realities of the crofting system. Local people who pointed this out were immediately branded as parochial and anti-conservationist by out-side 'experts' who had by then developed an interest in the Western Isles.

Ultimately however the biggest worry for the future is the loss of croft land, for once it has been removed from crofting tenure there is no way under the present legal structure that this land can ever be returned to crofting. Just compare the diversity – ecological, social, and economic – of a thriving crofting community in Lewis, with a single land-use mainland estate, whether it is under-used or smothered with blanket forestry or kept as mile upon mile of grouse moor. With the continuing fall in farm profits there is now a good case for dividing some of these under-used estates and large farms into croft-sized units and encouraging families to settle on them.

By injecting such vitality into our rural communities we would be supporting the conservation of rural communities as well as their wildlife. Already some Scottish local authorities outside the crofting areas are seriously considering such a proposal.

If our rural communities become even more depopu-lated then the land will fall into disuse, and in many cases the wildlife will also suffer. In communities where croft land has been neglected or abandoned the result-ing deterioration in the crofting system is often closely paralleled by a deterioration in the diversity of wildlife. Active resumption of traditional crofting practices and their modern equivalents will rejuvenate the land as well as the crofting community and the wildlife which depends on both for its survival.

*Iain MacIver,
crofter and community
education worker for the
Western Isles Council.*

2. THE CROFTER'S YEAR

What does a crofter do? How does the crofter's year run? Let's take the case of Iain MacIver, a crofter in the village of Lacasaigh in the island of Lewis, the largest of the Western Isles.

He has a ten-acre croft which is quite a large one for Lewis and which enables him to run a relatively large flock of sheep and some cattle. He is also a community education officer with the local authority. The combination of desk-bound council official and welly-booted crofter may seem odd but, in the crofting communities, people have many such contrasting roles and Iain MacIver finds no difficulty in combining both occupations satisfactorily. As a crofter, Iain's year is shaped by the natural cycle of seasonal activity on his land. It is the sheep which dominate the calendar. Throughout October and into November he must spend time selecting and separating his sheep for breeding. Blackface sheep used to be the favoured breed because of their ability to withstand the harsh winter conditions; nowadays, however, hill Cheviots are becoming more common because they provide a better financial return.

By December all the sheep will have been dipped and drenched for the first time in the season and most will have been put to the ram. Iain MacIver has his own breeding rams but some crofters prefer to hire one from The Scottish Office Agriculture and Fisheries Department. The rams are usually removed from the flocks at the end of the month and the pregnant ewes are put out to pasture. With the sheep turned out from the croft land to graze on the moor in January, Iain can turn his attention to the wintering of his eight cattle and their calves. The cows are brought in and housed in the byre where, depending on the weather, they will spend most of their time during the winter months. Feeding the cattle and cleaning out the byre takes up a lot of time and without the help of his father (who also runs a croft in the village) Iain would find it difficult to justify the costs and work involved. The land has to be kept drained, fodder and feedstuffs have to be provided and the stock has to be kept healthy. The difficulties might often appear to outweigh the benefits but with careful husbandry Iain MacIver has been able to maintain both the herd and a balanced budget. Although the sheep usually spend the winter on the moor, some crofters with smaller flocks will keep their stock close to the croft so that their rough grazing can be supplemented by daily feeding.

*Iain MacIver at work on his
croft.*

By March some of the earlier breeding sheep are having their lambs; this is one of the busiest times of the year for Iain. Supervising the birth of a new flock and playing midwife to many of the ewes is not an easy task. Difficult births need his constant attention, orphan lambs must be cared for and triplets must be fostered with singletons.

As the days get longer and the weather gets warmer many other chores have to be done. Many trailer-loads of peat for the next winter's fuel supply have to be sliced from the bogs – a back-breaking job – and stacked on the moor to dry before being brought home by tractor later in the summer. Potatoes and root vegetables must be planted in the good soil of the croft – enough to provide food for Iain, his wife and their two young children in the coming year as well as seed potatoes for the following season.

Labour-intensive jobs such as peat-cutting and potato-planting are often done communally, with other members of the township helping. By working co-operatively in this way the crofters can complete the workload of one household in a single day or evening.

The fast-growing spring lambs and their mothers are sent back to the moor to graze in June and the croft is rested to give the grass a chance to grow. Making hay takes up much of July, but before that the sheep have to be gathered so that their winter coats can be sheared.

Like his neighbours, Iain still uses hand-clippers to shear the sheep although more modern methods are employed for other work on the croft such as haymaking; in less than one generation this has moved from the hand-scythe to tractor-operated cutters through to mechanical baling. Haymaking is completed in August and the feed stored in stacks or in barns for the winter.

In September the potatoes are dug up and the first lamb sales take place; with the cattle and sheep sales in October the yearly cycle is completed. After all the hard work the price which the animals fetch at island markets often seems meagre recompense.

Throughout the year there are constant odd jobs to do as well, and maintenance is a never-ending chore. There are fences to be mended, roofs to be repaired and sheep to be kept from straying. Life on the croft is never luxurious and there is hardly such a thing as a day off; but for Iain and his like there is great satisfaction to be found in it.

Iain MacIver, for one, would maintain that the way of crofting is not nearly as parochial as it looks, and that in fact it demonstrates how Scotland's rural communities can be sustained and encouraged to the lasting benefit of both the people and the natural heritage.

Torcuil Crichton

The Isles of Eigg and Rhum from Elgol, Isle of Skye.

Glen Etive, Inverness-shire.

*Modern hay making on
Loch Ness-side.*

The Managing of the Land

ALAN MOWLE

Dr Alan Mowle is a specialist in rural affairs currently working on secondment to The Scottish Office from the Nature Conservancy Council for Scotland.

It may seem odd to think of Scotland's countryside as a garden, but almost every aspect of the land is already managed and cared for to some extent. In future, if we are to sustain our wildlife heritage, the beauty of the landscape and the productive capacity of the land, our countryside will have to be planned and tended to an even greater degree. So perhaps the garden analogy is not so inappropriate.

Scotland is a very green place; almost all of the land is countryside, since less than three per cent of Scotland's 48,000 square miles (124,000 sq km) have been built upon. The land is also relatively empty of people since, although Scotland has about one-third of Britain's land area, it has only ten per cent of the population. Moreover those people are heavily concentrated in the Central Belt, with nearly a third in the largest cities of Glasgow, Edinburgh, Aberdeen and Dundee alone. Only a fifth of the Scottish people live in communities of fewer than 5,000, the size of Dalbeattie or Huntly.

So the rural areas of Scotland are large, very thinly populated and, for the most part, free of the development pressures found in the south of England. Perhaps for these reasons the countryside is where we feel that traditional values and a quieter approach to life may still be found.

But country people have just the same aspirations as their urban cousins and all of us expect to share a similar standard of living as part of modern Scottish society. Town dwellers look to the countryside for much of their leisure and recreation. Thus the countryside means very different things to different people.

For farmers and foresters the countryside is a workshop, a factory floor, where they earn their living. They do not normally think of themselves as 'gardeners', although they are heirs to a long tradition of stewardship and husbandry. Their businesses are largely sustained by financial grants and subsidies from the rest of the urban community, channelled through a variety of government policy measures. One result of this has been the single-minded pursuit of farm and forest output at minimum cost which has damaged both social and environmental interests in the countryside.

For tourists the countryside is a place of beauty and a source of inspiration. Most of us visit the countryside for recreation purposes from time to time. Many country people derive part of their income from tourism, so they have an indirect dependence on the countryside beyond the direct dependence of farmers and foresters. But to date the tourism industry has contributed little to the management or conservation of the countryside upon which it actually depends. For those who want to climb, walk or ski in the countryside it seems perhaps more like a park than a garden.

Conservationists tend to regard the countryside as a giant nature reserve where our wildlife is protected and preserved. But we should never forget that most of our wildlife has survived by accident rather than as the result of deliberate management. The idea of 'gardening' may sound incompatible with the conservation of wild nature but, unless we start to tend the countryside with wildlife in mind, the destruction of habitat and loss of wildlife seen in recent years can only continue.

Of the three interest groups mentioned above, the management of the land and woodlands by the forester or the farmer in their role as 'gardeners' has the greatest impact on the landscape and wildlife, and the relationship between the gardeners and the garden thus deserves closer examination.

Blackface sheep in Glencoe; more than two thirds of Scotland's land is suitable only for rough grazing.

117

FARMING THE LAND

A glance at the crude statistics shows that over 80 per cent of Scotland's land is devoted to farming. The way in which farming is carried out is of critical importance both for the land and for the community. Farming has been transformed over the last half century into a commercial business capable of feeding urban markets.

The statistics conceal more than they reveal; over 70 per cent of farmland consists of unimproved rough grazing in the hill areas. Fertile arable ground is concentrated up the east coast where less than 12 per cent of Scotland's farmland produces nearly 30 per cent of total farm output: crops to a value of over £350 million per annum. In broad terms Scotland grows enough food to supply the population with temperate foodstuffs; and although there are shortfalls in horticulture these are counterbalanced by a large surplus of meat production.

But this impressive output of food is produced by a tiny labour force. There are only about 14,000 full-time farmers in Scotland (with another 6,000 part-timers) who between them employ roughly 21,000 full-time workers on about 10,000 holdings. Thus farming employs only 1.5 per cent of Scotland's working population.

However there are great contrasts in the size of farm businesses. A typical east coast farm will turn over more than £100,000 from an area of perhaps 300 acres (120 ha), mostly arable. At the other end of the scale a hill sheep farm may turn over less than £40,000 on a much larger area of over 3,000 acres (1,200 ha), more than 95 per cent of which is rough grazing.

Away from the east coast lowlands most farm businesses are small-scale and farm incomes are low. Nearly all farm output is in the form of livestock, mainly sheep and cattle, and the only crops grown on the farm are usually winter fodder for the animals. The European Community (EC) has designated most of Scotland a 'Less Favoured Area' (LFA) because of the natural disadvantages of its terrain, soils and climate; as a result special support measures are provided for farming in Scotland.

Friesian dairy cows at Dalcross, Ardersier, near Inverness.

The principal support for LFA livestock farms takes the form of annual headage subsidies for each breeding cow or ewe; these subsidies cost the taxpayer around £100 million per annum. This financial support provides perhaps a quarter to one-third of the turnover of the farm business and without it most farmers in Less Favoured Areas could not survive.

Direct subsidy of this kind is far less important for the arable farmer since cereal prices are held well above world prices by the European Common Agricultural Policy (CAP). Because this is organised on a community-wide basis within the EC the cost in Scotland is difficult to establish, but the two million tonnes of cereals produced each year by Scottish farmers represent about 1.2 per cent of the EC total. *Pro rata* these arable products attract roughly £50 million per annum of support in the form of intervention payments, storage costs and export subsidies. Without this support (Box 1) Scotland's arable farmers would also not survive.

After arable and sheep-farming the third important sector is dairy farming, where over-production led to the introduction of milk quotas in 1985. Each farmer has an annual production quota, a quantity which he must sell to the milk board at a fixed price. The quota system limits milk production and maintains the broad structure of the industry. Simply reducing the price paid for milk would concentrate production on larger, more efficient, farms and eliminate dairy farming altogether in some parts of Scotland where farms are smaller and less productive.

Taken together the various forms of public subsidy for Scottish farming channelled through a range of policy instruments cost the taxpayer around £300 million per annum: that is to say, something approaching a million pounds per working day.

One effect of the high level of farm subsidies has been to inflate land prices. On the face of it this makes owner-occupier farmers rich; the land on the 300 acre arable farm described above may be worth over £300,000 but this asset can only be realised when the farm is sold with vacant possession. The down side is that these high prices make it very difficult for would-be farmers to buy, and rule out land purchase based on borrowed money. High prices are also maintained by an increasing interest in land for 'hobby farming', especially near urban areas.

These high land values and all the other economic pressures have pushed farmers on to a treadmill, forcing them to work the land more intensively, chasing higher crop yields through increased use of chemicals and larger machines. Farmers who have resisted the pressure to join in have found themselves slowly squeezed out of business.

As farming has changed, so have the food processing and distribution industries with the development of supermarkets and increased processing of farm products for retail. One result of this has been a decline in the farmer's share of the retail food price, adding to all the other pressures. Many farm businesses now carry significant overdrafts; the accruing bank interest eats into farm income and for a significant number of farmers their asset value declines year by year (Box 2).

Farmers find themselves with less and less freedom in decision-making as their dependence on outside resources is increased. The farmer is increasingly tied to his banker, his accountant, his crop buyer and his suppliers of fuel, fertiliser and pesticide. Farming has become like any other industry but, unlike other industries, it happens to use most of the countryside as its main resource.

Farming is facing a crisis because there is simply too much food and the markets for produce are saturated. But farmers need to maintain their incomes like everyone else and will undoubtedly want to improve their crop yields in pursuit of even greater efficiency and profitability; as a result it is probable that present levels of crop production could be maintained on progressively smaller and smaller areas of land. But with a saturated market there is no point in increasing food production since we don't need any more food. Consequently large areas of land must come out of agriculture over the next twenty years if we are to limit food output to present levels. The crucial question is, which land will come out of farming?

One possibility is that marginal land in the hills will come out of farming as sheep and beef production is transferred to the more fertile lowlands. But since the level of stock which can be maintained per unit of lowland ground is much higher most of the hill areas would have to come out of farming altogether in order to balance supply with demand!

Taking the most productive arable land out of farming would minimise the area which we need to lose but it seems illogical to cut production on the best land we have, and most farmers would resist such a move. The most likely scenario is that land of intermediate quality will come out of agriculture as attempts are made to strike a balance of economic, social and environmental objectives through a reorientation of policy instruments. The creation of new woodlands on such land would be an attractive option if appropriate policy tools can be devised.

FORESTRY

More than 12 per cent of Scotland is covered with productive woodland, of which 92 per cent are plantations of exotic conifers. This contrasts markedly with the eighteenth and nineteenth centuries when Scotland was largely deforested. Nearly all Scotland's present-day forests have been created within the last century through the planting-up of bare ground.

After the last Ice Age most of Scotland below the

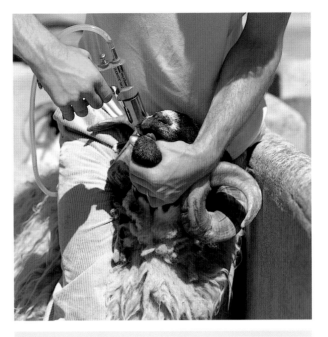

Drenching sheep is easier with modern equipment.

1. OILSEED RAPE

The way in which the Common Agricultural Policy shapes Scotland's countryside is exemplified by the huge increase in the area of oilseed rape grown on the arable land on the east coast of Scotland. Oilseed rape is the crop with bright yellow flowers so prominent in the countryside at springtime. Hardly any was grown in 1981 but by 1990 the area under oilseed rape had increased to more than 116,000 acres. Why did this happen?

In the early 1980s the European Community (EC) reviewed the pattern of food production. The Community was almost self-sufficient in most food products; but for vegetable oils, used in margarine and cooking oils, it was very dependent on imports. Very little vegetable oil was produced by the Community's farmers apart from olive oil grown in the Mediterranean states.

The EC member-states agreed to subsidise farmers to grow suitable oilseeds which could be crushed to extract the oil. But international trade agreements prohibit taxes on imports or direct payments to farmers, so a 'crushing-subsidy' is paid to processors for every tonne of Community-grown oilseed they use; the processors are thus able to pay a higher price for Community oilseed than they would pay on the world market for imported seed.

In Scotland oilseed rape grows well and produces about 1.5 tonnes of seed per acre. A crushing subsidy of about £150 per tonne therefore costs the European taxpayer over £200 an acre every year. Without this subsidy oilseed rape would never be grown.

Oil seed rape at Boghall farm, Pentland Hills Regional Park.

*The farmer's bill for
artificial fertilisers,
herbicides and pesticides is
now much larger than it is
for labour.*

2. FARMING TRENDS

Over the years farm incomes have been in long-term decline relative to the economy at large because, as living standards rise, we spend a lower proportion of our income on food. Suitable figures for Scotland alone are not easy to come by, but the same trends can be observed in any advanced economy. In 1967 UK farm production was worth about 0.5 per cent of UK Gross Domestic Product (GDP), while in 1987 it had fallen to 0.3 per cent of GDP. In fact the real value of farm output hardly changed over this twenty-year period, while GDP increased by 54 per cent.

For many years farming has responded to this pressure by trying to increase the value of output per farm and per acre. This can only be done either by increasing total output, reducing costs or having fewer but larger farms. Technological advances have enabled farmers to increase total food output. For example the area of cereals in Scotland has increased by only about 10 per cent over this twenty-year period, but average yields have gone up by about 70 per cent. This improvement in yield has been undermined by lower unit prices.

The number of farm workers in Scotland has fallen by nearly two-thirds since 1950, bringing a loss of over 60,000 jobs to rural areas. Over the same period the number of farms in Scotland has fallen by about a third, while the average size has increased as the land has been taken over by neighbouring farmers.

Looking to the future, the long-term pressure on farm incomes will continue. Any further increases in output will only add to surplus production. Farmers are already being paid to take land out of production in the cereal 'set-aside' scheme but much larger areas will have to come out of agriculture altogether and the number of farmers and farm workers will continue to fall. Many farmers will have to make part of their living outside farming if they are to maintain their living standards. All these changes will place continuing pressure on the Scottish countryside.

uniform, even-aged, close-packed trees understandably earn them the tag of 'blanket forestry'.

The creation of these commercial forests has been the greatest land-use change in Scotland's countryside this century. The taxpayer has footed most of the bill for this exercise even though many of the plantations are privately owned. Most planting until the 1970s was carried out by the Forestry Commission, creating a state forest of over 2,000 square miles (5,000 sq km); but changing policy instruments have swung the balance since then to the private sector.

The private investor turned to forestry because he or she could use afforestation to turn taxable earnings into a tax-free capital asset over a period of years. In addition generous planting grants helped to pay for the cost of establishing the new forest (see Chapter 5). Increasing controversy led to the abolition of these tax arrangements in the 1988 Budget. Although planting grants have again been increased, private investors' interest in afforestation has fallen away and people with high taxable incomes have gone looking for tax-shelters elsewhere.

As we enter the 1990s the forestry industry stands at a crossroads. Down one road we can see a continuation of the upland afforestation which has brought increasingly sharp conflicts with environmental interests. However the other road offers a shift of emphasis to new afforestation on lower, more fertile ground which may be coming out of agriculture.

The factors which led to planting of conifer forests in the uplands have now substantially changed. After the two world wars the need for a strategic reserve of timber was matched by an equal need for increased self-sufficiency in farming; covering good farmland with trees under such circumstances would have been clearly counter-productive. In the hills, however, unimproved land used for sheep grazing was cheap, reflecting its poor quality; so the uplands were planted with trees. As a result foresters adopted a low management-cost approach based on exotic conifers, principally Sitka spruce (Box 3).

Upland afforestation radically alters the landscape, and the impact can be made even worse by bad plantation design. If the lessons learned over the years are applied, many landscape problems can be avoided in present-day planting or in replanting after felling. But the ecological effects of afforestation are more damaging and difficult to avoid.

In a sense, modern forestry is an extension of the intensive cropping methods of modern agriculture into the least developed corners of the countryside. More than 90 per cent of new planting in Britain takes place in Scotland and nearly 62,000 acres (25,000 ha) of new trees every year displace the wildlife which once lived on open moorland. Large areas of heather moorland have been lost as a result, reducing habitat for birds of prey like the merlin and for waders such as the golden plover.

treeline was covered by the ancient wildwood of native broadleaved trees, consisting of oak, ash and elm in the Lowlands with the Caledonian pine forest north of the Highland line. A few rare fragments of the wildwood remain but the new conifer plantations bear little resemblance to these original forests. They are composed of different, often introduced, tree species and have a very different forest structure; their large areas of

When large areas are afforested over a few years the water and drainage patterns of the catchment area are disrupted. Flash floods become more common as new drains and deep-ploughed forestry furrows increase the rate of water run-off; in addition the sands and sediments caused by erosion can damage fisheries by suffocating the gravel beds where salmon and trout spawn. Acid rain deposits are also thought to concentrate in the dense foliage of the mature conifers; these deposits are then washed into the burns, destroying fish eggs and young fry as well as the invertebrate food supply of upland birds such as the dipper.

Therefore modern forestry, perhaps even more so than farming, is an industrial activity carried out in the countryside. Like farming it requires urban sources of capital, taxpayers' money, labour and fuel. Unlike farming, which still relies on a large number of one-man businesses, forestry is organised on a large-scale industrial model with gangs of workers employed, often on a contract basis, under the supervision of professional managers. The type of employment offered by forestry is radically different from that in agriculture and mechanised tree harvesting needs fewer and fewer workers.

The key to the future of forestry lies with the Forestry Commission, which has two distinct roles: that of a 'forest authority', disbursing planting grants and controlling felling, and that of 'forest enterprise', managing the state forest. As the original focus on timber production, to the exclusion of all other values, is replaced with a more balanced concern for social and environmental factors as well as economic objectives, the type and location of forestry must change.

Lowland forests using surplus farmland could deploy a wider range of native trees together with more varied designs and management. We can never recreate the original wildwood but new forests in the Lowlands could be more pleasing to the eye and much more environmentally friendly (Box 4).

THE PRICE OF WILDLIFE?

Some 94 per cent of Scotland is in the hands of farmers and foresters, and they are the major custodians of our countryside heritage. But the ways in which they manage the land are largely dictated for them by the subsidies and other financial supports on which they depend; these economic constraints have had a serious effect on our wildlife heritage (Box 5).

Scotland has a crucial role in conserving Britain's rich heritage of wildlife. But the rich variety of native wildlife is unevenly distributed across the countryside. A few species such as the kestrel are able to adapt to the changes in habitat brought about by Man, but most species are specialised and are relatively rare and restricted in their range.

Nature conservation aims to protect and conserve

Less than one percent of Scotland's original native pine woods survive today and almost no regeneration is taking place.

3. THE SITKA SPRUCE

Sitka spruce is a fast-growing conifer native to the western seaboard of North America and well suited to the oceanic climate of Scotland. It is typically grown on hill ground and cropped after about forty-five years; relatively little has yet been harvested because most plantings have taken place since 1950.

Before the 1950s upland planting involved a more diverse range of tree species and each planting scheme matched species to site characteristics of the area: larch for dry knolls, Norway and Sitka spruce for wetter soils, Scots pine for podzols, Douglas fir and other species for better soils. The predominance of Sitka spruce planting followed the introduction of deep ploughs, trailed behind crawler tractors, which create more uniform conditions across the planting site.

At the same time the objectives of forestry policy changed. The Forestry Commission was set up after the First World War to establish and maintain a strategic reserve of timber at the taxpayers' expense. A Treasury study in 1971 focused attention on poor financial returns; upland afforestation is inherently uneconomic so the new concern with 'minimising losses' required a low-cost approach. Sitka spruce offers the highest yields for the lowest expenditure and our hills are now covered with this tree as a direct result.

Because Sitka spruce grows so quickly its timber is light and relatively soft even for a conifer; as a result it has only a limited range of uses. Much of the production from Scotland's forests can only be used for pulp, paper or reconstituted board; when high-quality timber is required we remain largely dependent on imports.

Sitka spruce has been planted in vast swathes across much of the Highlands and Borders of Scotland, creating a dark, sterile habitat.

121

A dark tide of sitka spruce creeps up the mountainside at Loch Lunn da Bhra, near Fort William.

A new lowland forest could be created on derelict industrial land in the Central Belt.

4. CREATING A LOWLAND FOREST

The debate about the afforestation of Scotland's upland areas has diverted attention from the opportunities for creating forests elsewhere. But the need to take large areas of countryside out of farming to combat surplus production creates such opportunities.

The Central Scotland Woodlands Project began ten years ago and has now been superseded by Central Scotland Woodlands Limited (CSW). It is an exciting initiative which is exploring the possibility of planting trees on about 250,000 acres of land between Edinburgh, Glasgow and Stirling, a bleak landscape scarred by over 200 years of unplanned industrial development.

Although there is some high ground, most of the area is lower ground which is of higher quality than land normally used for conventional afforestation. This means that the CSW can plant a wider range of trees, including native broadleaves. At present there is tree cover of about 25,000 acres (10,000 ha); the aim is to extend this to 75,000 acres (30,000 ha) over the next twenty years. This will not result in a 'blanket' of trees as there would be tree cover on only about one-third of the land area – similar to that found elsewhere in Western Europe.

This new approach avoids the minimum-cost approach typical of upland forestry, tackling wider objectives of environmental improvement, job creation and economic regeneration.

CSW has been set up by the Secretary of State for Scotland in partnership with other public agencies, the private sector and the local communities involved. The company will not set up its own forest enterprise; instead it will facilitate tree-planting owned and managed by others.

A variety of planting schemes can be expected as the initiative gets under way. As most of the area is farmed, farm woodlands will make an important contribution. These may diversify sources of income for working farmers, or land may be sold to new owners who may be resident but with their main income from another source. There is scope for reclamation of derelict land for use as woodland and for restoration of land following opencast mining. Another important development will be the creation of community woodlands, giving local people a direct role in the management of the countryside.

our wildlife heritage by maintaining the range, variety and quality of habitats in the countryside; in particular it is important to preserve 'semi-natural' areas in which such wildlife can find refuge. In this way the wildlife typical of each place can continue to thrive across its traditional range. Recently attention has been focused on key sites which are managed as nature reserves or protected by some form of designation such as Site of Special Scientific Interest (SSSI) (see Chapter 16).

However these nature reserves and protected areas cannot, on their own, provide enough habitat to support viable populations of many plants, birds and animals. Over and above these key sites we need to sustain a much wider matrix of wildlife habitats throughout the countryside and to identify areas where the restoration of the natural habitat can yield positive results.

But how are we to gain the active involvement and co-operation of the custodians of our countryside – the farmers and the foresters? The countryside requires positive and sensitive management, and merely banning activities which may damage the value of an area for wildlife would be quite ineffective. A far more positive and creative approach is needed.

On some designated sites management agreements are set up with farmers and landowners. In return for accepting restrictions on the management of land the farmer is often offered compensation calculated by assessing the net profit which is foregone by managing the land for the benefit of wildlife. This approach seems reasonable but it is by no means perfect, because so many hypothetical calculations have to be taken into account in assessing the 'net profit foregone' by the farmer. The compensation payable is the difference between two financial forecasts: the first figure is the theoretical profit which the farmer could have made if no restriction had been placed on the use of the land; the second figure represents the reduced profit which might result with the restrictions in place.

The calculation for the hypothetical situation ignores all the risks taken by a farmer whenever a crop is planted; it is assumed that the imaginary crop will not be damaged by weather or pests, will produce good yields and will be harvested at a satisfactory price, and that no unforeseen expenditure will be incurred. In addition the calculation takes account of other forms of public subsidy as income. These factors tend to increase the apparent price of a conservation management agreement.

These compensation agreements have a place in some limited circumstances but, overall, they too are cast in negative terms. They aim to pay compensation to farmers and foresters for not carrying out activities which may damage the countryside; but they do nothing to reconcile conflicting policy measures. We need an integration of policy measures so that conflict is reduced; and more importantly we need an approach

5. THE EROSION OF THE HERITAGE

How can we measure the changes which have taken place in Scotland's countryside over the years? Without a time machine this is difficult, but photographs can help us explore what a particular place was like in the past and aerial photographs allow us to do this systematically. By comparing aerial photographs of selected sample areas we can estimate how the habitat has changed.

The National Countryside Monitoring Scheme (NCMS) has been doing this for each region in Scotland. Its first series of regional reports identify the principal changes from the 1940s to the 1970s; for some areas figures are available for the 1970s to the present day. Although these cannot tell us everything about the changes which have taken place they do quantify the most important.

The NCMS figures confirm that all over Scotland there have been serious losses of wildlife habitats since 1945. Broadleaved woods have been felled and replaced by conifer plantations (14 per cent in Dumfries and Galloway from the 1940s to the 1970s) or cleared for agriculture (20 per cent in Grampian from the 1940s to the 1970s). Hedgerows and treelines along field boundaries have been removed (41 per cent in Grampian from 1940s-70s, 40 per cent in Stirling District from the 1970s to the present day). Heather moorland has been planted with conifers (39 per cent in Dumfries and Galloway from the 1940s to the 1970s) or converted to poor grassland because of overgrazing by sheep (21 per cent in the Borders from the 1940s to the 1970s).

The NCMS is better able to estimate changes in habitats which cover a large area but, since many important areas for wildlife are fragmented and small, we have to turn to land-based surveys to check on their changes in detail. Surveys of these habitats have shown dramatic declines in area: for example over 90 per cent of lowland grasslands lost, 40 per cent of lowland heath, 50 per cent of native woodlands and 50 per cent of lowland peatlands (*Nature Conservation in Great Britain*, NNC, 1984).

These losses are particularly startling when compared with the original extent of some of these habitats. Until the last thousand years wetland and woodland covered most of lowland Scotland but these habitats have now been reduced to tiny fragments and even these small remnants are being lost or damaged. It is critically important that we protect what is left of these habitats for the benefit of the wildlife which cannot survive without them.

Bluebells among oakwoods in Perthshire; roughly 25% of all ancient semi-natural woodlands in Scotland have been lost since 1946.

The barn owl has declined dramatically through loss of its traditional habitat due to changes in modern farming.

based on positive management. Such an approach could well develop from the introduction of the system of Environmentally Sensitive Areas (ESAS) (Box 6). We must start thinking in terms of positive payments which encourage sensitive management and stewardship.

HOW ARE DECISIONS MADE?

It is an alarming fact that there is no single body or organisation with responsibility for co-ordinating the numerous decisions taken each day by public agencies which affect Scotland's countryside and its rural communities.

Each year huge sums of taxpayers' money go to support rural activities through a plethora of public agencies with little co-ordination. Each national agency pursues its statutory aims in deciding the application of the resources voted to it by Parliament and in deciding which projects should be supported or funded, without reference to the work of other agencies in the field.

The result is that the actions of a public agency in one sector such as agriculture sometimes conflict directly with the actions of another, such as nature conservation. But there is simply no framework or explicit basis for co-ordination among the agencies either at national or local level. Even local authorities, which are more geared to local circumstances, can only tolerate the operations of the national agencies in their areas.

Not only is there no framework for consultation but many public agencies are only loosely accountable to democratic control. No rural public agency is directly answerable to the community whose interests the agency can sometimes dramatically affect. Consequently the people living in the countryside do not have the opportunity to participate in many of the decision-making processes which affect their lives. No wonder some of the public agencies are treated with distrust!

If the public agencies do not co-ordinate their policies or consult the rural community, it is hard to see how collective, well-balanced decisions can be taken on issues such as which classes of agricultural land across Scotland should be given over to forestry. If the interests of landscape and wildlife agencies are to be taken into account as well as those of farming and forestry, the task becomes well-nigh impossible.

The need for some form of co-ordination among the various agencies is becoming widely recognised. So far the attempts to break down the compartments between the agencies have resulted in little but confusion. Creating a framework which can balance these diverse local and national interests remains the principal challenge for the 1990s.

WHO IS RESPONSIBLE?

It is not over-dramatic to say there is now a crisis in Scotland's countryside. There are many different agencies, interest groups and individuals, each with their own priorities and concerns; but there is no overall control and no integrated master plan. As a result the impoverishment of our natural heritage continues.

Most of the land is privately owned, a fact which is sometimes overlooked. What does this mean in practice? Some owners, fortunately a small minority, assert their right to do with the land as they wish; they make no distinction between land and other consumer goods which they own. But ownership of a washing machine does not carry with it any heritage or wider public responsibility, nor is there a framework of public policy and associated legislation and expenditure for the ownership and use of washing machines! In contrast, ownership and use of land carries with it a variety of rights and public obligations which constrain the use of the land to a greater or lesser degree. Responsible landowners will decide how they use their land against the background of those rights and obligations.

At the same time there is a sense, far from trivial, in which all citizens feel they have a justified stake in the countryside and, when the scale of taxpayers' support for farming and forestry is appreciated, this feeling is strengthened. It is this which leads to confrontations of private and public interests and inspires some people to advocate simplistic solutions of legislative diktat and land nationalisation. The real debate should be to assess these rights and obligations to secure an appropriate balance of public and private interests.

Recent years have seen an increasing reliance on the workings of market forces in the countryside as elsewhere. But the scope for achieving protection of Scotland's natural heritage through the unguided application of market forces is extremely limited. However efficiently a free market operates in the countryside there will always be a residue of non-market activities and 'goods', of which countryside conservation is one of the most important. For this reason we can expect to see conservation measures of one kind or another becoming more important determinants of public policy, with public money being directed towards private owners and occupiers.

For any landowner seeking to make a living from the land, government policies on agriculture and forestry dictate its management; but not all owners make a living in this way. For example there is a long tradition of landed estates in rural Scotland which rarely pay their way but serve as playgrounds for the super-rich with an interest in field sports (see Chapter 17). More such 'playgrounds' can be expected as interest in the recreational use of the countryside continues to grow. For such landowners, economic returns are a secondary consideration. Should such landowners have access to incentives designed for struggling farmers on low incomes? If not, then how can the public interest be expressed?

As far as our countryside heritage is concerned,

sensitivity in the continuing management of the land is essential. The motivation of landowners cannot be ignored; their co-operation must be secured. They must be offered various incentives with appropriate strings attached, securing their voluntary co-operation, with recourse to constraint by direction only as a long-stop against unreasonable behaviour.

AN EYE TO THE FUTURE

Many aspects of Scotland's natural heritage are threatened by the continuing changes in the countryside. These changes are driven by a combination of market forces and technology, modified by government policy and expenditure. Local communities are disenfranchised and have little influence over these instruments of policy. Meanwhile the urban majority is increasingly looking to the countryside for leisure and recreation and making its own views heard through an increasingly vocal environmental lobby.

This growing turbulence is exacerbated by the lack of any structure for co-ordinated action and by a reluctance on the part of the various factions involved to yield individual freedom of action for any common benefit. Yet our examination of the needs of Scotland's natural heritage and exploration of the many threats to its survival have shown that management for multiple goals must be the answer.

Market forces cannot provide a solution, however effective they may be as a mechanism for straightforward decisions on economic allocation. The many and unco-ordinated instruments of policy distort the market signals, persuading farmers, for example, to grow crops in European surplus by using methods which impose heavy costs upon the natural environment.

More importantly, market forces can only work with cash valuations. They fail to recognise that man does not live by bread alone, that civilisation brings with it leisure and a search for fulfilment of the spirit as well as the body. Conservation of our natural heritage is not a marketable commodity but a resource whose protection requires intervention by government, steering market forces towards activities which are more sensitive to the needs of the environment.

Our response to this must come at three levels. First, at the practical level – on the farm – the adoption of a managerial ethic is essential. Land management must be more systematic and taxpayer's support must be related to a farm plan (the cross-compliance principle). The business objectives of the farm need to be based on an audit of the natural resources available and the quality of the natural environment, alongside more conventional concerns of capital, technology and management skills. In return the farmer or forester can expect price and other signals which favour environmentally sensitive management while still responding to market forces.

Second, at the programme level, a structure of local and regional policy implementation is required which encourages flexibility of response and integration of purpose. 'Strategies' may help if they spell out relationships between different interests and provide a basis for local interpretations of policy measures sensitive to conservation and development needs. It is at this level that the needs and aspirations of local communities must be drawn in along with those of other 'players' including owners, managers and lobbyists. There is no room for sectoralism at this level and it is here that the elusive balance must be struck between local and national, personal and public interests.

Third, at the policy level, where overall goals are set and policy implementation is monitored: there is still a role for sectoral activity here, as agencies representing the different interests monitor and evaluate what they see on the ground. At this level, environmental standards defining acceptable management in agriculture, forestry and other countryside activities should be set for implementation at the programme level.

As we have seen, reality falls a long way short of these ideals. But unless we find ways of 'managing the garden' at all three levels, Scotland's natural heritage can only continue its long decline.

Below: the Eildon Hills, designated as an Environmentally Sensitive Area (ESA) in 1988.

6. ENVIRONMENTALLY SENSITIVE AREAS (ESAs)

Scotland has five Environmentally Sensitive Areas, covering more than 500,000 acres (200,000 ha). Breadalbane (the largest, with 300,000 acres between Loch Tay and Loch Rannoch) and Loch Lomond were designated in 1987, followed by the Stewartry area of Galloway, the machair (shell-sand coastland) of the Uists, and the smallest area (15,000 acres) at Whitlaw/Eildon, near Selkirk, in 1988. These experimental designations are the first serious attempt to involve farmers in positive conservation management of the countryside.

ESAs stem from a 1985 European Community Regulation which was enshrined into UK legislation in the Agriculture Act 1986. ESAs identify wildlife, landscape and archaeological aspects of the environment, and the management required to sustain them. Once the lessons have been absorbed from the early ESA designations the same approach (or something similar) could be adopted much more widely. Any area of countryside is in some way environmentally sensitive.

Farmers volunteering to enter the scheme must prepare a conservation management plan for their whole farm area. They receive payments in two tiers: the first relates to a number of general conditions applied to the whole farm and is calculated per acre. The second tier pays for the management of specified features of conservation value on the farm. The adoption of this plan means each agreement can be tailored to a particular farm and the ambitions of the individual farmer.

The general conditions aim to prevent farm operations causing damage to conservation aims and could perhaps deal with levels of stock, fertiliser applications and changes of land-use (e.g. farm woodlands). The second tier payments are linked to management prescriptions for features of conservation value such as herb-rich grassland, wetlands and field boundaries (both hedges and drystane dykes).

ESA payments are not large and form only a tiny proportion (less than one per cent) of taxpayers' support for agriculture, but they make a valuable contribution to farm incomes. They are not, and never will be, large enough to replace the income generated from farming, so they cannot become payments for 'doing nothing'. Instead they encourage the farmer to manage the land for a balance of objectives which include conservation of the wildlife and landscape features.

Stirling Castle

The Paths of Progress

JOHN HUME

John R. Hume is one of Scotland's leading authorities on industrial archaeology; a senior lecturer at Strathclyde University, he is now on assignment as an inspector with Historic Scotland.

FROM PATHS TO ROADS

As soon as the first nomadic people began to settle in Scotland they began to create access routes to their sources of food and fuel, as well as to vital materials such as wood, stone, clay and, later, metals. These early pathways to the sources of such commodities became tracks which became more heavily used as communities grew. In places where ground conditions were difficult, or where the climate was poor, these routes could be critical to the survival and growth of individual settlements. In such circumstances water ways became more important and sites at the heads of navigable rivers, or with natural harbours, were particularly valued.

Such factors were already at work in prehistoric and early historic Scotland; places like Dumbarton, Dunadd (Argyll), Edinburgh and Stirling became important because they were sited near navigable water as well as having natural defensive heights. By Norman times water routes were well developed and land routes were becoming an essential part of social and economic life. The feudal system depended upon centralised political control which required good communications. Similarly the organisational structure of the Church – with its parishes, diocesan centres, pilgrimage churches and abbeys – relied upon inland transport and stimulated its growth in turn.

The economic dimension of this burgeoning society can be seen in the establishment of burghs as centres for trade and craftsmanship. The growth of towns created central administration which, together with the religious function of the larger burghs, helped concentrate resources for the building of bridges, the laying out of proper through routes and the construction and improvement of harbours. At a local level the building of corn mills by feudal lords also helped to create smaller trade networks.

In the later Middle Ages and in the early modern period these trends were complemented by the growth of industry and by the larger towns developing strong overseas links. During the seventeenth century successive Scottish administrations encouraged industrial growth, laying the foundations for the expansion of trade and commerce that followed the Act of Union of 1707.

The early and mid eighteenth century saw improved communications begin to transform the face of Scotland. Following the Jacobite Rising of 1715, General George Wade was ordered to construct a system of metalled military roads in order to police the southern Highlands. These roads opened up what was largely untracked land and required the construction of forty 'Wade' bridges built of stone. As an added bonus these roads allowed travellers access to the more remote parts of Scotland for the first time.

One of the best examples of a hump-backed Wade bridge. Built in 1732: it crosses the river Fechlin on the east side of Loch Ness.

Field Marshal George Wade: painting by Van Diest.

The growth of the cattle rearing trade in the Highlands, and the need to drive beasts south to market, created a network of drove roads through the glens and mountain passes. Many of them were simply tracks across unimproved ground, but wide grassy roads were also laid out in order to allow the cattle to graze on the surrounding land during the journey; this was especially so in the southern uplands.

Industry had grown considerably by the late eighteenth century, stimulating the demand for new and improved roads. Transport was making a visible impact on landscape and townscape by this time. But while the new roads may have made intrusive cuts through the landscape, nevertheless by channelling traffic they reduced the tendency of animals and vehicles to take a way round a miry track. Better communications encouraged land improvement and enclosure of common land. Enclosure, in fact, gave definition to the evolving road system by surrounding open fields with new stone walls and by planting boundary hedges and trees along roadsides.

Coach services were now being started but road surfaces were still very poor, making journeys long, uncomfortable and unreliable. However coach services expanded rapidly and communication centres became more important as the wealthier classes began to travel for pleasure to a much greater extent. Landowners built inns for travellers on their estates and writers and poets began to extol the aesthetic value of remote scenery and romantic ruins. These early literary tourists were the harbingers of today's mass migrations (see Chapter 17).

In the early nineteenth century Thomas Telford (1757–1834) revolutionised Scotland's road system; from 1801 he constructed more than 1,000 miles (1,600 km) of road as well as 1,200 bridges. It was Telford who built the prototype road which was to become the A9 of today (Box 1). With new road surfaces such as those developed by John Loudon McAdam (1756–1836) horses could pull carriages at high speeds provided that gradients were kept to a minimum; levelling of the road bed was achieved by the techniques of embankment,

The A9 crossing the Kessock bridge, Inverness.

Telford bridge at Craigellachie

1. THE A9

Of all the roads ever constructed in Scotland the grandest in conception and execution is the A9 to the north of Perth. Its predecessor was for most of its length built by Thomas Telford as part of the government's policy of opening up the Highlands to stem the flood of people migrating south. In the far north some parts of the A9 still follow Telford's route, but since the early 1970s most of it has been completely rebuilt to carry more traffic at higher speed. This has involved major engineering work, dwarfing Telford's achievements in bridging the Tay at Dunkeld, the Beauly at Beauly, and in constructing the causeway across the Fleet estuary known as the Mound.

The most spectacular pieces of engineering are the great dual carriageway in the Pass of Killiecrankie which is carried on concrete legs and the bridges over the Beauly Firth at Kessock and the Cromarty Firth at Foulis. These are immediately and obviously notable achievements, as are the smaller bridges at Bonar Bridge and elsewhere. What is less obvious is the care taken by the road's designers not just to build a road capable of carrying heavy traffic but also to make a road that is fit for the magnificent scenery through which it passes. Telford's road lasted for about a century and a half with minimal alteration; its successor may well be called on to do the same, in much more arduous traffic.

cutting and bridge-building. By 1830 Telford's roads had systematically opened up the Highlands, extending and improving the eighteenth-century military roads for the growing civilian traffic. Telford also built the major Glasgow–Carlisle Road as well as key bridges such as Glasgow Bridge, the Dean Bridge in Edinburgh, Lothian Bridge and Pathhead Bridge. Owing to the development of the railways, which absorbed a great deal of road traffic, most of these roads remained practically unaltered for a century.

The new roads undoubtedly improved travelling conditions but they were not used for mass transport of people and goods since they were expensive and could only cope with limited traffic. However they proved vital for the transport of goods, postal communication and the middle-classes, since they created an integrated economy in Scotland for the first time.

Environmentally the easy lines, noble bridges and select clientele of the new roads made them relatively acceptable but, in addition, the economic possibilities which they opened up proved a powerful stimulus to the building of railways. However before the railway boom came the heyday of canal-building.

THE WATERWAYS

Inland waterways had always provided a smoother and more reliable form of transport than roads, and from the late 1760s various schemes were advanced for canals and river improvements. Roads were much cheaper to build, however, and the rate at which canals were built was restricted by shortages of capital and technical ability. The 35-mile-long Forth and Clyde Canal, from Grangemouth to Bowling, took twenty-two years to complete (1768–90) and a government loan was needed to pay for the final section.

The Forth and Clyde Canal, which was closed to navigation in 1962, was designed to allow coastal trade to cross the Central Belt of Scotland and was thus an important link in the shipping industry. The canal's own passenger and light goods trade was linked by road services to places much further afield. On the other hand the Monkland Canal from Glasgow to Airdrie and Coatbridge (constructed in 1761–90) and the Saltcoats Canal were primarily designed for the transport of coal.

The use of the early canals and river navigation encouraged the growth of towns, but after the first shock of the water channels being cut the across rural landscapes their impact on the countryside was limited. Only one Scottish canal was built to serve agriculture and rural industry, namely the 18-mile-long Aberdeen-shire Canal which ran from Aberdeen harbour to Port Elphinstone (1807), but it was not a commercial success. Some early nineteenth-century canals like the Crinan Canal (Box 2) and the 60-mile-long Caledonian Canal (built by Thomas Telford in 1803–22) crossed from sea to sea with little or no inland traffic; while

others were just extensions of the Lowland canals system, like the Glasgow Paisley and Ardrossan (which reached Johnstone by 1811 but was never completed), and the Edinburgh and Glasgow Union (1822).

The Paisley Canal was historically important in

2. THE CRINAN CANAL

Before steamships were invented, voyages by wooden sailing vessels round exposed headlands were fraught with danger. The voyage round the north of Scotland through the Pentland Firth was fearsome and so was that round the Mull of Kintyre, where vessels were exposed to the mountainous seas and high winds of the Atlantic. Additionally, in times of war, foreign warships and privateers could attack merchantmen without undue risk.

As commerce grew during the eighteenth century and inland waterways developed, the idea of cutting canals across narrow parts of Scotland emerged. The first planned canal was the Forth and Clyde (1768–90). The second, across the head of the Kintyre peninsula, which came to be known as the Crinan Canal, was projected by John Knox in 1784, as was the third, through the Great Glen: the Caledonian Canal.

The Crinan Canal was only nine miles long and was built relatively quickly. It was designed to take the small vessels engaged in the West Highland trade and was really promoted to benefit the people of the west coast rather than to make money. An Act of Parliament was obtained in 1793 and most of the capital came from private sources. It was completed in 1801 with a loan from central government and when it was in operation it came to rely on the state. It was formally taken over in 1848 and has been improved from time to time to take deeper vessels.

From the 1840s to the 1930s the canal was a link in a passenger service from Glasgow (later Gourock) to Oban, Fort William and even Inverness, the so-called 'Royal Route' after Queen Victoria used it in 1849. It was much used by puffers and still serves as a base for the VIC 32, the last operating steam puffer.

Today the canal's main importance is as a link for yachtsmen between the Clyde estuary and the west coast cruising area, perpetuating its original technical intention; and by bringing revenue to the coastal harbours of Argyll it fulfils something of the wishes of its promoters. It fulfils these functions quietly, efficiently and charmingly: Scotland's miniature canal.

pioneering cheap short-range passenger transport, enabling large numbers of Scots to use public transport for the first time. By that time, however, improvements in railway construction made further canal construction an unattractive proposition. Boats could only travel quickly on the canals if these were free of locks; but lock-free canals required level routes and the number of such routes in Scotland was very limited. The heyday of canal-building was over, and Thomas Telford was already turning his prodigious talents from the construction of waterways to the construction of road-systems.

THE RAILWAY AGE

The wooden rails of Scotland's early horse-drawn railways were exclusively built to carry coal from the mines to local consumer markets or to junctions with water transport for transfer to more distant customers. Thus the very first railway, built in 1721, was built to link pits at Tranent with the harbour at Cockenzie. But it was not until the 1770s, over fifty years later, that wooden railways became popular in central Scotland.

Horses could pull heavier loads on railways than they could on roads and this was the reason for using what were, in effect, specialised roads. The later invention of iron rails and wheels inspired new developments since they enabled horses to pull even greater loads and reduced maintenance costs.

Iron rails were first used in Scotland on the Kilmarnock and Troon Railway, which the Duke of Portland promoted as a coal-carrying line; this line used smooth wheels and flanged cast-iron rails, unlike today's railways, which conversely use smooth rails and flanged wheels. It became the first public railway in Scotland to pioneer passenger services using a steam locomotive.

Many schemes for railways were devised from the early years of the nineteenth century but it was not until the 1820s that improved technology produced a recognisably modern system. The critical invention was the wrought-iron rail, first produced in North-East England. It proved much better than the cast-iron tramplate and was used on both the famous Stockton and Darlington Railway and the more modest horse-drawn Monkland and Kirkintilloch Railway (opened in 1826).

Even if steam locomotives had not been improved from their early nineteenth-century origins, railways would still have multiplied; but in 1829–30 the Liverpool and Manchester Railway successfully demonstrated that locomotives could haul speedy passenger trains as well as freight. The potent combination of steam locomotives and wrought-iron rails had a dramatic effect on the evolution of rail travel.

The viaduct over the River Almond: painting by David Octavius Hill.

Within ten years central Scotland had a basic system of arterial railways and within twenty years the railway system had been extended as far north as Aberdeen, with three routes linking Scotland to England.

3. THE EDINBURGH AND GLASGOW RAILWAY

The cities of Edinburgh and Glasgow have been in rivalry for many centuries. For most of this period Edinburgh dominated as a centre of population, power and commerce. In the eighteenth century the Clyde became important owing to its relative proximity to North America, and its merchants were very effective in establishing trading links with what became the southern United States and with the West Indies. This stimulated the rise of industry throughout west central Scotland, creating a base for much larger-scale industrial growth in the nineteenth century. In consequence Glasgow grew to rival Edinburgh in population and to become the more important commercial centre. Edinburgh, however, was the seat of government, of the legal process and of banking, and thus there was a need for speedy communication between the two cities.

There were coach services from 1768, a canal link from 1822, and a part-rail part-canal route from 1840. But the Edinburgh–Glasgow route was an obvious choice for a first-generation main-line railway. As completed in 1842 it was superbly engineered, with three major tunnels, long and deep cuttings, lengthy viaducts and marvellous overbridges. Its curves were gentle and its gradients slight, except for a rope-worked incline at the Glasgow end.

Apart from an extension at the Edinburgh end and the abandonment of rope haulage from 1908, the Edinburgh and Glasgow Railway is virtually as built after nearly 150 years of operation. It remains a most noble and effective monument to the generous intentions of its promoters and to the capabilities of its engineers (Grainger and Miller). In its day industry grew round it but most of this has now gone, and its interference with the environment is minimal; indeed, as on railways generally, its cuttings and embankments are havens for plants and animals otherwise threatened. The Edinburgh and Glasgow Railway remains an effective argument for wise and generous provision of public utilities.

At first the locomotive-hauled railways had to be as level as possible, with cable-assistance on gradients if necessary, as at Cowlairs on the Edinburgh and Glasgow Railway (Box 3). But as steam locomotives became more powerful and reliable the massive civil engineering works required for the early lines became less necessary. By that time the advantages of railway communication were obvious, and although roads and canals remained important locally they were in all respects secondary to the railways. In the Highlands and some other areas railways were promoted primarily to improve communications rather than as profitable ventures.

The architects and engineers who built most of these pioneer railways considered it a matter of pride that they should design stations, bridges and viaducts as substantial and dignified structures. But the scars of large railway works aroused public antagonism and there were fears about the effects of steam engines on farm animals and the countryside. To minimise nuisance from smoke, only coke was burned in locomotives until the 1860s when improvements in boiler design allowed the use of coal.

Overall the effect of railways on the environment was complex and striking. They certainly encouraged the growth of towns and in the later nineteenth century were the main factor encouraging the spread of the suburbs. They also enabled the middle classes to spread out from the industrial and commercial centres to commute from select dormitory towns such as Kilmacolm, Bridge of Weir and Troon in the west; while North Berwick, Gullane and Peebles became the equivalents in the east. Rail transport encouraged farmers to specialise in certain products – beef in the north-east, sheep in the Highlands and Borders, dairying in the south-west and cereals in the south-east. They made it easier to exploit coal, ironstone and oil-shale deposits over a large part of Lowland Scotland and fostered the smelting of iron for processing into wrought iron and steel. Railway communications allowed the shipbuilding and heavy engineering industries of west central Scotland to develop on a very large scale.

From the early 1840s large numbers of people began to use the railways for excursions to the Clyde coast, and towns such as Helensburgh, Gourock, Largs, Troon and Ayr, along with towns on the east Fife coast, became popular resorts for day trippers. Rail travel enabled the more affluent tourists to visit Oban or to use the many golf courses which proliferated from the 1880s.

From the 1880s the railways became even more

4. CLYDE STEAMERS

The Clyde estuary was a natural area for the development of steam navigation. In France and in the United States the broad navigable rivers provided something of the same stimulus but early experiments in France proved abortive. The line of development started in Scotland with William Symington (1763–1831), the Leadhills-born inventor and engineer, in the 1780s and was taken up in the United States on the Hudson River by the American engineer Robert Fulton (1765–1815). It resulted in the development of shallow-draught river steamers.

The physical topography of the Clyde, with its islands and long sea-lochs, created a need for water-based communication and its sheltered waters provided an ideal environment for the safe development of steam propulsion.

Henry Bell's 30–ton steamship *Comet* was built at Port Glasgow in 1812 as the first steam-propelled vessel to operate on a navigable European river. It began a process of evolution which culminated in transatlantic liners and world-wide commercial network of steamships; locally in the Clyde it led to the creation of a system of water-borne passenger transport without parallel in the United Kingdom. There was every kind of water transport, from short cross-river ferries, through bread-and-butter routes linking communities on the estuaries, to medium- and long-range excursions.

Steamers catered for all classes of society quickly, efficiently and quietly. It was a fiercely competitive business, as evidenced by the service from Ardrossan on the Ayrshire coast to Brodick on the island of Arran; here the Glasgow and South Western Railway and the Caledonian Railway challenged each other with fast boat trains and speedy steamers and all for minimal traffic rewards. At stake, ultimately, was control of the trade of Ayrshire; the Arran competition was merely a gambit – but what a glorious one. Both companies built fine, fast steamers for the trade. The Glasgow and South Western vessel, the *Glen Sannox*, was arguably the most beautiful Clyde steamer ever built. The fastest steamer time between Glasgow and Brodick in 1893 was 80 minutes; today, with the existing car ferry, the fastest achievable time is 115 minutes.

Henry Bell's Comet, the first steam propelled vessel on any European river.

The first steamboat on the Clyde; painting by John Knox

important in that they allowed cities to go on expanding. The price of this was the construction of expensive underground routes in Glasgow and the development of street railways (tramways); at first such trams were horse-drawn or steam-powered but they were later driven by cables and electricity. The construction of suburban railways resulted in the concentration of new houses and shops around stations; tramways encouraged ribbon development along tram routes as well as more intensive development of inner city sites.

The large number of horses which pulled the trams and other transport (especially in Lanarkshire) needed large amounts of fodder and increased the local demand for oats and hay. This altered the economy of some farming areas by creating a new market for native wheat which had suffered because of competition from imported wheat. Electric tramways eliminated this horse-economy although horses remained numerous in cities until after the First World War.

Electric tramways made mass urban transport both cheap and popular; routes were extended far from town centres, giving many people better access to the countryside. The publication of guides and travel booklets encouraged ramblers to take advantage of this new facility. More importantly the trams encouraged suburban development for the less well-off and gave both professional and labouring workers a wider choice of workplace.

STEAMING AHEAD

In parallel with the rise of railways and tramways, steamship services also grew and became locally significant. Although the first practical steamship in Europe – Henry Bell's *Comet* of 1812 – was not a commercial success, steamships quickly proliferated in the sheltered waters of the Clyde (Box 4). The size and power of such vessels grew rapidly and within a decade coastal services began to operate. From then until the 1840s, when long-distance routes were opened, steamers were

increasingly important for passenger services around the coasts of Britain.

However it was in the Clyde estuary and in the western Highlands and Islands that steamers proved permanently valuable. In the Clyde, steamers had two main effects: they allowed middle-class families to live permanently or seasonally in coastal resorts and they permitted large numbers of working-class excursionists to visit holiday places which catered for them. Rothesay and Dunoon became favourite 'Doon the Watter' destinations enjoying a popularity which we can scarcely imagine today.

Although at first steamers operated from the centre of Glasgow, combined rail-steamer services developed rapidly once the railways became integrated and by the later nineteenth century most steamships were operated by the three railway companies which served the area. The competition between the companies encouraged a high quality of both service and comfort. Faster steamers could work longer routes, enabling people to commute greater distances, but the development of large-scale coastal suburbs was confined to the upper Firth of Clyde and the island of Bute. The island of Arran would have been intensively developed but for the opposition of the principal landowner, the 12th Duke of Hamilton.

In the western Highlands and Islands the effect of the steamboats was different. Local communities were only marginally affected by incomers and commuters. In-stead steamers benefited isolated island and mainland communities by allowing them to develop and specialise. By providing cheap travel they encouraged people to move from remote areas to central Scotland but they also made lowlanders aware of conditions in the Highlands. Some lowlanders invested in land, with mixed results, but other more socially minded people tried to support the highlanders in their struggles with a harsh environment. The development of the whisky distilling industry on Islay, Jura, Mull and Skye was purely commercial, but the Harris Tweed industry was organised partly for benevolent social reasons.

Steamships greatly encouraged tourism in the southern Highlands; Fort William, Oban and Campbeltown all partly owed their economic rise to the tourist trade. And of course the rapid improvement of rail and steamer services gave a dramatic boost to another major aspect of the Highland environment: namely the sporting estates (see Chapter 17).

AFTER THE WARS

The First World War was a real turning point in the character of land-use in Scotland, as in so much else. The war began a process of democratisation of wealth and power and of control of the means of transport, which no administration since has been able to gainsay.

Many soldiers also gained experience in motorised transport during their service, and this encouraged the

133

civil use of motor vehicles to expand rapidly in the 1920s and 1930s.

Immediately after the First World War bus and lorry services began to develop, linking urban communities with each other and with the country. Within twenty years the rural railways were dead or dying; electric trams had vanished from all but the four cities and a network of new arterial and improved local roads had been built. These made motor transport much more attractive to the general public and greatly enhanced the use of motor car.

Cars were glamourised in novels, in the cinema and by press advertising which encouraged people to buy them. The old bounds on large-scale settlement imposed by transport difficulties were burst and new suburbs came into being. Ribbon development, which had begun with the tramways, was extended by motor transport. Motor touring in buses and cars opened up more of the Highlands, hastening the decline of the Gaelic culture which was also being swamped by the English-language radio.

The Second World War did not have such a dramatic effect on the Scottish environment as the Great War. Scotland was strategically important during both world wars and the remains of military sites are still with us, some of them now recognised as important monuments to epochal events. So far as post-war developments were concerned perhaps the most important was the development of air transport which had started to make a small impact with internal commercial services in the later 1930s. In the years after the war transatlantic aviation was at first centred on Prestwick airport; it led to a great increase in the number of American visitors, whose spending power had a definitive effect on the tourist trade, especially in the Highlands. It also encouraged government-sponsored investment in Scottish manufacturing industry.

The further expansion of aviation throughout the world badly affected the Scottish shipbuilding industry, which was further damaged by the concentration of freight into bulk carriers and container ships. The decline of Scottish shipbuilding was made even worse by the development of nuclear weapons which sharply reduced the demand for conventional warships.

Railways were badly affected by post-war trends, especially the increased use of personal cars. Many rural railways were closed for passenger services during the 1950s and in the 1960s most of the remainder went as part of the Beeching cuts. Services to the north and west Highlands were subsidised for social reasons but elsewhere the cuts were severe, involving closure of almost all railways in the Borders and in Galloway. Further expansion of road transport through massive road improvement schemes since then has slashed freight traffic on the railways. However in the west of Scotland conurbation rail transport is still much used, and towns in the Central Belt which have good rail services have grown faster than other comparable settlements. In recent years the re-opening of passenger services on some lines and the building of new stations have been a notable feature; it may well be that the railway age is due for a revival.

Meanwhile Scotland has been gaining a very fine road network. This has allowed large numbers of people to move away from the inner cities to housing developments in suburban and semi-rural areas; this is especially so in west central Scotland. The mechanisation of agriculture and the dwindling population of farm workers released many buildings in the countryside for other uses, and in a 50–60 miles radius around cities many farm properties have been converted into homes for city commuters. Only strict planning controls have prevented large-scale building in the 'green belts' around the cities.

The pattern of shipping round the coast of Scotland has also been influenced by the dominance of motor transport; coastal freight services have almost all disappeared. Ferry services across sea lochs, which were once numerous, have now been reduced to a handful of minor locations. Similarly what were once fully-fledged shipping services to island and mainland piers have been replaced by car ferries on the shortest possible routes – if necessary with overland road links as on the Outer Isles service operated via the Isle of Skye. These changes have put more vehicles on island roads, creating a traffic pressure which is likely to result in the building of a toll bridge to replace the Kyle of Lochalsh to Kyleakin ferry, thereby opening up Skye to still more tourist and heavy vehicular traffic.

But today's transport is in some ways more environmentally friendly than that of the nineteenth and earlier centuries. Aviation traffic, especially at peak holiday times, has brought with it considerable noise pollution on the flight paths into Glasgow and Edinburgh airports. But no palls of smoke hang over railway stations or harbours and the noises of steam engines and clanking wagons no longer disturb the sleep of town dwellers. On the roads cars have cleaner exhausts and are quieter.

But the vast tracts of land swallowed by new roads and car parks threaten people's quality of life in both town and country. Improvements in public transport are likely to have little effect except in the Central Belt, where traffic congestion and parking difficulties are already encouraging people to leave their cars at home for the journey to work.

There is now a real crisis of urban traffic which must urgently be addressed. The towns and cities that grew and prospered because of transport improvements are now in danger of becoming suffocated by the very traffic they have engendered. It is hard to see how this crisis can be resolved without a revolution in social attitudes. There are no major new transport developments on the horizon that compare with the dramatic innovations of canals and road-improvements in the eighteenth century, of steam railways and ships in the nineteenth century, and of the motor vehicle and aeroplane in the twentieth century. The only likely development is towards a retrenchment in transport improvement: actually reducing mobility rather than increasing it.

In the wider countryside, in the absence of convenient and flexible public services, personal transport is so well-suited to the needs of the majority of the population that it is likely to survive anything other than a very massive rise in fuel costs.

Meanwhile, as so often happens, projects and schemes which had ceased to be commercially viable in their day are being revived for nostalgic and other reasons. Abandoned canals are being brought back to life by enthusiasts who find in them a serenity and environmental charm that modern developments lack. Disused railway tracks are being converted into walkways and tracks for ramblers and cyclists.

And even modern developments have their environmental side-benefits too: new motorways are being constructed with broad verges which, with a minimum of maintenance, quickly become valuable wildlife habitats in their own right. And by their very nature these new 'nature reserves' are inviolate sanctuaries because they are just about the only areas in Scotland where Man is kept strictly in his place – on the road!

THE POST OFFICE – *Keeping in touch*

The succession of revolutions in transport and communications has played a vital role in the evolution of modern society.

The Proclamation of Charles I in 1635 'for the settling of the Letter Office of England and Scotland', linking 'Edenburgh' and the 'City of London' in a return journey of five days, is regarded as the start of a public communications service. But throughout the troubled seventeenth century and well into the next, all the post in Scotland was carried on foot, with the exception of the single route between Edinburgh and Berwick, en route to London.

The failure of the 1745 Jacobite Rebellion resulted in much official attention being given to roads and bridges in Scotland. These Highland roads and the march of the Turnpike Trusts paved the way for a major impetus to the development of posts. They also heralded the arrival of that most romantic of postal conveyances, the mail coach. The first arrived in Edinburgh from London in 1786; and by the end of the century coaches also plied between Edinburgh, Aberdeen and Glasgow.

It was Robert Wallace, the member of Parliament for Greenock from 1832, who was instrumental in securing Parliamentary support for the sweeping reforms of the Post Office which were carried out by Rowland Hill. The most famous of these was the universal Penny Post of 1840, with mail being charged by weight not distance and prepaid by means of the 'Penny Black' stamp. The

impact on public communication was immediate and dramatic. In 1839 just over 7.5 million letters were delivered in Scotland; the next year recorded 18.5 million letters and within ten years this figure had doubled. The mail coach could not have coped, but steam trains could.

As the nineteenth century progressed, so the rate of scientific and technological change accelerated. The age of steam was followed by electricity, with the telegraph being a splendid example of response to that change. But the telegram was doomed by the product of still newer technology: the telephone, destined to become one of the great icons of the twentieth century.

When telecommunications were split from the Post Office in 1981 to form British Telecom, it also heralded for some the imminent arrival of 'paperless communication'. With well over a thousand million letters now being posted in Scotland and even more delivered, the opposite has turned out to be true.

Post Offices have gradually become the local representatives of a state increasingly involved with the lives of its citizens. What with dispensing pensions (since 1908), TV licences and 150 other transactions, the 2000 post offices in Scotland have a vital and central role to play – particularly perhaps where they underpin the viability of remote rural and island communities.

MARTIN CUMMINS   The Post Office

Waterfall at Jenny's Lum,
River Kendrick, Fintry Hills.

Water lilies at the RSPB
reserve, Loch Garten.

The Streams of Life

PETER MAITLAND

Dr Peter S. Maitland is a specialist in freshwater ecology and fish conservation, and runs his own consultancy based at the Fish Conservation Centre near Stirling. He has been on the staff of the Universities of Glasgow and St Andrews, as well as the Nature Conservancy and the Institute of Terrestrial Ecology.

The lochs and rivers of Scotland are famed all over the world in poetry and in song as a national resource of breathtaking beauty and inestimable value. The *bonnie, bonnie banks of Loch Lomond, Sweet Afton,* the *Silvery Tay* and many other references all conjure up waterside images of peace and beauty. There is a practical side too: pure water from Highland springs is an essential ingredient in the production of that other celebrated liquid, *uisge beatha,* the Gaelic for 'water of life' – Scotch whisky; and fresh Scottish salmon grace restaurant tables on every continent. In addition the mystery of Loch Ness and its alleged monster has drawn visitors from every part of the globe. No image of Scotland can be properly conjured up without including her lochs, her lochans, her rivers and her burns.

In times of critical water shortage in other parts of Great Britain, Scotland is fortunate in having vast amounts of high quality water: Loch Ness alone contains more water than all the lakes and reservoirs in England and Wales put together. Yet although we value Scotland's fresh waters highly for their beauty we often undervalue them as a key national resource; indeed substantial damage is being done to some waters by various human activities.

Much of the physical nature of the lochs and rivers of Scotland has been shaped by ancient land movements and in particular by the action of ice during the last Ice Age which came to an end some 12,000 years ago. The grinding action of huge glaciers which gouged out many of our loch basins and river valleys, the kettle holes left after the melting of huge ice blocks, and the damming of river valleys by terminal moraines – these all left behind a varied but barren landscape as the great ice cap finally retreated.

Many people think of Scotland as being a very wet country yet the rainfall in some parts of the east (Moray and East Lothian, for example) is low, with only about 20 inches (50 cm) of rain each year. Some parts of the west, on the other hand, make up for this and well over 80 inches (200 cm) of rainfall each year is common in some of the mountainous areas of the west coast.

Running water has formed much of our landscape as it is seen today and our freshwater resource in terms of the number of lochs and rivers is an impressive one. Recent counts have shown that Scotland has a total of well over 31,000 lochs and lochans and over 5,000 rivers and burns. These include some of the most spectacular freshwater bodies in Great Britain as well as the largest: Loch Lomond (Box 1) is the greatest by area at 27 square miles (70 sq km); Loch Awe is the longest at 25 miles (40 km), and Loch Morar the deepest at 1000 ft (300 m), while Loch Ness has the greatest volume – 26 billion cubic ft (735 million cubic metres). The River Tay (Box 2) is the largest river with an average flow of 5,614 cubic ft (158 m)per second, more than twice that of the River Thames.

At the height of the last Ice Age no wildlife existed in Scotland and practically all our present plants and animals have managed to arrive over the last 10,000 years or so. Clearly this is not too difficult for plants with airborne seeds and for birds and flying insects, but the problems of immigration and dispersal are much greater for purely aquatic invertebrates and for fish. Actually fish are still slowly moving northwards to invade Scottish waters perfectly suitable for them,

Water sculpted rocks and giant kettle-holes at Glen Orchy.

which they have been unable to colonise as yet. People play an increasing role in transporting such organisms and there have been many changes in our aquatic wildlife in recent times.

WATERS OF HISTORY

Historically Scotland's fresh waters have been of critical importance to human settlement and culture. The words of the famous song *The Road to the Isles* ('by Tummel and Loch Rannoch and Lochaber I will go') show how the larger lochs and rivers were vital for transport at a time when there were few roads and much of the country was covered by impenetrable forest. The major routes across Scotland were, and still are, along the larger glens and river valleys, notably the lochs and rivers of the Great Glen and the Rivers Forth and Clyde in the central Lowlands. The value of these two routes was further enhanced by the construction along them of Scotland's two major canals – the Caledonian Canal and the Forth and Clyde Canal – both of which were extensively used for transport at one time (see Chapter 11).

Water has also determined the siting of human

1. LOCH LOMOND

Loch Lomond, famous for its scenic beauty and 'bonnie banks', is the largest area of fresh water in Great Britain (see Chapter 1). It is also vitally important for wildlife and parts of the shoreline and islands have been protected as a National Nature Reserve for nearly three decades. The loch has been studied intensively for some time and the ecology is now quite well documented.

Several uncommon plants are found around its edge, the most notable being the Loch Lomond dock; a few rare invertebrates also occur. At the turn of this century a small worm discovered in the mud at the bottom of the loch was found to be a species new to science and was named after the loch: *Arcteonais lomondi*. It has since been recorded in Loch Morar but appears to occur nowhere else in Great Britain.

No fewer than nineteen species of fish occur in Loch Lomond – the largest number of species known from any Scottish loch. The rarest species in national terms is the powan. Second in rarity is the unusual black dwarf race of river lamprey which feeds mainly on powan. The combination of the powan and the river lamprey is unique in the British Isles. In the last ten years several new fish species have been introduced to the loch, including the ruffe; four of these are now established and abundant in some places.

Much of the loch's water catchment is natural moorland or woodland but some areas are substantially affected by farming and forestry. Fertilisation of the land has polluted local burns with nutrients which have eventually leached into the loch. In addition schemes to improve drainage by ploughing and ditching have caused more silt to be washed into the loch; they have also made burns more liable to sudden spates as well as causing them to be drier during droughts.

There is now substantial demand for the water within the loch and its catchment, and considerable volumes are piped away for use elsewhere. Perhaps even more seriously, recreation is becoming a major industry on and around the loch because of its proximity to Glasgow; a wide variety of activities attracts increasing numbers of people. In summer thousands of visitors bathe in the loch, or picnic along the beaches. The resulting noise and litter are the main difficulties arising, but actual erosion of the shore is also evident.

Loch Lomond is an ideal centre for boating and, with more and more boats using the water each year, pollution from rubbish, oil waste and sewage has increased. Boats also cause problems because of noise and interference to wildlife as well as to anglers and bathers. There are increasing problems among boat users themselves, causing friction between, for example, water-skiers and anglers. Sport fishing is controlled by the Loch Lomond Angling Improvement Association which has about 1,000 members, many of whom have boats on the loch.

Loch Lomond is probably Scotland's most important loch. Its high amenity value should mean that changes detrimental to its water quality are opposed. However people with interests in tourism, camping, boat hire, cabin cruising, power boating, water-skiing, canoeing, bathing, picnicking, natural history, angling, research, conservation and water supply are increasingly involved in profound conflicts of interest. The problems can only be successfully resolved if a management strategy for the integration of different uses is developed for the loch and its catchment area. In addition it is vital that more effort goes into conserving the quality of the loch rather than simply attracting more people into the area.

settlements from earliest times, since almost all dwellings were built near suitable sources of drinkable water. In addition water was an important element in the defence strategy of early settlers who built their homes on small natural or artificial islands in lochs; these 'crannogs' were sited offshore for greater safety (see Chapter 7).

Salmon (Box 3) and sea trout migrating into Scotland's waters each year provided a marvellous and abundant source of food and it is evident that these were captured in various ways from earliest times. In some places they could be (and indeed still are) caught by hand but other methods were developed, including the use of spears, traps and nets. Wildfowl of all kinds must also have provided an important part of early Man's diet in Scotland.

Sources of water for power also affected the siting of later settlements and many derelict old mills and 'mill towns' all over Scotland are testament to this. Alongside them we find the mill dams, built of stone and earth, which held back the water in many burns and rivers and diverted it down a new water course (the mill lade) to drive a mill wheel. Several of these mills have been kept in working order and can still be seen today: Preston Mill on the River Tyne in East Lothian is an excellent example.

OUR AQUATIC WILDLIFE

One of the great features of our fresh waters is the marvellous variety of habitats they provide for wildlife between mountainous source and sea estuary. Up on the high tops of our mountains, where the ptarmigan and golden plover live, there are innumerable shallow peat pools and small burns. Most of them cannot support fish but they do have fascinating plants, like the carnivorous bladderwort, as well as many interesting invertebrates. The deep lochs of the mountain corries may hold isolated remnant populations of arctic charr. Lower down in the straths are larger lochs and rivers, which support important salmon and trout (Box 4) populations in addition to many other fish as well as a wide variety of plants and invertebrates, including the large pearl mussel.

Most of these waters are very pure chemically and naturally slightly acidic, but in areas of limestone (e.g. Durness or the island of Lismore) the waters are alkaline and so clear that light can penetrate deep, giving the lochs a lovely bluish appearance.

As they approach the coast the rivers reach their maximum size and flow into firths or estuaries where the animals and plants of the freshwater communities change dramatically to salt-loving ones. All round the coast are small saltwater pools and creeks with similar species.

There is a wealth of plants and animals above and below the surface of these undisturbed waters. Pond-

weeds and stoneworts grow in the depths, lilies float on the surface, while irises, marsh marigolds, bulrushes and many other plants add grace and colour to the banks. Bright damselflies dart among the rushes and dragonflies hover in the sun, catching other insects, while whirligig beetles and skaters slide around on the water's surface film. Beneath the surface the nymphs and larvae of dragonflies, mayflies and stoneflies, as well as water boatmen, shrimps and snails, provide ample food for fish. Indeed more than fifteen species of fish may be found together in some of our larger waters. Scotland has fewer species of freshwater fish when compared with the natural communities that occur further south in Europe. Nevertheless forty of the fifty-five British species are found here and the number is slowly increasing as more move up from the south. Taking the starting point of our fish communities as the closing stages of the last Ice Age, it is clear that the fishes of our estuaries, many of which come into fresh water to spawn, had no difficulty invading new waters as the ice receded. Thus sturgeon, shads, sparling, sea bass, gobies and mullets must have lived in our estuaries for thousands of years.

The only fish which were able to colonise truly fresh waters permanently as the ice receded were those capable of living in both salt water and in the ice lakes and glacial rivers of those times. There were probably no more than twelve species capable of this at that period; most notable among these were lampreys, salmon, trout, arctic charr, powan, eel, sticklebacks, flounders and the vendace (now probably extinct in Scotland).

By 1790 only another five species had been added to the Scottish fauna, namely pike, minnow, roach, stone loach and perch. How they arrived here is uncertain; some probably came naturally, carried as eggs on the

Loch Ness; the greatest volume of freshwater in Britain.

Dragonflies, damselflies and many other freshwater invertebrates are acutely threatened by pollution and loss of habitat.

feet of wildfowl for instance, but others may have been brought by humans.

By 1880, ninety years later, another five species were known to occur in Scotland: brook charr (from North America), grayling, tench, bream and chub (all from England). The main agents of dispersal during this and

2. THE RIVER TAY

The flow volume of the River Tay makes it Britain's greatest river.

Many fine waters could lay claim to the title of Scotland's premier river; but the one with most justification is probably the River Tay. Its catchment area of 2,000 square miles (5,000 sq km) is the largest in Scotland and it has the greatest flow of any river in Great Britain; this exciting water is at one and the same time a most attractive and valuable resource.

Rising as a small trickle at a height of 2,050 ft (620 m) in the west of the country, near Beinn Laoigh, the source water tumbles down the mountainside to join with other burns, forming the River Cononish. Further downstream, near Tyndrum, the Cononish becomes the River Fillan which passes into Loch Dochart and Loch Iubhair and emerges as the River Dochart; this flows east and eventually passes over the lovely falls at Killin to enter Loch Tay, one of Scotland's many large and beautiful lochs.

Emerging from the loch as the River Tay, at Kenmore, it flows down a magnificent wooded strath to Ballinluig where it is joined by the River Tummel, which doubles its size. Now a major river it flows steadily towards Perth, joined by the Rivers Braan and Isla. At Perth it becomes tidal as it enters the firth and is joined by the River Earn before reaching the open sea beyond Dundee. During their journey from Beinn Laoigh the waters have travelled 92 miles (148 km).

The river shows many ecological changes along this course. Starting as a cascading mountain burn with few nutrients and very few plants or animals, it slows to become a rocky Highland river full of mosses and other weeds as well as many invertebrates and fish. As it enters the strath it slows further and meanders, with many deep pools and extensive areas of gravel. This stretch, surrounded by farmland, is very rich and has an abundant aquatic wildlife. Finally it moves into the estuary and merges with salt water, providing yet another varied habitat for aquatic life.

An obvious feature on the river is Loch Tay itself, which forms almost one-sixth of the total river length and whose deepest point at 508ft (155 m) is well below sea level. There are many other lesser lochs within the catchment (574 are shown on the 1 : 50,000 map) and several of the larger of these have been harnessed for hydro-power. As a result the pattern of flow in the river is somewhat erratic, being related to changes in power demand rather than immediate rainfall. Some of the water in the River Tummel has actually been transferred from the River Spey.

In Scottish terms the fish which live in the River Tay form a diverse community and the river's twenty species are of considerable conservation interest. There are no fish at all near the river's source, but trout soon appear downstream and are joined by salmon and eels, all of these occurring throughout the main river to the sea. Some thirteen species are common in the middle reaches but one species, the arctic charr, is found only in Loch Tay.

As the river moves into the estuary and salty conditions take control, some fish such as minnows disappear; but these are made up for by other species like sparling, which make up a varied estuarine community here.

The salmon fishery on the River Tay is a famous one. Huge numbers of fish are caught each year: usually about 50,000 by the commercial netsmen near the mouth and 10,000 by anglers upstream. In the modern river, salmon making their way upstream must not only pass these hazards but also surmount several hydro-electric dams. Fortunately they are helped at each one by a fish ladder, and built into the ladder on the Faskally Dam at Pitlochry is a viewing chamber in which the public can see these magnificent fish move upstream (incidentally recording themselves on an electronic counter as they do so).

The largest salmon ever caught by rod and line in Great Britain was taken in the River Tay in 1922 by Miss Georgina Ballantine; it weighed just over 64 lb (29 kg).

As well as being a pearl among Scottish rivers the River Tay is also famous for its production of fine freshwater pearls. These rare lustrous gems are formed around stray particles of grit which lodge in the mantle of the pearl mussel *Margaritifera margaritifera*, once common in the River Tay and other Scottish rivers, but now becoming rarer owing to changing land-use, pollution and overfishing.

later periods were people and there are many records of deliberate introductions of these and other species around this time. This was a very busy period for the translocation of fish and many landowners introduced new species to waters on their Scottish estates, including several from North America.

By 1970 another eight species were known to have become established in Scotland: rainbow trout (Box 4), carp, goldfish, gudgeon, rudd, orfe, dace and bullhead, and humans appear to have introduced all of them. The latest character in this saga is the ruffe, a small perch-like fish which appeared in Loch Lomond in 1982, probably introduced by anglers from the south. This species has thrived in the loch and is now one of the most common fish but its impact on the ecology of the loch is still uncertain.

Many other fish have been introduced over the last 200 years but without success; these included large-mouth and smallmouth bass (introduced to Loch Baa by the 8th Duke of Argyll in 1881), and cutthroat trout released into a small loch on Shetland. Between 1920 and 1930 several foreign species were introduced to ponds on an estate in Fife, including the American lake charr, dolly varden, mudminnow, bleak, bitterling, Danube catfish (which can grow to a length of ten feet!), brown bullhead and pumpkinseed. None of these species is known to exist in Scotland today.

Thus our present fish are a mixture of natural immigrants from the sea and from further south, along with many more recent arrivals which people have brought from England, continental Europe and even North America. The situation is by no means stable and we can expect other newcomers in future years. These will certainly add to the diversity of our fish communities but may also bring with them the threats of disease, competition and predation on our more sensitive and valuable native fishes.

EXPLOITING THE WATERS

The ever-increasing standard of living in Scotland (and many other countries) has entailed heavy demands on freshwater resources and made conflicting demands on the available water. We urgently need to develop schemes for integrated water resource use on a regional and national basis, but it is a course which planners and politicians have been slow to take.

To make the best use of water resources, especially in areas with low or variable rainfall, adequate reservoirs for the storage of rain water have to be constructed. These form an important part of most water supply systems and in areas of Scotland such as the Kilpatrick Hills, the Ochils and several other upland areas close to the Central Belt there are now more reservoirs than natural lochs. Unlike some of the enormous reservoirs which we see abroad, these artificial systems have usually merged well with the local landscape and ecology.

Arctic Charr from Loch Doon have survived since the last Ice Age but are now threatened by acidification.

Powan are now one of Scotland's rarest fish, being found only in Loch Lomond and Loch Eck.

The availability of copious amounts of clean water played an important role in the development of the whisky, steel and paper industries, all of which use large volumes of water. In modern times it is not so crucial for industries to be close to the actual source, since aqueducts have been built to carry water from one part of the country to another. The pipelines linking Loch Katrine to Glasgow, and Loch Lomond to Grangemouth, are good examples.

Although historically important, few waters in Scotland are now used for navigation, apart from the Caledonian Canal, which is still used by fishing boats travelling from one side of the country to the other. However many pleasure boats, particularly canoes and yachts, still use the old canal systems as well as lochs and rivers and a few of the larger lochs still have small pleasure steamers on them – an echo of Victorian times (see Chapter 11).

Scotland is very fortunate in having the basic resources for the production of hydro-electricity, namely a mountainous countryside and lots of rain, much of which falls in winter when demand for electricity is greatest. Many hydro-power stations have been built in Scotland, sometimes harnessing the water of natural lochs but more often damming lochs to enlarge them or creating entirely new reservoirs by damming glens. The water in these reservoirs is often augmented by supplies brought in from neighbouring catchments via aqueducts; such auxiliary supplies are also used at

Rainbow over the papermill at Corpach.

trout for the stocking of lochs and rivers. Fish-farming has expanded rapidly in recent years and the production of rainbow trout for the table and young salmon for rearing in sea cages has been especially rapid. The main requirements for salmon and trout farms are large supplies of cool high-quality water as well as an adequate area for ponds and reasonable transport to markets. More and more fish are being reared in floating cages in lochs (see Chapter 2).

The fish which live in Scotland's lochs and rivers, especially salmon and trout, give pleasure and recreation to many thousands of anglers each year and constitute a major national resource worth many millions of pounds. Most of the commercial fisheries for salmon and sea trout do not take place in fresh water but in estuaries or the sea, when the fish are moving upstream into fresh water to spawn. In addition to salmon and trout angling there is also an increasing interest in fishing for perch, pike and other coarse species.

People's increasing leisure time places an enormous demand on the remaining areas of natural countryside; our lochs and rivers are the focus for a tremendous variety of recreational activities such as sailing, power-boating, water-skiing, fishing, wildfowling, birdwatching, bathing and general picnicking (see Chapter 17). It is unfortunate that the most valued waters for these activities are rarely found in urban areas; understandably, people prefer to enjoy themselves among clean lochs and rivers set in attractive countryside.

THE THREATS TO OUR WATERS

The unusually dry summers of recent years have certainly made many people more concerned about water supplies; not only were many lochs and rivers in Scotland shallower than normal but reservoirs were lower, gardens were drier and cars were dirtier as a result. Is there really a problem? How can there be, when we actually use only a small percentage of our valuable water resources directly? With all that available water there should be enough for every need; yet there is an enormous range of demands which often conflict with each other.

For instance we each use about 22 gallons of water a day for our domestic needs: drinking, cooking, washing, bathing, toileting and so on. Industry too has huge demands: the Grangemouth petrochemical complex alone uses 3–4 million gallons of Loch Lomond water every day. Hydro-electricity, fish farming, domestic sewage, recreation of all kinds – they all make their insistent demands on our water resources.

Naturally all these pressures bring problems; many of our waters have been so misused that they are unfit for either people or wildlife. We do many things which affect water even before it gets into our lochs and rivers; land-users are particularly important in this respect.

pumped-storage schemes at Foyers on Loch Ness and at Cruachan on Loch Awe (see Chapter 13).

Regular irrigation is practised only in a few of the drier agricultural areas in the east of Scotland; there it has proved useful for watering vegetables during the growing season and swelling new potatoes just before they are lifted. Water is usually pumped from a nearby burn, or a borehole, and sprayed over the fields. Most water used in this way is immediately lost by evaporation or transpiration by the crop and very little ever finds its way back to the burn. Irrigation requirements are usually very seasonal, but unfortunately demand tends to be highest in dry periods when rainfall and reserves are lowest.

Although people have farmed or cultured fish for food from ancient times it is a relatively new idea in Scotland. Many of the early efforts were centred on 'stew ponds' associated with the monasteries. Later, fish hatcheries were built to produce salmon and brown

Fisherman on Loch Na Keal, Isle of Mull.

The use of fertilisers, herbicides and pesticides in agriculture and forestry means that many of these chemicals or their residues end up in nearby water courses; and the spread of pollution is often enhanced by the draining and ditching of land which causes water to drain faster.

Many lowland lochs such as Loch Leven have suffered algal blooms caused by over-enrichment from agricultural fertilisers; when these blooms peak, the algae die and their decomposition suffocates fish from lack of oxygen. Domestic and industrial pollution can be even more severe and may completely kill all aquatic plants and animals, as has happened in parts of the Rivers Clyde and Forth. These stretches of extreme pollution, devoid of oxygen or poisoned by chemicals, act as a barrier to migrating fish which cannot cross them to reach stretches of clean water further upstream.

Weirs and dams on rivers act as barriers in the same way. Airborne pollution, such as acid rain, can also have a devastating effect and several of our hill lochs which had healthy trout populations a century ago are now too acid for fish to survive. People have also created other problems, for example by introducing alien plant or fish species; and recreational activity by the waterside can destroy vegetation and disturb wildlife.

The larger waters often hold the limelight, yet one of the saddest things over the last hundred years is what has happened to our smaller lochs, burns and ponds, especially in the Lowlands. Virtually all the small streams in Lowland agricultural areas have been ditched, canalised and piped to such an extent that there are virtually no natural examples left. With small ponds the situation is even worse, for they have been gradually drained and filled in over the last century or so and even the few which remain are degraded or threatened. There is an urgent need in many areas for a review of what still remains in order that the most important small waters can be saved.

LOOKING TO THE FUTURE

Surely with so many lochs, rivers and burns in Scotland there are enough to go round? The real answer is yes, but there are many problems and conflicts to be resolved. Our present national planning is quite inadequate.

What we need is a national framework and planning policy for all our lochs and rivers. We must look at their distribution, quality and value in relation to the demands we place upon them. Some are clearly vital for major uses such as hydro-electricity or water supply,

3. THE ATLANTIC SALMON

The life cycle of the Atlantic salmon, the largest British salmonid, is well established: adults return from the sea to spawn in the river of their birth around November in nests called redds (see Chapter 2). The eggs hatch in the spring to give young called alevins which quickly develop into small fry and then into well marked 'parr'. After two years or more these become silvery 'smolts' which migrate downstream to the sea and thence to their rich feeding grounds in the North Atlantic. There are approximately 400 different stocks, or local races, of wild salmon in Scotland.

The stocks of Atlantic salmon in Scotland have declined over the last few centuries. Whereas most river systems formerly contained populations of salmon, these disappeared from some rivers with the onset of the Industrial Revolution because of pollution and artificial barriers. However in some places where salmon have been absent for decades, recent improvements in water quality have been such that stocks are recovering naturally (from adjacent stocks), as in the River Clyde.

Superficially at least the Atlantic salmon is economically the most important of our three

native salmonids (salmon, trout and charr) and it is certainly the one which receives most attention politically. Wild fish were formerly the most important; about 1,000 tonnes a year are caught by anglers and by commercial netsmen. However the development of salmon farming has rapidly overtaken this and the production of farmed fish is currently about thirty times that of wild fish. Some netsmen have gone out of business in recent years; this trend seems likely to continue and eventually most wild fish will be taken by rod and line.

Attempts have been made at various times to estimate the value of the fisheries for Atlantic salmon and sea trout; these estimates vary widely according to the method used. One recent estimate gave a value of £50.4 million to the rod fishery (with 3,360 permanent jobs) and £1.8 million to the commercial fishery (with 390 permanent jobs). One of the highest values recently placed on Atlantic salmon was for the sale of fishing rights on a stretch of the River Beauly, where the value was assessed on the basis of £12,000 per fish caught annually.

Atlantic salmon migrating upstream to spawn.

Loch Duntelchaig Reservoir near Inverness.

and this must be the overriding priority although minor uses may fit in with this. Other waters may be of such tremendous wildlife importance that their conservation should be paramount. Several of our largest waters are so nationally important that an individual management plan is needed for each one in order that the needs of recreational or agricultural users do not conflict with the primary aim of maintaining the quality and value of that water. In all these cases people who use our water resources must be prepared to compromise and even renounce their claims in some cases – if not on one water then on another.

Such a master plan for our waters could integrate national requirements with local needs. Given an appropriate national framework (probably relying on a computerised database of some kind) the extent, value and role of each part of our water resource could be assessed. Rational judgments could then be made about the best uses for each loch or river; these could range from 'wilderness waters', where no human activity would be allowed, to urban waters which people could use intensively. Some water-activities are perfectly compatible with others, and on certain lochs or rivers one can plan different zones of use: for example at Loch Leven and Linlithgow Loch, boating, angling, nature conservation and recreational use of the water's edge are all satisfactorily integrated. However on other waters, even ones as large as Loch Lomond and the River Tay, there are increasing conflicts among user groups and these problems can only be resolved by the introduction of a sensible local management plan. The earlier such strategies are introduced the better so that Scotland can take full advantage of her natural heritage of abundant pure water.

Brown trout; the two top fish have been crippled and deformed by acidification of their loch. The healthy fish is from a nearby burn.

4. TROUT

The brown trout varies enormously in form and colour and this has resulted in many local names. There are two forms, the brown trout proper and the sea trout; both spawn in fresh water in October or later and the young develop there, rather as salmon do, for a few years. Thereafter brown trout stay on in fresh water (often moving into a loch to mature) but sea trout become silvery smolts and descend to the sea. Here they feed in estuaries and coastal waters before returning to the rivers of their birth to spawn. The number of different stocks of sea trout in Scotland is probably only slightly more than that of salmon, but the different stocks of brown trout must number several thousand.

The rainbow trout was first introduced to Scotland from North America about a century ago and is now a very common fish in places. However although rainbow trout have been released in many waters throughout the country, the species has become established in only a few places and most stocks are maintained by regular introductions for angling or by escapes from fish farms. All too many farmed fish escape or are released, whereupon they compete with native fish for space and food. Many farms, for both trout and salmon, have imported foreign strains of fish and are developing domestic races with characteristics unlikely to be advantageous in the wild.

There has been concern recently over brown trout but this has probably been over-emphasised, for there are still many thousands of individual stocks in Scotland and some at least are likely to be pristine. Nevertheless there have been many losses, and some extinctions are at present masked by substantial annual stockings from hatcheries. There have also been some recent losses due to acidification and there is no doubt that the current decline in the stocks of sea trout on the west coast of Scotland is real and substantial.

All electricity, whether made from nuclear fuel, fossil fuel or wind and wave power, is ultimately derived from the sun.

146

The Power of Scotland

JOHN BUTT and JOHN TWIDELL

Professor John Butt is Professor of Economic History at the University of Strathclyde, and Dr John Twidell is Director of the Energy Studies Unit, also at Strathclyde. Separately, they have published a number of books on the industrial archaeology of Scotland and on energy.

Scotland's energy resources have always been formidable. The sources of energy are very diverse and include peat, oil, oil-shale and coal as well as wind and water power, which have all been exploited by the talent of her scientists and engineers. Nevertheless for much of Scotland's history the brawn of humans and animals was the main source of energy.

Until the nineteenth century, people in Scotland lived in close harmony with their immediate environment and their activities were strictly conditioned by the energy supplies available locally. Then the power of fossil fuels – coal, oil and gas – was released and exploited to such an extent that the environment itself was drastically affected. We cannot of course turn the clock back but we must return to the notion of a 'sustainable' energy lifestyle, while endeavouring to maintain our quality of life but on a higher plane.

Conservation of energy has always played some part in the thinking of energy producers – if only for economic reasons; but today we live in an age which should be totally committed to energy efficiency aided by a full range of advanced modern technologies. For instance just as peasants once used the endlessly renewable energy of the sun to bleach and dry cloth, today we should be looking at 'solar friendly' buildings,

using the sophistication of computer-aided design and microprocessor-based energy control.

Scotland's energy riches have been released as a consequence of human determination, inspiration and ingenuity. But nature's gifts have not always been so easily available as today; the environment and geology of Scotland have often contrived to make it difficult to harness the resource in question. Moreover political involvement with England since the Act of Union in 1707 has meant that for practical purposes Scottish energy has not been, and is not still, master in its own house. The development of Scotland's energy, therefore, is an exciting, significant and unfinished story.

PEAT

If the ground temperature happens to be less than 5°C, dead plants do not decompose as they would normally; in much of Scotland's cold, damp and largely treeless environment the old heather, mosses and bracken do not completely decay as in warmer latitudes. Instead they are compressed by their own weight to form peat: a wet, dark brown organic mass that excludes oxygen. Peat was laid down in Scotland over many thousands of years, forming beds several metres thick. Indeed some of the earliest remains of Neolithic man in Scotland have been found in peat bogs dated to 6000 BC.

Crofters in the west of Scotland normally cut peat with spades; the peat pieces are stacked for drying and then used as fuel. Commercially it is scraped or extruded by tractor-driven 'ploughs' today. This peat is exactly the same material as that which is sold in garden centres for improving the soil of suburban gardens.

Over the centuries peat has been used to roof houses and burned for domestic heating and cooking. But it has had industrial uses, too, such as for the commercial extraction of salt in the thirteenth century, for firing pot stills for the distilling of whisky, and for the production of iron in ancient 'bloomeries'.

In recent times there have been frequent attempts to

Peat cuttings near Lochinver with Suilven in the background.

147

exploit peat on a commercial scale. From 1951 to 1961 the North of Scotland Hydro-Electric Board developed a two-megawatt, peat-fired, gas-turbine electricity generating station at Altnabreac in Caithness. However this project, like many others, was a commercial failure. The basic problems of using peat as an energy source remain: the extraction is labour intensive (even with modern machinery); the peat beds are often remote from roads; the fuel must be dried before it can be burned, and even then its calorific value is low. Moreover the removal of vast amounts of peat has implications for ecology, since peat bogs are vital wetland habitats for rare plants and birds, and if the peat is removed the habitat is destroyed.

The laws of Scotland have always provided Scots with the right to obtain fuel for basic warmth and cooking. In the Middle Ages it was a common obligation for 'bondsmen' to cut and supply a prescribed amount of peat for their feudal lord. However everyone still had the basic right to cut their own peat from designated areas of common land. Rights to property, pasture, peats and personal protection are essential components of Scottish traditional life. These laws survive in modern times in the Crofting Acts which safeguard property and peat-gathering rights throughout northern and western Scotland, including the Islands. The hereditary owner of a croft is allocated an area to dig peats sufficient for a continuing supply from year to year; and a week's hard work in the summer can provide a family with a year's supply of peat for home use.

TIMBER

Scotland's forests and woodlands have been exploited from prehistoric times for timber and fuel. Oak was a favourite wood for construction, whether it was for the beams of a great hall in a castle, for furniture or for shipbuilding. Beech was also used, particularly for early milling machinery, while Scots pine found many domestic and industrial uses. Farmers took their toll of woodlands by felling in many areas but especially in the central Lowlands. The prevalence of goats, cattle, sheep and deer throughout Scotland made the survival of seedlings and saplings unlikely. The grazing of domesticated animals and wild deer had a major impact in clearing the land of trees and keeping it barren.

In early modern times vast amounts of timber were burned to produce charcoal for industrial users, particularly the ironmasters. Charcoal was the main fuel for industries where quality or purity of the product was critical to commercial success. But the destructive distillation of wood itself produced other useful products besides charcoal such as pyroligneous acid, blacking, resins and pitch. Moreover the armaments industry used charcoal as a basic raw material in the production of gunpowder.

The blast furnaces had an insatiable appetite for charcoal; indeed Scotland's relatively cheap timber reserves caused English and other ironmasters to move their works to forested areas of the Highlands in the seventeenth and eighteenth centuries. If no suitable local Scottish iron ores could be found it was cheaper to transport the red Cumbrian iron ores to the source of charcoal in Scotland than to export the charcoal to furnaces near the iron ore mines of the Lake District. Sir George Hay, one of King James VI and I's favourites, was closely involved in founding several ironworks: near Loch Maree at Letterewe, at Talladale and the Red Smithy.

Other early ventures are associated with Urquhart in Inverness-shire, Edzell in Angus and Cameron of Lochiel's lands in Argyll.

Developments during the eighteenth century are easier to trace. In 1723 a blast-furnace was operating at Achray in the parish of Aberfoyle, fuelled by local supplies of birch wood, and it was still operational in 1738. The York Buildings Company, leasing Grant's woodlands in Strathspey in 1728, bought 60,000 fir trees and established a furnace and forge at Coulnakyle using ore from the Lecht just over a dozen miles away. Glenkinglass (1727), Invergarry (1727) and the much more significant Bonawe (1753) and Furnace (1755) are other instances of investment in the charcoal iron industry. The furnaces at Bonawe near Taynuilt remained 'in blast' until 1866 and operations in the area by the Lorne Furnace Company, as it became known, carried on until 1874.

There is a common notion that the furnaces of the English and Irish ironmasters and charcoal-burners consumed much of the ancient Caledonian forest. However two factors cast doubt on this: first, many of the areas where ironworks were established remain heavily forested today – and this is not as a result of plantings by the Forestry Commission, extensive as they have been; second, ironmasters, according to recent research, were much more committed to coppicing of woodland than is usually supposed. Coppicing was the method the wood cutters used to harvest the young tree-growth on a five or ten year cycle; when they cut down the trees they left the stumps and roots in place to grow more coppice poles because young wood produced the best charcoal.

This system also required careful woodland management and regular replanting. Thus the longevity of the Bonawe furnaces simply does not square with the idea of wasteful exploitation of the forests. If the ironmasters had simply burned up the surrounding woods they would have gone out of business, so sustainable coppicing made perfect economic sense. The common goat and the Blackface sheep may have more responsibility for the destruction of young saplings and the disappearance of woodlands than the ironmasters ever did.

In modern times trees are planted overwhelmingly as

forestry monocultures. Quick-growing softwoods are raised for paper production and the building trade. Landowners have received significant subsidies and tax benefits to create and sustain plantations over farmland, hillside and peat bog alike. However these plantations are not natural forests and do not sustain common plants and animals. Even worse, unique wilderness areas of the countryside are being blotted out for the production of trivial newsprint.

WATER POWER

The technology for using water power as an energy source for milling grain was first brought to Scotland by the Vikings and later by the English. The earliest machines were meal-mills using horizontal waterwheels on a vertical axis. These were most common in areas where Norse influence was strongest and remains and restorations of such mills can be seen in Shetland and Lewis today. They were simple easily built structures and they served local purposes well. More complex waterwheels, with a vertical wheel on a horizontal axis, were built throughout the country and were probably introduced by the Normans. A few were tide-mills (usually known as sea-mills) but most used the power of freshwater rivers and streams.

The use of such mills for grinding corn became widespread and one estimate suggests that about 4,000 of them were in active use in the two centuries before 1870, scattered throughout the country. Large mill complexes were created in the towns, including Glasgow's mills on the River Kelvin, Edinburgh's on the Water of Leith, and those at Perth which used an intricate city-centre lade system.

The textile industry also made use of water power; the earliest application, in the fourteenth century, was for the 'fulling' or softening of woollen cloth, known in Scotland as 'waulking'. It is probable that this technology was copied in the early paper mills which pulped rags for making paper. These mills were the prototypes for later developments in the flax, linen, cotton and woollen industries which began in the early eighteenth century and culminated in the great cotton factory villages of New Lanark (Box 1), Deanston, Stanley and Catrine. The classic feature of industrialisation, the concentration of production in large factories, represented an initial victory for water power.

There are many other instances of the application of water power during the early phases of industrialisation. Landowners developed sawmills to increase their incomes and improve their estates. Water engines were used to drain the early undersea coal workings at Culross in Fife, and the mining areas around the Forth provided the best opportunities for these expensive innovations. The crushing and smelting of ores, particularly in the lead-mining districts of Leadhills and Wanlockhead, also attracted state-of-the-art water power: water-driven stampers broke up the ore and the same installations drove the air-bellows at the smelting furnaces.

In the eighteenth century, water-powered machinery was to be found at the iron furnaces and forges, improving the blast and driving the trip and tilt hammers. After 1750 there were considerable improvements to the design of waterwheels and to their installation. The resulting improvement in efficiency supplied much of the increased power demanded by the

1. NEW LANARK

New Lanark, 20 miles (32 km) to the south-east of Glasgow, is recognised by world heritage bodies as one of Britain's outstanding industrial monuments: a classic factory village, designed to produce cotton cloth in the first phase of Scotland's Industrial Revolution. The newly invented English cotton-spinning machinery of the late eighteenth century required water power, and the River Clyde was tapped by an extensive water-lade tunnelled through a hillside to provide water for New Lanark. When David Dale (1739–1806) and Richard Arkwright (1732–92), the patentee of the water-powered cotton-spinning frame, visited the area in 1784, Arkwright thought Lanark could be turned into a new Manchester.

The first mill was built in 1785–6 and spinning began in March 1786, but this building was consumed by fire before a second mill was completed in 1788. Undeterred Dale replaced it and ultimately built four mills as well as housing for the workers. This remained the world's largest water-powered cotton-mill complex until its closure 180 years later. It was a very substantial investment by the standards of the time and New Lanark became the model for enlightened management practices under Dale's ownership and that of his son-in-law, Robert Owen (1771–1858).

Robert Owen's name is strongly linked with New Lanark because he managed to combine profitability with scientific management and a concern for humanity, at a time when these attributes were rare and usually regarded as incompatible. He was a pioneer of factory reform, education, enlightened labour relations and co-operation, and became a messiah of utopian movements in early-nineteenth-century Britain and America. The village where he worked and wrote *A New View of Society* (1813) is one of the most complete survivals from the era of early industrialisation and has been the object of a massive and successful conservation effort.

The mills at New Lanark built by David Dale were the largest working water-powered complex in the world until closure in the 1960s.

Preston Mill at East Linton restored to full working order by the National Trust for Scotland.

Hydro-electric power house at British Alcan, Fort William.

Industrial Revolution – so much so that the contribution to the Revolution attributed to the arrival of steam power has probably been overstated. In fact large and small industries in Scotland continued to use water power on traditional lines until relatively recent times.

The total power available from water resources increased dramatically with the coming of hydro-electricity. The generation of electricity from coils attached to a rotating shaft became realistic for public supply from the 1880s. The question was, what power source should be used to turn the shaft? The first generators in New York and London were driven by steam engines but in Scotland water power was an obvious alternative. At this time Glasgow was the 'second city of the Empire' and arguably the world centre for engineering and commercial development. Here Lord Kelvin exerted his dominant influence in science and engineering (Box 2) and was soon joined by other great engineers. Hydro-electric power was proposed not only for Scotland but also for north-eastern America, using the Niagara Falls. The first commercial electricity generated in Scotland was from hydro-power at Greenock in the period 1892–95; then, in 1896, Lord Kelvin was a key figure in the opening of the British Aluminium Company's hydro-electric plant at Foyers on Loch Ness and in the encouragement of hydro-electricity as advancement for rural populations.

The use of hydro-power to generate electricity for urban areas on a significant scale required the creation of a national distribution grid. In 1927 Central Scotland was the first area in the UK to be designated by the government for such transmission; this provided the economic base for a scheme to generate power from a series of lochs in Galloway which in 1935 became Britain's first large hydro-power system with a capacity of 100 megawatts. The capital cost was £30 per kilowatt capacity and the electricity output generating cost was 0.11 old pence per kilowatt hour (kWh). Fifty-five years later the scheme is now operated by Scottish Power; the generating stations still function efficiently and have a long life expectancy. The generating cost has decreased in real terms to about 0.3 new pence per kWh, classically proving the importance of investing in sustainable, pollution-free energy sources.

2. LORD KELVIN
(WILLIAM THOMSON, 1824–1907)

Professor William Thomson of Glasgow University was made Lord Kelvin in 1892 in recognition of his outstanding contributions to fundamental physics and practical engineering. His prime concerns were the theory and applications of energy. His reputation has continued to grow after his death and he is now honoured world-wide as the most outstanding applied physicist of all time. The author of more than 600 technical papers, his name was given to the fundamental unit of temperature (the degree Kelvin), to the derivation of the Second Law of Thermodynamics, to the invention and commercial production of many instruments, to the beginnings of hydro-power engineering, to the first transatlantic communication cable and to the establishment of science for commercial engineering practice.

He was born in Belfast into a family of seven children and his mother died when he was only six years old. Two years later his father moved with the children to continue his work as a mathematics teacher and writer at Glasgow University. William was obviously of outstanding intellect and was tutored by his father in mathematics; by the age of ten he had entered the university himself, first graduating from Glasgow and then from Cambridge. After careful planning by his dominant father, he returned to Glasgow University as Professor of Natural Philosophy when he was twenty-two. He remained loyal to Glasgow throughout his life, creating the world's first modern physics laboratory just off the High Street.

His relationship with the technical and commercial cultures of Glasgow was profound and his patents and commercial inventions made him a wealthy man; the city stimulated him and he stimulated it. On his death in 1907 he was buried in Westminster Abbey, with his name ennobled throughout the world by his discoveries; his reputation brought honour to the name of Glasgow, the city in which he blossomed.

Hydro-electricity generation at Laggan Dam, Roy Bridge.

A further bonus has been the success of the original consultant engineering companies in large hydro-power schemes world-wide.

The next significant hydro-power development in Scotland produced a system of ten times greater capacity. This arose from the North of Scotland Hydro-Electric Board's construction schemes from 1943 to the 1960s. During the Second World War the socialist Secretary of State for Scotland, Tom Johnston, persuaded the Westminster government to create Britain's first nationalised power Board and to initiate the capital intensive programme needed to harness the water resources of the Highlands.

The 1943 Act establishing the Board was noteworthy in several respects: first, it was the forerunner of the 1947 Act, nationalising 300 separate companies and co-ordinating electricity supply throughout the UK; second, it had a long-term vision of economic development in the Highlands and Islands; third, it was the last major Act of Parliament relating to the 'right' of citizens to receive energy: section 2.3 of the Act, the 'Social Clause', made it a duty of the Board to supply new consumers in rural and island areas as a requirement 'for economic development and social improvement' at rates which would otherwise be uneconomic. In 1990 this requirement for social service, rather than profit making, ceased with the privatisation of electricity supply.

The 1,064 megawatt hydro-electric capacity of the North of Scotland Hydro-Electric Board (now Hydro-Electric plc) is based on nineteen main power schemes and several smaller generating stations in the Highlands and Islands. In addition the Board had 700 megawatts of pumped storage at two stations. Care has been taken to protect the environment despite the obvious ecological disruption of water dams in blocking salmon runs; however small run-of-the-river schemes are less disruptive. The network is now almost entirely linked by overhead and undersea cables which merge the electricity from hydro-power with energy from the gas-fired station at Peterhead.

The cable network also integrates the pumped storage dams of Loch Awe and Loch Ness with wind power on Orkney and with the rest of Britain's national grid. In addition there are about fifty private generating schemes, all of small capacity, which sell their excess power to the competing Hydro-Electric grid. The Mackenzie Report of 1962 foresaw a total hydro-electric potential in Scotland of more than 1,964 megawatts. This would represent a 70 per cent increase over our present hydro-electric generating capacity, so the story of electricity from water power is far from over.

WIND POWER

The windmill was a relatively late arrival in Scotland and the earliest reference we have is to a mill at Largo in Fife during the mid fifteenth century. The idea was probably introduced from the Netherlands, or from East Anglia, where windmills were common. Many were constructed in the mid and late seventeenth century but the greatest building activity took place in the late eighteenth and early nineteenth century when a book on cereal production stimulated technical developments in milling.

By 1850 steam-driven mills, operating mainly in towns, had begun to eclipse the Scottish windmill. A few survived by converting to steam, for example at Carluke, and a few more resisted modern pressures until the early twentieth century. Survivals indicate a technical progression from the simple post mill to a variety of increasingly sophisticated tower mills. Most were constructed by local millwrights and masons, and the more limited the use the more simple the design. There were possibly no more than a hundred Scottish windmills of which the great majority were in the east of Scotland, stretching as far north as Orkney.

Windmills were more expensive to build than horse-mills or watermills and were rarely a sound economic proposition in a country where both water and horses were plentiful. Most commonly windmills were used for threshing and grinding grain, peas and other cereal substitutes; a few were used for pumping water or drainage, as for example at Strathbeg; one at Leith was used to grind metal ores brought from the Earl of Hopetoun's mines at Leadhills; and another at St Monans pumped sea water into storage tanks for the saltpans.

Modern wind turbines are very different from the historical windmills described so far. Today's wind turbines are used almost entirely for generating electricity although very occasionally they are used to pump water for cattle troughs. The idea of using electricity for lighting, and later for power, arose from the scientific discoveries and engineering developments of the late nineteenth century. In the 1880s, while Lord Kelvin opted for water power to drive electricity-generating turbines, and others used steam engines, James Blyth considered wind power.

The 60 metre diameter wind turbine at Burgar Hill, Orkney, generates more than three megawatts of electricity.

151

Professor James Blyth was an engineer at Anderson's University in Glasgow (soon to become the Royal Technical College and later Strathclyde University). Blyth designed and built what was possibly the world's first patented wind turbine for generating electricity. His patent of 1891 was for a 16–metre (52 ft) diameter machine, constructed at his family home in Montrose; this produced electricity for twenty-four years until the First World War, when Blyth had to stop work. After the war the development of wind-power generators ceased apart from the use of very small machines such as the Lucas 'Free-lite' which was used for battery charging for lighting on remote farms. Such machines were used through the 1930s and 1940s and the remains of some can still be found in the Highlands and Islands.

The next significant wind-power development in Scotland was the 100 kW, 14-metre (46 ft) diameter experimental turbine built on Costa Head, Orkney, in 1951. Commissioned by the North of Scotland Hydro-Electric Board, it was constructed by John Brown's of Clydebank, who also built the great liners, *Queen Mary* and *Queen Elizabeth*. Yet as many established engineers have found, wind power is not as straightforward as shipbuilding. The experiments continued for six years until the machine was dismantled in the face of the competition from cheap diesel fuel. The development could have continued but the rapidly falling price of oil in the 1950s and 1960s prevented further interest. It took the shock of the 1973 OPEC oil price rise to cause a renewal of activity.

When looking for alternative energy supplies, it is not difficult to realise that Scotland has the best wind-power potential in the whole of Europe. The writer W.H. Murray has described life on the Western Isles as being akin to living on an aircraft carrier in mid-Atlantic! In the light of this potential, UK government and industry co-operated with the North of Scotland Hydro-Electric Board from 1982 to develop other machines on Orkney. These include the large 60–metre (197 ft) diameter, three-megawatt turbine on Burgar Hill which can produce more power than any other windmill in the world because of Orkney's strong winds. Three machines of this type could supply electricity to satisfy all of Orkney's needs (Box 3).

Elsewhere in Scotland modern wind turbines are used for commercial power. Some are manufactured in the UK while others have been imported from Denmark or the Netherlands. They all use modern composite materials and microprocessor-based controls. The wind turbine on Fair Isle, Shetland, erected in 1982, has perhaps had the greatest impact; this produces power for about 80 per cent of the lighting, cooking and heating needed by the island community. Other machines in Scotland are used on fish farms and conventional land farms where farmers can earn extra income from selling electricity.

Throughout Scotland great care is taken to protect

Energy efficient house at North Ronaldsay bird observatory, Orkney, uses maximum insulation, wind power, solar heating and heat recovery systems.

3. ENERGY ON AN ISLAND

Nothing concentrates history as much as the analysis of a small island. North Ronaldsay is the most northerly and nearly the smallest of Orkney's inhabited islands. The seas around produce riches from oil but life on the island has had to follow its own way. In 1529 the priest John Bellenden noted that the islanders' only fuel was dried seaweed and cattle dung, having no local peat beds or woodland. In the nineteenth century various mills were used, including small household windmills; a large windmill that became the last traditionally operating post-mill in Britain when it ceased rotating in 1905; horizontal horse-driven mills; and even some hydro-powered mills that obtained a head of water despite the island being so flat. Around 1900 coal became a staple fuel imported during the annual visit of the steamer, affectionately called the 'puffer' throughout all the islands of Scotland.

Lighting in homes was usually derived from oil. From early times until the 1850s imported whale oil and natural oils were used in wick lamps. Then paraffin oil from mainland Scotland became available. Small battery-charging wind turbines were used in some houses by the 1930s before small diesel engine generators became the norm in the 1970s. These engines are still kept for emergencies even though the island was connected to the Orkney electricity grid in 1983.

Today the island has a 'low energy house' built by the local general practitioner, Kevin Woodbridge, which is none the less thoroughly warm. This house, part of the North Ronaldsay Bird Observatory, depends for its warmth on the use of thick insulation, the capture of solar energy (especially into the large south-facing conservatory), forced ventilation heat recovery and, most importantly, the use of a modern wind turbine to generate electricity for heat. The house temperature stays above 20°C all year, proving that there need be no fear from the eventual exhaustion of fossil fuels.

the environment and so far the careful siting of wind turbines has not caused complaint. However despite the large wind-power potential and the success of wind farms in other countries, notably Denmark, only a few machines have been installed in Scotland. This is because we have so much surplus generating capacity from coal-fired, gas-powered and nuclear power stations; this surplus of electricity is also reflected in the very low price offered to small private generators.

However wind power and water power create none of the pollution associated with coal-, oil- and nuclear-powered generating stations, and they are sustainable for as long as we have wind and water. In the very long term these factors may come to be appreciated and we may see a full development of Scotland's wind- and water-powered potential.

COAL AND STEAM POWER

The continuities in the development and exploitation of energy resources are nowhere more evident than in the story of the coal industry. As we have already heard, steam engines were used for water drainage at some collieries and Newcomen's steam engine, later radically improved by James Watt (Box 4), was used at a few others.

Most of the leading coalmasters in 1750 were also owners of saltpans and the Firth of Forth was the major area for the production of both coal and salt. The demand for coal diversified greatly in the next hundred years: household use increased very considerably and industrial demand grew even more. The population growth of Edinburgh and Glasgow – and the general spread of towns – after 1780 provided secure but fluctuating home markets for collieries in surrounding areas.

4. JAMES WATT (1736–1819)

James Watt was an inventive genius whose ideas transformed society throughout the world during his own lifetime. Born in Greenock in 1736 into a moderately prosperous family, and educated at the local academy, he demonstrated an early aptitude for making and repairing mechanical devices.

After training as an apprentice in Glasgow and London he became the 'Mathematical Instrument Maker to the University of Glasgow' in 1757. Staff and students interested in science and mechanics gravitated towards his workshop, since all the latest discoveries were discussed there. Watt made lifelong friendships with many professors, including Joseph Black, the theorist of latent heat and John Anderson.

To illustrate his lectures Professor Anderson had a model of a Newcomen steam engine, as used to drain mines. However he could not make it operate successfully, and it was this failure in 1763 which changed the course of Watt's career and thereby the course of world engineering. A full-scale Newcomen engine functioned by creating a partial vacuum in a cylinder below the piston. First the cylinder was filled with steam, then cooling water was sprayed into the cylinder to condense the steam and create a partial vacuum. The model stimulated Watt to try to understand the working principles, so he began careful measurements for a quantitative analysis. As a result he became the first scientist to measure the energy (the latent heat) required to turn boiling water to steam and realised how large an amount of energy this is

(about six times the energy needed to heat the water to boiling point.)

Watt realised that the heat losses from the small-scale model were proportionately much greater than from the full-scale Newcomen engines, so the model would never operate efficiently. In thinking about the essential inefficiency of cooling the whole cylinder at each cycle of movement, he realised that the steam should be condensed outside the main cylinder in a separate condenser. Thus the cylinder could be kept hot, resulting in greatly improved efficiency. Transferring this idea back to full-scale engines Watt embarked on his lifetime work as the developer of the modern steam engine.

The Watt engine took ten years to perfect and was manufactured as a significantly more efficient and reliable engine than Newcomen's. Watt's patent was obtained in 1769 after trials at Dr John Roebuck's colliery at Kinneil near Bo'ness. Roebuck's financial difficulties led Watt to seek a new partner in 1774, and this he found in Matthew Boulton (1728–1809) of Birmingham. The technical efficiency of Watt's engine depended upon accurately machined cylinders and other components, and over the following years Birmingham workmanship and Scottish engineering made the fortunes of Boulton and Watt. Further inventions and modifications greatly extended the practical uses of the steam engine, laying the foundation for much of Britain's pre-eminence as the workshop of the world in the nineteenth century.

Many landowners and tenant farmers were improving their soil by spreading lime which was produced in local coal-fired kilns. The development of the glass and chemical industries, including town gas, required huge amounts of coal-gas as did the expansion of the breweries and distilleries; the great growth of the coke-based iron industry, beginning with the foundation near Falkirk of the Carron Company in 1759, also demanded a constant supply of coal.

Coal production was approximately 460,000 tonnes in 1700 but had possibly reached two million tonnes by 1800. In the nineteenth century coal was king as the heavy industries of the West of Scotland came to dominate the economy. By 1850 output had climbed to about 7.6 million tonnes, the peak being reached in 1913 when 43.2 million tonnes were mined.

From 1800 to around 1870 the ironmasters determined the commercial fortunes of the coal industry since they tended both to own the collieries and to be their own best customers. Coatbridge, dominated by the ironworks of Bairds of Gartsherrie, was a stereotype of classic industrial pollution in the age of coal:

> dense clouds of smoke roll over it incessantly, and impart to all the buildings a peculiarly dingy aspect. A coat of black dust overlies everything. . . .
> (David Bremner, *The Industries of Scotland*, 1869).

After 1870 the expansion of output was dependent on changing markets for coal; overseas exports increased from 1.4 million tonnes to 10.6 million tonnes by 1913 and ships' bunkers took about 3 million tonnes, while demand from the ironworks stagnated at just over 2 million tonnes. The railways and the merchant navy brought steam power to the fore and there was a close association between the design and manufacture of the world's locomotives at Springburn in Glasgow (Scotland's railway-building capital) and efficient marine engines for the Clyde's great shipbuilding firms.

From 1913 the path of the coal industry and steam power was ever downward. By 1945 output was just over 21 million tonnes. Deep mining was fraught with all the problems of a 'robber economy': the more coal was extracted, the more costly it became to extract the remainder. When the Scottish coal industry was nationalised in 1947 it was employing 81,000 miners, working 237 collieries, with an output of 25 million tonnes per year. However in the 1980s it became increasingly apparent that Scottish deep mines were in decline owing to the difficult geology of the narrow coal seams and the shrinking of Scottish heavy manufacturing industry. There was also competition from bulk deliveries of cheaper imported coal and from nuclear power.

Moreover gross pollution of the air and the land became a severe handicap for all coal production industries. From the 1950s there were increasing restrictions on the use of ordinary coal for domestic heating and industrial purposes in cities and towns. During the same period North Sea gas became available – offering a cleaner fuel without the polluting gases of sulphur and nitrogen oxides which arise from coal burning.

So by 1988 output from 2,000 miners in the three remaining deep mines had dropped to 2.4 million tonnes per year; and this was almost entirely for use in coal-fired power stations. The deep-mined output had been overtaken by increasing opencast mining output from sixty-two sites, forty-nine of which were privately owned. It was the closing of an age for Scottish mining.

SCOTLAND'S OIL

Scotland has a unique place in the modern story of the exploitation of oil, mainly because of the discovery of huge oil fields in the North Sea. However in the 1850s Scotland had established a land-based mineral oil industry based on extraction from oil shales; this shale-oil industry developed the technology from which modern methods of refining have evolved, and which will forever be associated with the name of James 'Paraffin' Young (Box 5).

Natural oils had of course been used by Scots from prehistoric times, principally for lamps, but industrialisation created a large demand for new lubricants since whale oil and vegetable oils tended to fail when used on hot fast-moving machinery. James Young established a new oil industry, at Bathgate originally, which quickly spread into other areas in the 1860s during what became known as the 'Scottish Oil Mania'.

American petroleum became a serious competitor in that decade and the later exploitation of major finds at Baku in the Caucasus area of southern Russia, and in the Middle East, ushered in the age of the giant multinational oil firms. Yet the Scottish shale-oil industry survived through a combination of scientific efficiency, diversification of products and its proximity to raw materials and markets. The last plant only closed in the 1960s when the exploitation of the North Sea's oil fields was about to occur. 'Paraffin' Young's shale-oil industry has left us with the imposing landmarks of the great red shale bings which scar the landscape of West Lothian and the Central Belt of Scotland.

The first fossil fuel to be discovered offshore from the UK was natural gas in the southern part of the North Sea. This was in the early 1960s when the northern sea off Scotland was not expected to yield any supplies. Then in 1969 the Phillips Petroleum Company struck oil about 250 miles (400 km) due east of the Firth of Forth. This was the Ekofisk field, where drilling had to be carried out under 400 ft (120 km) of stormy sea.

Thereafter all the UK's oil finds were off the east and north-east coasts of Scotland, especially off the islands

Oil production platform, North Sea.

of Shetland. The names of the fields read like a Scottish roll of honour: Duncan, Clyde, Montrose, Buchan, Claymore and Ninian amongst them. British oil was, in territorial terms, Scottish oil.

When the 1973 oil crisis was triggered by a doubling in price of Middle East oil it was clear that these Scottish resources would provide not only all the UK needs but would also, with Norway, ensure the supplies of Western Europe. By 1984 Scottish oil production was running at 2.5 million barrels per day (125 million tonnes per year). This bonanza provided ten per cent of the UK government's tax revenue and five per cent of the UK total business output, and the excess production of 0.5 million barrels per day (25 million tonnes per year) above national consumption was a major export earner.

In addition natural methane gas, often associated with oil production, has been an economic resource of great importance. A national grid of gas pipelines fans out from North-East Scotland, supplying both homes and industry as well as a major power station at Peterhead and a huge chemical works at Mossmorran in Fife. Tragically the revenues derived from the use of these capital resources have been frittered away by the Westminster governments without any express purpose. Only Shetland and Orkney, whose councils had the wisdom to obtain special Acts of Parliament, have managed to turn these non-renewable resources into buildings, roads, sports centres, schools and other long-term developments.

Aberdeen became the oil city of Western Europe in the 1970s and was transformed from a city with a fishing and regional business economy to an international centre of subsea oil exploitation. However without any special Act of Parliament the long-term effect on Aberdeen's economy is difficult to predict for, when the oil price dropped in the late 1980s, Aberdeen's economy quickly suffered, with little sign of any intrinsic strength that could have been developed in the preceding years of substantial oil wealth.

History will probably see Shetland as the community that has best succeeded in taming the oil barons for its

Turbine hall, Torness nuclear power station.

NUCLEAR POWER

The commitment of the Scottish electricity boards to nuclear power has been distinctive and total. By 1990 over half of Scottish electricity was being generated from nuclear power stations; moreover the reactors used to produce the power are of unique British design: the Magnox and the Advanced Gas-Cooled Reactors (AGR). The ownership and the operation of the reactors were the responsibility of the pre-privatisation South of Scotland Electricity Board (SSEB). However the North of Scotland Hydro-Electric Board co-operated with financing and with agreements to buy the power as a priority.

The first reactors in Scotland were built by 1964 at Chapelcross in Dumfries-shire (41–megawatt capacity) and Hunterston in Ayrshire (360 megawatt); these were of the Magnox design. The very considerable over-capacity of electricity generating plant in Scotland by 1989 resulted in electricity from Chapelcross being diverted to England before privatisation, and the Hunterston-A station was closed down as uneconomic in 1989 towards the end of its life.

The main nuclear stations have been the later AGR installations. The first of these was also built at Hunterston, the B reactor (1,320 megawatt), and the second at Torness (1,364 megawatt). The Hunterston-B reactor has proved to be one of the most efficient nuclear power stations in the world and the Torness installation is one of the most noteworthy. In deciding to build Torness the SSEB stated their faith not only in more nuclear power to the detriment of coal but also in the British design as against the American Pressurised Water Reactor (PWR) design favoured in England.

We have yet to see whether the SSEB's predictions of the costs of nuclear power are fulfilled. Originally nuclear power was thought to offer the cheapest electricity costs after hydro-power and potentially to be the main strength of a privatised industry. However when privatisation was being planned, the City financiers decided otherwise and refused to contemplate buying the reactors for the privatised electricity companies. They had decided that by the standards of commercial accounting, and with the need to charge for decommissioning and waste treatment, nuclear electricity was the most expensive form of power. Therefore Scottish Nuclear has remained as a nationalised board and is not a private company.

The UK Atomic Energy Research Establishment decided to build its most developmental nuclear reactor – the Fast Breeder Reactor – far away from major population centres, near Thurso in Caithness. Hundreds of nuclear physicists and engineers came to settle with their families at Dounreay looking across the Pentland Firth to the inspiring cliffs of Hoy on Orkney. The creation of this new community has been extremely successful, so much so that when the closure of the Fast

own benefit. In 1974 the Zetland County Council Act gave the Council the rights to charge taxes on oil developments and shipments. With a resultant income of more than £50 million per year the 20,000 citizens of the Shetland community have had the benefit of capital development and special programmes for elderly and disadvantaged people. Throughout the islands, houses were restored or newly built, school finance and staffing prospered, roads were widened and surfaced, harbours were improved and the fishing fleet strengthened. The falling oil prices in the late 1980s cramped the style of the council, who may never see the full realisation of their heady dreams of the early oil bonanza. Nevertheless as the price of oil increased again in 1990 the hopes returned.

Breeder Reactor and its associated 300—megawatt electricity station was announced in 1989 few families wanted to leave. This closure was another casualty of the reality of electricity privatisation and Dounreay had to diversify or perish.

The top management wish to diversify into using the plant as a spent nuclear-fuel depository, while others see opportunities to change to wind-power generation and to general research and development. The future of the establishment is thus far from assured at present.

THE FUTURE

The future development of energy supplies in Scotland is handicapped, surprisingly, by an embarrassment of established sources. The capital supplies of offshore oil and gas meet ten times Scottish needs by supporting the whole UK. Sadly nothing of this wealth is being garnered to prepare for the future when the treasure has all been sold. A near 100 per cent over-capacity of electricity-generating plant discourages both small generating companies and private individuals from selling electricity. England does not have such an excess of conventional resources and the government is favouring plans for more renewable energy supplies, for greater use of gas and for the generation of energy from waste materials.

Yet we know that Scotland has even greater resources of clean and renewable energy and the technology for the efficient use of energy. Scotland has Europe's greatest potential for wave and wind power and there is still more hydro-electric and tidal power waiting to be exploited. In addition landfill-gas (methane from rubbish), combined heat and power, forestry waste and passive solar heated buildings are all poised for sustainable economic benefits. The sum total of all these 'rational' forms of energy utilisation means that the energy needs of Scottish homes and industry can be sustained indefinitely if we use common sense, moderation and advanced technology.

Thus the ultimate future is exceedingly optimistic if only the present income from the North Sea capital assets is used to develop the technology for harnessing renewable energy resources. At the moment we are 'selling the family silver' and using the income for temporary benefit. It is imperative that we invest quickly in technology appropriate to the lasting value of Scotland's natural and human environment.

5. JAMES 'PARAFFIN' YOUNG (1811–83)

James Young was born in Drygate, not far from Glasgow Cathedral. James first worked in his father's carpentry business and attended evening chemestry classes at Anderson's (now Strathclyde) University.

In 1837 Young moved into industry at St Helens on Merseyside. Lancashire was the major centre of the chemical industry at that time, and there were many opportunities for bright young men to advance their careers.

His opportunity came when a natural oil spring occurred at a coal mine in Derbyshire; Young was called in as consultant and in 1848 he set up the world's first oil refinery to process petroleum for lubricants and lamp oil.

The scale of the Derbyshire oil seepage was never large enough to make Young's fortune but it did lead him to question its origins and thence to distill coal. After two years of experiments he finally managed to produce oil from selected *cannel* (candle) coals. His friend Hugh Bartholomew, manager of the Glasgow City and Suburban Gas Company, sent him a barrel of the newly-mined cannel coal, known as Boghead, which had been discovered on the Torbanehill estate near Bathgate. Boghead coal turned out to be the richest oil-bearing mineral ever discovered – neither a true coal nor an oil-shale, but a unique geological freak which had characteristics of both.

In 1851 Young moved to Bathgate and began Scottish oil production there, armed with his patent of 1850. Despite Young's attempts to keep operations secret the profitability of this operation became known, which constantly tempted businessmen to infringe his patent. Fortunately Young won all his court battles to defend his monopoly.

However the oil-shales of the Lothians, which gave much lower yields than Boghead coal, were gradually exploited from 1859, particularly near Broxburn. When Young's patent ended in 1864 there was rapid investment in the industry and ninety-seven firms were soon established. Young meanwhile had created a new plant at Addiewell and his firm remained the largest public company.

Despite intense foreign competition large-scale exploitation of Scottish oil-shales continued. In the 1890s, for instance, more than two million tonnes a year were being mined and processed into saleable products. The major achievement of the industry, however, was the creation of the refining technology which led to the development of the world's petroleum industry.

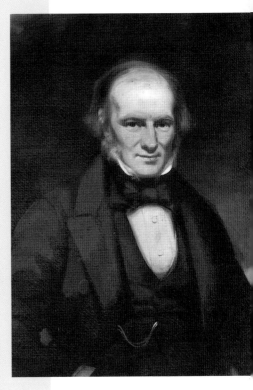

Remnant Caledonian Pine,
Inveroran, West of
Scotland.

The Conservation of Nature

ALASTAIR SOMMERVILLE

Dr Alastair Sommerville is the Conservation Officer of the Scottish Wildlife Trust.

The conservation of buildings, or of art involves people taking action to prevent damage, whether it be to an Adam house or a Wilkie painting. For example if we want to conserve a medieval tapestry, we clean it carefully and then store it away from damp and air pollution so that no further deterioration can take place. In wildlife conservation, however, our tapestry is the countryside and the patterns are the fields, mountains, rivers, lochs and woodlands – an intricate fabric of natural and man-made habitats. However we cannot preserve such a living tapestry of animals and plants as simply as we can in the case of a woven tapestry. The ecological system of our countryside, the breathing and reproducing fabric of its life, can only be safeguarded through the complex process we call nature conservation; only through our own efforts can the diversity and balance of nature be retained.

Nature is never static; it is forever changing, like a running stream of life which we must understand if we are to preserve it. Wildlife conservation is the practical art science and skill of understanding such rapidly changing systems and looking after them to ensure their survival amidst the unthinking exploitation of the world by humans.

Wildlife conservation as we know it today, involving the systematic protection of the places where plants and animals live, is a very recent development. It developed from nineteenth century legislation intended to control the commercial exploitation of wild animals. During the Victorian period there was growing concern at the wholesale slaughter of birds, and vigorous campaigns led to a series of bird protection Acts from 1869 onwards, each one adding to, or improving on, the previous one. During this time the issue of importing tropical birds' plumage, including egret and ostrich feathers for hat decoration, led to active women forming a pressure group to stop the trade.

This group eventually became the Royal Society for the Protection of Birds (RSPB) which celebrated its centenary in 1989; the importation of plumage for the millinery trade was eventually banned in 1921. The final version of the Act, giving full legal protection to British birds and their eggs, was eventually passed in 1954.

The idea of setting aside protected areas as nature reserves, to conserve the animals and plants living in them, took a long time to develop (Box 1). The Society for the Promotion of Nature Reserves (SPNR) was formed as early as 1912 to survey Britain and identify wildlife habitats that should be conserved. The SPNR decided at the start that it would not purchase land but would encourage other people, particularly the National Trust, to buy and manage selected sites as nature reserves. However this was not a popular idea at the time; most people believed that wildlife could best be protected by passing laws to protect individual species.

In 1926 SPNR's initiative resulted in the foundation of a local body, the Norfolk Naturalists' Trust, which acquired some of the first and most important nature reserves in the country. After the Second World War the Yorkshire Naturalists' Trust was formed, followed by the gradual spread of 'County Naturalists' Trusts', of which there are now almost fifty throughout the UK. In Scotland the Scottish Wildlife Trust (SWT) was founded in 1964 to cover the entire country, and the Trust now acts for SPNR's successor, the Royal Society for Nature Conservation (RSNC).

OFFICIAL NATURE CONSERVATION

The early voluntary naturalists had to carry out much more exploration of the British countryside, particularly of Scotland, before conservation became official. The government's own agency, the 'Nature Conservancy' was created only in 1949; it was renamed the Nature Conservancy Council (NCC) and in 1991 the Scottish branch was given independence as the Nature Conservancy Council for Scotland (NCCS).

The original body was given the duty of setting up a series of National Nature Reserves (NNRs) which would preserve examples of the wide range of habitats found in these islands, together with their plants and animals. The NCC also had to identify a much larger number of smaller Sites of Special Scientific Interest (SSSIs) which would give protection to wildlife and geological places of particular importance (see Chapter 16). Additionally the NCC was instructed to carry out research to ensure the effective management of the

Grey Heron.

3. A BIRCHWOOD REBORN

A study of old air photographs showed that the birchwoods around Loch Muick on the Balmoral Estate were dying rapidly. There were plenty of seedling trees at ground level, but every time they grew above the tops of the heather they were bitten off by browsing red deer. To save this woodland the SWT put up a six-foot-high deer fence around the remnants of the original birchwood leaving plenty of room for it to expand. Parties of volunteers carried the fencing materials up the hill and dug deep holes in the peat to anchor the posts. Other SWT members grew thousands of tiny trees from the seed of these trees to be returned to the finished enclosure and planted. In forty years from now the 'new' Glen Muick birchwoods could rival their Speyside counterparts.

warden to stop people stealing eggs or foxes taking chicks. An old Highland birchwood trying to regenerate itself naturally must be protected by a tall fence if all the seedling trees are not to be eaten by red deer (Box 3).

Wildlife site management requires normal estate, agricultural or forestry practices to be combined with new conservation techniques based on the application of scientific advice. Members of the wildlife organisations provide much labour themselves but there are also specialist groups like Scottish Conservation Projects Trust (SCPT) and its affiliated groups which specialise in this type of work.

4. THE WATCH OZONE PROJECT

Ozone is a very reactive gas which is highly desirable in the upper atmosphere but very poisonous at street level; it is invisible, very difficult to measure and causes a range of lung and health problems in human beings. It does have a strong damaging effect on plants and in particular it causes leaf spotting to a relative of the tobacco plant, *Nicotiniana*. The amount of damage to the leaf surface indicates the amount of ozone present. The WATCH club have devised a foolproof way of monitoring ozone pollution that can be done by children using a pack of *Nicotiniana* seeds with a standard way of growing them. Sampling the air from all over Scotland and the rest of the UK, children will produce the first really detailed maps of the concentration of low-level ozone pollution. If you would like to get involved, simply contact WATCH at the Scottish Wildlife Trust.

Bill Oddie and children on the WATCH Ozone Project with Nicotiniana plants.

Sadly there are many places where our wildlife has been severely damaged and major efforts are required to reinstate the original habitat. Habitat creation can involve planting wildflowers, grasses and trees to improve a neglected woodland or to landscape a barren industrial tip. However one cannot instantly re-create the complex ecology of plants and animals found in a natural habitat which may have taken hundreds of years to evolve.

Nevertheless many common plants, insects and mammals will quickly establish and thrive in such 'new' sites. Habitat creation like this has largely been undertaken by conservation bodies in the past but recently local authorities, and even industry, have realised the value of this approach for nature conservation – even just in economic terms.

THE THREATS

The wildlife of Scotland is still under severe threat today. The entire countryside bears the scars of the original forest clearance; of the incessant grazing of sheep and red deer; of the intensification of chemical agriculture in the Lowlands and of the industrial wastelands of the Central Belt; and the damage continues.

In addition to these long-standing problems new pressures have come on a massive scale. Vast areas of the Scottish uplands have been planted with 'monocultures' of conifers transforming the habitat dramatically (see Chapter 10), blanketing the upland moors with a dark and sterile habitat which acidifies the lochs and causes the silting up of rivers. There are some temporary benefits to wildlife from such modern forestry, as the young plantations are colonised by some of our common woodland birds; but we undoubtedly lose many rarer birds of the open hill such as the golden plover.

Another series of habitats of similar importance for wildlife is found in the coastal seas around Scotland. These include sheltered sea lochs, muddy estuaries, rocky shores, sandy beaches, underwater cliffs and reefs, kelp forests, tidal races and sandy plains. Most of this underwater world is still unexplored, but we know that it contains all manner of strange communities of brittle stars, dense colonies of solitary corals and sea squirts and the largest groups of breeding grey seals in Europe. These wildlife riches result from the clean water brought to our shores by the North Atlantic Drift (see Chapter 2).

Many of our rivers and coastal waters are grossly polluted by sewage and chemical effluents (Box 7), but a major new environmental threat to Scotland's waters has arisen in the last decade. The unique sea lochs of the west coast, which are akin to the fiords of Scandinavia and are found nowhere else in mainland Britain, have suddenly been transformed by the rapid expansion of marine fish farming (see Chapter 2).

In the Lowlands the few isolated wildlife sites that remain are gradually being eroded. The pressure for housing and industrial development means that the green spaces in and around towns are vulnerable; this is particularly so in river valleys which in themselves add amenity value for housing. Open areas outside towns, which could well be managed for wildlife, are increasingly targeted for waste dumps, for opencast coal mining or peat extraction. Roads, pipelines and rural industrial estates can appear anywhere and, even if designed with sensitivity, such developments add to the fragmentation of wildlife habitats. Most of the sites are already very small and, unless there are 'nature corridors' to similar sites nearby, many will not survive in the long term unless we make a great effort to keep them; many sites may gradually lose their wildlife interest altogether.

Contrasting with the decline of these important Lowland wildlife sites there is a steady increase in the number of sites of relatively low wildlife value. Old railway lines, bings (coal tips), abandoned factory sites and urban fringe farmland are being recolonised by wildlife, with the natural regeneration of trees and scrub, but they can never develop the wealth of species which are found in a natural habitat.

CONSERVATION AS A FORCE

While large-scale land-use changes are going on it is essential that the voice of the conservation movement is properly heard. The NCC for Scotland, the government's own advisory nature conservation body, administers the statutory controls over SSSIs and gives wide-ranging guidance on nature conservation matters. If any development is proposed on a SSSI which would conflict with the wildlife conservation interest of the site, and no compromise can be reached with the landowner, then the NCCS will defend the site through the legal means available to it. The NCCS offers advice and opinion on a wide range of land-use changes including forestry, fish farming, agriculture and planning; however the agency is limited in how far it can press its views. Luckily in Scotland there is a close and constructive working relationship between the statutory NCCS and the voluntary wildlife conservation bodies. The Scottish Wildlife Trust (SWT), the Royal Society for the Protection of Birds (RSPB) and the World Wide Fund for Nature (WWF) are the main bodies concerned with the wider issues involving wildlife, and all three are active at many different levels.

Of the three, only the Scottish Wildlife Trust is entirely Scottish. It was founded in 1964 as a single trust to cover the conservation of all plants, animals and habitats throughout Scotland via a national network of branches and support groups. The principle of the SWT is to involve local volunteer members in practical nature conservation but the Trust also uses them to survey and

5. WORKING FOR WILDLIFE

Even the most unpromising urban sites can become important wildlife areas. Bawsinch lies along the shore of Duddingston Loch in the heart of Edinburgh; it was a vehicle scrap yard when it was bought by the SWT but it has been transformed into 16 acres (6.4 ha) of superb woodland, scrub, grassland and wetland habitats. Over the course of twenty years volunteers have planted trees, dug ponds, maintained grasslands and monitored the wildlife to produce one of the finest city wildlife sites in Scotland.

Bawsinch wildlife reserve in the heart of Edinburgh was once a vehicle scrapyard.

monitor what is happening to wildlife in their area. Today the SWT has 10,000 members, eighty-four reserves and a WATCH Club of more than a 1,000 children (Box 4).

There are many other organisations in Scotland which have a more specialised interest but also are involved with wildlife conservation. Mountaineers and ramblers are an important sector, as are the various organisations involved with woodlands, otters, marine conservation and environmental education. Several of these bodies successfully co-operated in opposing the plan to extend skiing facilities at Cairngorm across to Lurcher's Gully (see Chapter 17). The obvious success of working together led to the creation of a regular forum of all voluntary conservation bodies, the Scottish Wildlife and Countryside Link (SWCL), to discuss and act on conservation matters of the day.

A WINDOW ON THE FUTURE

Earlier chapters have illustrated what Scotland's environment was like in the past; but it is equally important to envisage and plan for what it could be in the future. The basis of this future vision must be centred on the concept of integrated land-use, which simply means using any one area of ground in the best

6. THE COMMON FROG

Frogs are still common and widespread in Scotland despite the dramatic reduction in their numbers in parts of England. However their habitat has been decreasing, especially in Lowland Scotland, as ponds are drained, filled in or polluted by chemical run-off from farmland. The presence of the humble frog and its tadpoles is therefore a valuable indicator of the health of our remaining freshwater habitats.

The common frog is increasingly uncommon in many parts of Britain due to water pollution and draining of ponds and wetlands.

way possible taking into account all the interests involved.

Land-use interests comprise not only nature conservation but also the forestry industry, farming, tourism and recreation. In practice, integrated land-use might require a decision not to plant commercial conifer woods on areas of grassland which wildlife needs for its survival, or it might involve leaving broad corridors alongside a stream running through a commercial plantation in order to encourage waterside plants and animals.

To do this we need to develop long-term strategies for everything that humans do to the land or in the marine environment. Such policies would be based on the principle that any use of the resources of the land or sea must be sustainable. For example the trees in a wood could be cut down for timber but only if there were a long-term plan to replace the felled trees with new seedlings, at the same time ensuring that there was no lasting damage to the rest of the wildlife of the wood (Box 5). Similarly when we decide how many fish may be taken from a river or fishing ground it would be very stupid to destroy the long-term stability of the fish stocks by taking too many at once.

Linking theory to practice requires a more sensitive and ecologically sound approach to all development proposals. Already we have some useful methods, for example the technique of Environmental Impact Assessment (EIA), which involves looking at the many different possible effects of a development proposal through consulting people about it and combining these findings with the most expert ecological opinion. This can be done very professionally and in an unbiased way to provide the information on which a sound judgment can be made.

However wildlife is only part of the entire ecosystem which supports us all; damage to any part of it can affect both man and wildlife. It has at last been recognised that the major way in which industry causes damage is by pollution to air and water. The long-distance effects of acid rain have been discovered by establishing that factory gases from Germany kill trees far away in Scandinavia. The role of pesticides in the food chain was first exposed when it was shown that DDT, used to control insects on crops, accumulated in lethal concentrations in sparrowhawks and peregrines. But we are only just beginning to appreciate the potential global impact of these pesticides and other chemicals – and heavy metals and radioactivity – through transmission in the world's oceans.

The suspected damage caused by chloro-fluoro-carbons (CFCs) to the ozone layer of the upper atmosphere has forced governments to devise new and urgent approaches to pollution control. Some steps have been taken recently to try to control these poisons at source and to force the different regulating agencies to act co-operatively. However in the future there must be far better processing and disposal of waste products by the producer, and a separate environmental agency to monitor all the other agencies in order to ensure a comprehensive pollution control mechanism.

In an ideal future, nature conservation itself would be an accepted part of every development, supported by local and national government, national agencies and private companies alike. Every developer or industrialist would have to show what impact his plans would have on the environment and what measures he is taking to safeguard wildlife. The network of National Nature Reserves would be managed alongside local reserves, with sufficient resources being allocated to ensure that their quality was maintained. Every country park and town park would have a policy to maximise its wildlife potential. All public land would be covered by local authorities' nature conservation strategies, which would be part of their overall environmental strategy (see Chapter 15). The huge increase in native woodland would be supplemented by agricultural and forestry grants given for the land to be managed for wildlife.

The true value to the human spirit of green space and of exposure to the variety and richness of the natural world would be universally recognised. Environmental education would be a fourth 'R', and improving the quality of our surroundings would be an important vote winner for all politicians. Substantially greater help for the conservation of wildlife in the Third World would mean a much wider appreciation of the way in which the earth needs to be treated to make sure that it survives the next million years.

This is not a Utopian ideal. All it needs is the will to achieve the goal. If people believe passionately enough that Scotland's natural heritage must be conserved for future generations, and become actively involved towards that end, it is a crusade that cannot fail.

WHAT YOU CAN DO

The general recognition of the need to conserve the

7. WATER POLLUTION

Industrial complexes such as Grangemouth on the Forth estuary have serious problems in disposing of their waste products. Modern pollution control legislation insists on cleaner discharges to the air and sea, both of which have been used to dump immense amounts of chemicals. However many companies now realise that they must set more stringent standards for environmental pollution and are using their own technical expertise to find new ways of reducing the amount of pollution they produce.

environment, both locally and globally, has been the result of persistent campaigning by a relatively small number of people. Large conservation bodies have considerable influence today but the role of the individual is also vital to the process. The fate of all the world is literally in all our hands and taking action ourselves is an essential and effective way of influencing what happens.

• Get to know your local area. Looking after the wildlife around you is a basic step as your local knowledge may well be the key to any action being taken. Look at your local map, go for walks, ask local people about what is already known to be special in the area. No matter whether you live in the Highlands or in the inner city, the environment where you live can be valuable not only for human beings but for wildlife as well.

• Fight for your own green spaces. If threats to any wildlife area are known to you, you can do something about it. If it is a planning matter which requires the local council to initiate public consultation, make your feelings known to the local authority and encourage your friends to do the same. Even a matter involving a local farmer can be resolved if you talk to those concerned. Damage is often done to wildlife sites by people who are completely unaware of the results of their actions but who would be quite prepared to accept a compromise if one were offered.

• Learn more about the natural world. Understanding the way in which the wildlife habitats work is essential if you want to be able to influence what happens. Luckily there is an increasing number of clear readable books available to explain the ecology and natural history of our native wildlife. A better knowledge of the subject will give you confidence and add authority to your views and suggestions.

• Make your views known. Public pressure is the most effective way of getting both local and national government to take notice, and every voice counts. The 7,000 letters to the Secretary of State for Scotland protesting about the Highland Regional Council's proposal to encourage the expansion of skiing at Cairngorm into Lurcher's Gully was quoted by him as one reason for refusing to countenance that particular development.

• Understand environmental issues. Most of the major national papers and the weekly 'green' magazines devote a lot of space to what is going on with regard to environmental issues, both local and national. Many of the conservation bodies can help by supplying details or expert opinions about the facts relating to local disputes and planning issues.

• Join your local group. Actions speak louder than words and getting involved with your local conservation group will make them more effective and give a focus to your own energies. You might take on physical work like planting trees or clearing out an overgrown pond, for which training of several sorts is often available; but you could also be counting butterflies,

watching bats or even rattling a collecting box! All of these activities add up towards making the conservation movement in Britain the envy of the world.

8 . ST ABBS HEAD: WORKING TOGETHER FOR WILDLIFE

This superb site on the Berwickshire coast illustrates a unique partnership between the Scottish Wildlife Trust, who first set up the reserve, and the present owners, The National Trust for Scotland. St Abbs is famous for the vast numbers of seabirds which nest on the cliffs but it also lies within the St Abbs and Eyemouth Voluntary Marine Reserve. The rich and varied sea life found in the clean waters is protected by the collaboration of fishermen, conservationists and divers, all working together.

St Abbs Head provides nest sites for many thousands of kittiwakes, guillemots and razorbills.

Great Sundew, a carnivorous plant of the wetlands.

9 . A PLACE FOR WILDLIFE

Each generation faces different threats to the wildlife habitats which surround it. Today lowland peat bogs are particularly vulnerable not only to commercial extraction of peat but also from opencast coal mining and the use of the land for afforestation. The specialised plants which live in peat bogs cannot survive elsewhere and rarities like the Great Sundew can only hang on in more remote western peat-bogs.

SIR FRANK FRASER DARLING (1903–79)
Profile of a Pioneer, by Dr J. Morton Boyd.

Any account of nature conservation in Scotland must include the story of one of the pioneers of the ecological and movement in Scotland. Frank Fraser Darling was an Englishman, but he always felt himself to be half-Scottish. During his student days he had travelled in Scotland and fallen under the spell of the country and its people and he conceived a desire to make his professional mark as a scientist in Scotland.

So he came to Edinburgh to see F. A. E. Crewe, the Professor of Genetics there, whose work he greatly admired, and was offered a PhD studentship to work on the fleece characteristics of Blackface sheep. It was a hard decision to make for he already had a wife and child to support; but Fraser Darling seized the opportunity eagerly.

After graduating PhD he became Chief Officer of the Imperial Bureau of Animal Genetics at Edinburgh but he soon became disillusioned with administrative work. He had just spent three years with the sheep in the uplands and islands and had imbibed the rough beauty and freedom of these solitudes; but there were no opportunities now for ventilating the enormous enthusiasm for active research which had brought him to Scotland.

So he abandoned the comfortable salaried life in Edinburgh and took to the mountains and islands, complete with family. He wrote industriously for a living: *A Herd of Red Deer* (1937), which brought him a DSc from Edinburgh University, was both scientific and romantic in style. By choice he occupied the area between ecology and animal behaviour; his quest was for the underlying truth in natural processes. His main bid for a breakthrough in 'hard' science was in the studies of bird flocks. He developed a hypothesis of a mechanism which drives gregarious behaviour but he was not quite able to demonstrate it from the meagre data he assembled from gull colonies in the Summer Isles. None the less, students of animal behaviour and physiology still feel that such a mechanism may exist; and in biology textbooks it is called the 'Fraser Darling Effect'.

It was through his books, *Island Years* (1940) and *Island Farm* (1943), taken almost verbatim from his journals of life in the islands, that he first made his name with the general public. They were charming idylls of family adventure, laced with science and philosophy, in the glorious settings of Coigach, Treshnish and North Rona. But his aspirations in 'hard' science were ended by the outbreak of the Second World War, when he returned to his 'island farm' on Tanera in the Summer Isles.

The war years saw a change of direction which brought him to the path of conservation, which he followed for the rest of his life, in Scotland, the USA and Africa. He became the great exponent of 'nature in the round'. His agricultural training and his natural instincts made him unusually sensitive to the relationships between man and nature, and his interests shifted from wildlife *per se* to the impact of human beings on natural resources. With his island croft as his working frame he wrote a series of articles for the local press publicising his theories on self-sufficiency; later these articles were published as *Crofting Agriculture* (1945), which remains a little classic.

National recognition came in 1943–4 with his appointment to a Scottish National Parks Committee and its subordinate Wildlife Conservation Committee. The outcome was the setting up of National Parks in England and Wales, but not in Scotland (to his intense disappointment), and the establishment of a Nature Conservancy for the UK, *inter alia* to set up and manage National Nature Reserves.

He also became Director of the West Highland Survey to study the causes of population and economic decline there. Although the survey was completed by 1950 the report was not published until 1955, mainly because of a deep difference of opinion with officials in the Scottish Office who could not come to terms with his perception of Man's responsibility in the sorry tale of land-use in the Highlands. The sub-title of the report – West Highland Survey: An Essay in Human Ecology – betrayed the thrust of his thinking.

Sir Frank Fraser Darling, ecologist and conservationist (1903–79)

Loch Beinn a Mheadoin in Glen Affric

In the 1950s Fraser Darling was living in the south of England but kept in touch with Scotland as Director of the Nature Conservancy's Red Deer Survey, which led to the Red Deer (Scotland) Act 1959 and the setting up of the Red Deer Commission. But he had fallen from favour in Britain and was now active in the newly-formed International Union for the Conservation of Nature and Natural Resources (IUCN, now the World Conservation Union), where he became a dominant figure at international conventions throughout the world.

His main endeavours were now devoted to surveys in the US National Parks, the Game Department of Northern Rhodesia (now Zambia), and the Masai-Mara Game Reserve in Kenya. In these surveys he saw a restatement of the travesties of Man's misuse of the environment, and spoke out vigorously in exposing greed and self-interest. He could be tactless to a fault when it came to presenting the facts as he saw them. His uncompromising report on the US National Parks was well received, but those from Northern Rhodesia (Zambia) and Kenya were not, and ran a similar gauntlet as the West Highland Survey had done at the Scottish Office.

In the 1960s he spent much of his time in the USA as a vice-president of the Conservation Foundation in Washington DC – an ambassador extraordinary for nature conservation throughout the world. In the many situations he looked at, from tropical Africa to arctic Alaska, his instinc-tive perception of Man's interdependence with nature took him straight to the core of the problem. Red deer in Scotland, caribou in Alaska, elk in Washington and elephant in Tsavo all had a different ecology but a common place in the human mind; and having perceived the guiding principle he was able to communicate it to the common man.

It was that gift of communication which came to the fore when he was invited to give the Reith Lectures of 1969. To those who knew him in his early days, when he was afflicted by a shuddering stammer, his delivery of the lectures was well nigh unbelievable. It was symbolic of his entire life, which he described as 'the hole out of which I have climbed', that in the end he should emerge so triumphantly into the sunshine. The lectures were published as *Wilderness and Plenty* (1970), and in that same year he was knighted.

He retired to the Laigh of Moray where he looked back with melancholy on the battles he had fought (and mostly lost) in the face of the implacable self-interest of his fellow man. In a man-centred world he saw nature as the elemental stuff of which we are made – sacred beyond compare, yet debased by us on a colossal scale. What he had to say is even more relevant to the conservation of nature today.

Dr J. Morton Boyd is a former Director of the Nature Conservancy Council in Scotland (1971–85). He knew Fraser Darling well, and is the author of many books, including *Fraser Darling's Islands* (1987) and *The Hebrides* (1990)

*Edinburgh Castle and the
Nor' Loch: painting by
Alexander Nasmyth.*

The Greening
of the Cities

GRAHAM WHITE

Graham White is the founding Director of the Environment Centre in Edinburgh. He is the author of the first *Scottish Environmental Handbook* (1990).

The pattern of our early towns and cities evolved without planning and was superimposed on the existing landscape of woods, fields, rivers and lochs. In many cases man's activities changed the original landscape beyond all recognition, but relics of these original landscape features and wildlife habitats still survive within our towns and cities. The rivers and streams which run through a town may have followed their courses for thousands of years and within our cities isolated fragments of ancient woods, moors and wetlands remain.

If we could view the world through the eyes of a bird, a butterfly or an insect, we would probably see the town as just another place to live, albeit a rather different place from the countryside. Certainly within the city there is scarcely an inch of space, from the attics and roof gables of our houses to the sewers beneath our feet, that is not made use of by some plant, insect, bird or animal. In this sense wild creatures make little distinction between town and country; they simply occupy any habitat which can sustain them.

Some animals and plants are specialised and require special habitats such as sand dunes, marshes or ancient woodlands; other more adaptable creatures thrive just as well on the brick wall of a factory or on the clinker bed of a disused suburban railway. In fact, far from being empty of wildlife, the streets of Edinburgh, Glasgow and Aberdeen are patrolled at night by urban foxes, while the grass verges of our motorways are quartered by kestrels during the day. There are even reports of peregrine falcons hunting above central Glasgow. One day perhaps they will even nest there, as they have done in the cities of Czechoslovakia and Eastern America.

However we tend to place greatest value on the animals and plants which we find in the countryside and undervalue those which are adaptable enough to survive in our towns. Nature also refuses to stay put and crosses man-made boundaries with ease: animals, birds and plants move around the planet on journeys which dwarf our own tourist excursions. The Red Admiral butterfly in your town garden may have travelled a thousand miles from the shores of the Mediterranean to get here. The swifts, which fly and scream around the church spires and tower blocks of our inner cities, have journeyed all the way from the mountains of North Africa to be our summer guests. The plants of our towns and cities are similarly nomadic: the purple flowers of buddleia (a plant from northern China), the pink rosebay willowherb (an American invader) and the golden Oxford ragwort (a plant from the slopes of Mount Vesuvius in Sicily) now blanket demolition sites and wasteland in our city centres. Their seeds are carried on the wind, while others arrive by water, on our car tyres or on the soles of our shoes.

For most people, however, the words 'nature' and 'wildlife' are associated largely with the countryside; they relate to that green landscape which exists in our imagination, somewhere out there beyond the edge of the town, past the green belt and the barley fields, among the mountains, rivers, sea lochs and nature reserves of Scotland. This automatic association of wildlife, nature and countryside is deeply ingrained within our minds and has profound implications both for nature conservation and education.

Until the late 1970s many nature conservation organisations in Britain seemed to view the world through a pair of 'rural' spectacles. Conservationists were not generally interested in towns or cities because the plants which grew there were largely 'weeds' and the birds and animals which lived there were just 'common or garden'. Wildlife groups were rarely concerned with the human environment as such and did not seem to see the relevance of urban areas to nature conservation.

Indeed until very recently the history of nature conservation in Britain was synonymous with the preservation of natural habitats and wildlife in the countryside. But the strategy of trying to conserve our natural heritage by simply putting a fence around it and keeping people out has been a colossal failure, with a large proportion of important wildlife habitats having been lost since 1949. In 1984 the NCC published *Nature Conservation in Great Britain*, which catalogued the mass destruction of ancient woodlands,

Edinburgh's Old Town from Calton Hill.

heaths, herb-rich meadows, lakes, fens, bogs and grass-lands, as well as the extinctions or near extinctions of many plants, birds and animals.

Gradually many people have become aware that nature conservation centres upon the relationship be-tween people, their activities and wildlife and, as such, the need for mass education becomes the focal issue. Consequently environmental education has to start where the majority of people live and work, in the streets and parks of their towns and villages, and it is inevitable that it will broaden to address other en-vironmental issues besides those of wildlife conserva-tion.

Foxes have adapted well to life in towns.

Oxford Ragwort and Rosebay Willowherb, The Shore, Leith

Paradoxically many of the urban creatures which we now regard as common or garden were once seen as rare, valuable and exotic. We seldom stop to consider that every creature or plant we now see in the town was once exclusively a countryside dweller. For instance the blackbird of our parks and gardens is in fact a relatively recent urban immigrant and only became common in urban Britain in the mid-nineteenth century as it extended its range from the woodlands of Europe.

Similarly the starling, which we now regard merely as a pest, was once an admired rarity. In a letter to *The Times*, written in 1894, a proud birdwatcher claimed the first sighting of a pair of starlings roosting in London's Hyde Park. Roosts of up to 50,000 birds soon became common in major cities and bird droppings created serious environmental health problems. Despite our contemporary scorn the starling is in fact a strikingly handsome bird with a remarkable ability for formation

1. WHAT WAS ONCE COMMON IS NOW RARE

The red kite, or *gledd* as it was known in Scotland, is a beautiful bird of prey that the RSPB is trying to re-introduce to remote countryside areas of England and Scotland (see Chapter 5). However it was once very much a town-bird and was a common scavenger in the streets of Edinburgh and Glasgow, as it was in London at the same period. In Scotland it was condemned to extermination: an Act of King James II of Scotland in 1457 decreed that 'gledds' were among the birds of prey which should be destroyed. In London at a similar period, however, people were specifically prohibited from harming kites because of their value as street cleaners. In fact the extinction of the red kite in Scotland is linked to the period of agricultural improvements in the eighteenth century, when the new husbandmen and gamekeepers destroyed virtually all birds of prey which threatened their farmyard chickens and the laird's pheasants.

The polecat is now extinct in Scotland but it too was once extremely common and lived in the streets of Edinburgh. It was widely distributed in both towns and villages, where it fed on rats, mice and voles. It was the most common member of the weasel family in Scotland until the 1860s. Records from the Dumfries Fur Market in the *New Statistical Account of Scotland* state that in 1833 so many thousands of polecat skins were offered for sale each week that they were 'a drug on the market'. But the agricultural improvers and gamekeepers saw polecats as enemies and began a systematic extermination. By 1847 the *New Statistical Account* notes that their skins were available only in small numbers, and by 1858 they were 'very scarce'. The last one offered for sale was in 1866. In less than three decades the most common carnivore in Scotland had been exterminated by fur-trappers, farmers and gamekeepers.

flying. Its original habitat was countryside meadows but it has found richer pickings on the mown grass of our parks and school playing fields; additionally the warmer winter temperatures of our cities are more to its liking.

Our rural prejudices are not just confined to birds; to many people the golden Oxford ragwort is simply an urban weed that is too abundant; like the exotic purple buddleia or the shocking pink rosebay willowherb it is 'not native' and is an 'alien immigrant' to boot! In our botanical xenophobia we often overlook the fact that every plant, tree and flower was once an alien immigrant and that they all arrived in Scotland within the last 12,000 years. The new urban plants are of course recent arrivals and their impact is dramatic and often detrimental to previously established species. But it all depends on what timescale one uses: the 'Scots' pine is virtually regarded as a national symbol these days, but

The site of the original botanic garden, the Physick Garden at Trinity Hospital, in Edinburgh's Old Town.

10,000 years ago it was itself an alien invader which blotted out trees that were unable to adapt to the developing climate and habitat of Scotland.

To summarise: we create an artificial split between town and countryside; we tend to undervalue plants and animals that are common, and overvalue those which are rare; we often distrust that which is 'alien' or new, and cherish that which is 'native' and old. In short we project all our human values, prejudices and parochialism on to the natural world which surrounds us.

Fortunately, since the 1980s, our attitudes have begun to alter with the emergence of a broader-based environmental movement which focuses more on the quality of life which both we and wild creatures enjoy or suffer in both town and country.

EDINBURGH: A CAPITAL ENVIRONMENT

To examine the history of Scotland's urban environment in depth would require the contributions of many experts to a number of volumes, but Edinburgh presents us with a cross-section through Scotland's urban history. Indeed the environmental history of Scotland's capital illuminates many of our attitudes to the town, the country, parks, urban green space and wild creatures. People living in the town of Edinburgh in the medieval period were still close to the countryside; prints of the time show the houses of the Canongate, each with its own vegetable garden or orchard, running

down from the central spine of rock into the countryside beyond.

The country surrounding the Royal Mile had much more wetland than today, with a large loch (the Nor' Loch) occupying the site of the present Princes Street Gardens and the Borough Loch filling the area where the Meadows now exist. These wetlands attracted a different variety of wild creatures from those we see today and we have some written evidence of this:

> ... in the year of our Lord 1416 ...a pair of Storks came to Scotland, and nested on the top of St Giles [Cathedral] of Edinburgh and dwelt there throughout a season of the year; but to what place they flew away thereafter no one knows.
> (*Scotichronicon*).

The drainage of these sizeable lochs and the bogs which carpeted much of Edinburgh's environs was paralleled by similar drainage schemes throughout Scotland as land was reclaimed for agriculture and roads.

The capital was also surrounded by the great forest of Drumsheugh which was gradually cleared to make way for farmland. Along with the forest went the roe and red deer, the wolves, wild boar and other creatures that lived there.

The human ecology of Edinburgh has also undergone radical changes along with the natural ecology. The Old Town was not planned as such; it grew piecemeal, as more and more tenement closes were added to house the growing population. Living conditions within the walled city thus became increasingly cramped and unsanitary throughout the seventeenth and early eighteenth centuries, with frequent epidemics of cholera, typhoid and even bubonic plague. There was no piped water supply or sewerage system and the gutters of the Royal Mile literally ran with the filth of the overcrowded town. Hemmed in by its defensive walls, Edinburgh was suffering what today would be called a chronic environmental crisis.

Eventually, Lord Provost Drummond and the city fathers rose to the challenge. In 1752 a document entitled *Proposals for Carrying on Certain Public Works in the City of Edinburgh* proposed to bridge the Nor' Loch, providing access to the site for a spacious 'New Town', which could relieve the environmental pressures of the Old Town. This development was to be built on the broad ridge of land lying to the north, across the loch. A competition for the layout of the New Town was arranged and the plan submitted by James Craig was successful; Craig was awarded the freedom of the city and a gold medal as his prize (Box 2). His scheme solved Edinburgh's environmental crisis but only for those rich enough to afford the leap from the Old to the New Town.

As soon as the New Town was completed there was an exodus from the Old Town. The nobility and professional classes decamped from the filthy and overcrowded environment of the Royal Mile to the airy spaces and classical buildings of the New Town with their piped water supply and carefully engineered sewers. There was then an increasingly dramatic contrast as the Old Town slipped into decay and the cholera epidemics of the eighteenth century, which decimated the Canongate, barely touched the citizens of Princes Street and Charlotte Square.

The environment of the Royal Mile continued to decay until relatively recent times, when the growth of modern town planning and tourism created a civic renaissance (Box 3).

A VERY URBAN COUNTRY

Scotland is a very green place, but more than 80 per cent of the people are crammed into the small triangle formed by Edinburgh, Glasgow and Stirling. Most Scots are born, educated and spend most of their working lives and recreational time in towns. This has important implications for the way in which teachers and nature conservationists should try to inform people about the nature of Scotland; essentially, we must start from where people are rather than where we want them to be. Most of us can recall some simple experience in our childhood which triggered our love of wildlife and the natural world. Perhaps the seeds were sown during those trips to the local pond to feed the ducks and swans. Or maybe it was fishing for sticklebacks in the old canal and trawling for the jellied masses of frog spawn in spring time. Many will recall wandering along the disused railways to harvest luscious blackberries. Others will remember their delight in the scarlet

James Craig's winning plan for the New Town of Edinburgh.

2. EDINBURGH'S NEW TOWN

James Craig's plan for the spacious New Town included gardens in St Andrew Square and Charlotte Square as well as proposals for two wide bands of formal parkland for the areas now occupied by Princes Street Gardens and Queen Street Gardens. The later additions to the New Town emulated these enclosures of private garden spaces, following the *rus in urbe* trend created in Craig's plan; today there are no fewer than sixty private or council-owned gardens in the New Town Conservation Area. The large amounts of green space within the city have undoubtedly contributed to Edinburgh's reputation as having the 'highest quality of environment' in Britain.

At the time of the building of the New Town the land to the north of Queen Street was open fields, and the boundary between the town and the country was both gradual and diffused. Lord Cockburn wrote in his memorials:

> How can I forget the glory of that scene!...on the still nights in which I have stood in Queen Street and listened to the ceaseless rural corn-craiks, nestling happily in the dewy grass.

This paints a strikingly rural picture of Edinburgh even after the building of the New Town; and it is fascinating to learn that the corncrake was a common bird of the meadows stretching from Queen Street down into Stockbridge. The corncrake is now seriously threatened even in its remaining habitats in the Western Isles and is in every sense a rare bird; it is hard to imagine that it once lived in the heart of Edinburgh.

Municipal housing: the 'banana flats', Leith.

enamelled carapace of a ladybird or the painted master-piece of a Red Admiral butterfly found in the school playground.

These formative experiences point to the common ground shared between people and wildlife in towns; the quality of life for both is strongly affected by the amount of green space which survives. Such green oases are often nineteenth-century parks and gardens but these are generally of limited value for wildlife, since wide expanses of mown grass provide little food for birds or insects. In addition, parks are often sprayed with weedkillers to suppress 'weeds' (or wildflowers) and may have been doused with insecticides which poison bees and butterflies, as well as the intended leatherjackets and aphids. Similarly, foreign trees and shrubs such as rhododendron offer little sustenance for our native wildlife.

In contrast the unplanned and accidental wildlife parks which have evolved along our disused railways or canals, on derelict pieces of wasteland and in over-grown cemeteries are generally more valuable for birds, insects and plants. In his book *The Wild Side of Town* (1986), Chris Baines highlighted the 'unofficial coun-tryside' of the towns and made a plea for the enrichment of the urban environment through placing a new value on such wild areas.

NATURE CORRIDORS

Many of Scotland's canals and railways have lost their original functions but acquired new value as urban green space (see Chapter 11). The Union Canal flows into the very heart of Edinburgh, while the Forth and Clyde Canal runs through Maryhill in Glasgow, form-ing linear urban nature reserves. These two canals,

3. SIR PATRICK GEDDES (1854–1932)

The name of Patrick Geddes stands out like a beacon in the environmental history of Edinburgh as the champion for the improvement of social conditions in the Old Town. As the pioneer of many aspects of modern town planning he was a 'synthesist' who developed many ideas which today we would recognise as ecology, sociology and environmental education. He realised that people needed green open spaces, fresh air and contact with nature just as much as they needed warm houses, wholesome food, proper sanitation and meaningful work.

He was born in Ballater, the youngest of five children, and studied botany at Edinburgh Univer-sity. However he found the system restrictive and moved to London to study under the biologist T.H. Huxley. He later studied at the Sorbonne in Paris and in Mexico, and for the next ten years worked as a demonstrator in the botany department at Edinburgh University.

In Edinburgh he and his wife moved their family back into the slums of the Old Town where they set up home in the Grassmarket and later in James Court. Geddes was appalled at the environmental conditions of the Old Town and set about rehabili-tating properties and creating green spaces as gardens and vegetable-growing areas.

He created the Outlook Tower on the Royal Mile which was an early attempt to merge ideas from sociology, town planning, ecology and what we today would call 'environmental education'. Geddes was one of the strongest advocates of 'greening the city' and he carried out one of the first 'open space surveys' of the Old Town, during which he recorded at least seventy-six open spaces on the Royal Mile. He believed that education and the study of nature should be combined and he organised local school children to work on twelve of the open spaces which he had identified, creating gardens on these sites. The site of one of these gardens survives on the land below Johnston Terrace and in 1982 the Scottish Wildlife Trust developed this as a wildlife garden. Geddes went on to become Professor of Civics and Sociology at the University of Bombay in 1919, but in Scotland he has never been given the regard which he is accorded throughout the world as a pioneer of environmental education and town planning.

A Patrick Geddes Centre has now been estab-lished in Edinburgh's Outlook Tower, linked to an educational trail which runs the length of the Royal Mile, exploring sites connected with Geddes.

along with the Caledonian Canal, make up part of the 150-mile (240 km) length of Scotland's remaining industrial waterways which form our largest unofficial nature reserve. Countryside Rangers on the canals have recorded 400 species of land plants, 100 species of water plants, 500 types of insect, 15 species of fish, 130 species of resident or migratory birds, 15 kinds of dragonfly and 30 resident or visiting butterflies.

The Beeching cuts of the 1960s created many miles of disused suburban railways which often run from the very centre of the town out through the urban fringe into the countryside. The tracks were simply torn up and the clinker beds were left for nature to reclaim; many of them now sport a dense growth of birch and willow scrub which supports a great variety of insect and bird life. In the early 1980s many district and regional councils began to look again at these green corridors in terms of their recreational potential since they offered mile upon mile of cyclepaths, walkways and green open space at very little cost.

THE URBAN CONSERVATION MOVEMENT

The Nature Conservancy Council (NCC) played an important part in inspiring the birth of urban nature conservation during the late 1970s. A landmark publication by the NCC at that time was *The Endless Village* (1978, by W. G. Teagle) which documented the surveying of open spaces and wildlife resources in the city of Birmingham and the Black Country. In this report the NCC listed priorities for improving the wildlife habitats of the West Midlands. These included: the identification of the remnants of the ancient plant and animal communities of the area; improvements to the entire area in terms of management of public land, parks and recreational spaces; and the creative use of derelict land reclamation projects so as to create new urban living space for wild creatures and plants.

More than anything however the report stressed the need to interest local people in their wildlife heritage and in the environmental quality of their lives in towns. It concluded by stressing that planners, ecologists, landscape architects and local authority staff all had a part to play in working with ordinary people to create better urban environments for people and wildlife.

The work that led up to the publication of *The Endless Village* inspired a group of people in Birmingham to take a greater interest in the quality of their urban environment. They carried out ecological surveys of open spaces and campaigned for the conservation of the wildlife which lived in them. This group evolved into the Urban Wildlife Group which was founded in 1980 and renamed as the Urban Wildlife Trust in 1989. Three more urban wildlife Trusts quickly followed during 1980–1: the Avon Wildlife Trust, the Cleveland Trust and the London Wildlife Trust.

The people who initiated this new movement were

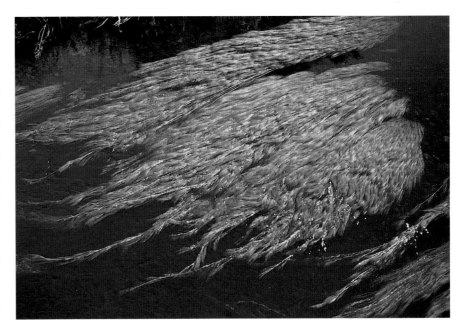

often teachers, planners, or landscape architects; more often than not they were simply local people who were concerned about their community environment. But they tended to be rather different from the kind of people involved in traditional nature conservation organisations: 'people-oriented' rather than passionate botanists or birdwatchers, concerned with the quality of the urban environment for both people and wildlife. They were also interested in wider planning and environmental issues including traffic, pollution, recycling and so on.

The movement was also stirring in Scotland at this time. In 1974 a new organisation, the Volunteers Environmental Resource Centre, was formed in Edinburgh to promote conservation and environmental education in the broadest sense. This charity rapidly grew and was reconstituted in 1984 as the Environment Centre, which from the outset advocated a 'people-centred' approach to the environment and conservation. There are now more than sixty urban wildlife groups in Britain but only a handful in Scotland. The first in Scotland was the Glasgow Urban Wildlife Group, initiated in 1981 as an umbrella group for local planners, conservation groups and representatives from the Nature Conservancy Council.

Brook-lime weed in the Water of Leith, Warriston, Edinburgh.

Newts being rescued from a development site near Edinburgh airport.

175

Glasgow's parks are among the greenest in Europe but the city centre has been razed by urban motorways.

The Lothian Urban Wildlife Group was formed by the Environment Centre in 1986 as the first such group with full-time staff in Scotland. The conservation world in Scotland is becoming increasingly aware of the issues of urban conservation and environmental quality in towns. In 1987 the NCC funded 'phase one' ecological surveys of open spaces and wildlife habitat within the city boundaries of Aberdeen, Dundee and Edinburgh. A phase one survey, in the urban context, simply means that every single open space, garden, disused railway, cemetery and derelict site in these cities is looked at and then classified by habitat type.

Also in 1987 the NCC published another significant document, *Planning for Wildlife in Metropolitan Areas*, which advocated the inclusion of wildlife and the natural aspects of urban environmental quality for unitary development plans in England and Wales. In the same year the Department of the Environment and the Welsh Office issued Circular 27/87 entitled *Nature Conservation*; paragraph 38 of this circular noted that:

> Local authorities are required by section 11 of the Country-side Act 1968 'to have regard to the desirability of conserving the natural beauty and amenity of the country-side'. This duty embraces the conservation of flora, fauna,

geological and physiographical features and extends to urban as well as rural areas. Councils are particularly urged to ensure that, where they own or hold land for any purpose, their own estate management practices take nature conservation considerations fully into account.

The Act of 1986 imposed a duty on local authorities in England and Wales to take conservation into account in urban areas. However this Act did not apply in Scotland, and the corresponding Scottish Development Department Circular 1/1988 made no reference to nature conservation in planning. Nevertheless the developments in England have had an effect north of the border and many Scottish local authorities are now carrying out wildlife surveys and preparing 'nature conservation strategies' for inclusion in their Local Plan.

The NCC has supported the growth of the emerging urban wildlife movement by the publication of *Urban Wildlife News*. Recently this support was reinforced by the NCC's publication of *Nature Conservation in Towns and Cities* (1990), number five in their *Urban Wildlife Now* series. This booklet provides local authorities with a strong framework for action by describ-

Princes Street, Edinburgh—the finest street in Europe is often a fume-filled jam.

ing a number of successes where planning departments have rescued derelict land, created nature parks and generally enhanced the environment for people and wildlife. The NCC has also funded urban nature conservation projects in towns, including wildlife gardens and study areas in school grounds, through its Community Nature Scheme.

Nature Conservation strategies are a great step forward for the saving of green open space in Scotland's cities and for the conservation of wildlife in towns (Boxes 5, 6, 7 and 8). Fifty-two such strategies are already being prepared by local authorities for both rural and urban areas of Britain, using NCC guidelines, often with direct support from the NCC.

The conservation strategies being prepared for Scotland's major towns and cities will, it is to be hoped, conserve the wildlife which survives in our towns; but it is equally important that they will help protect many of our parks, playing fields, disused railways and canals for the enjoyment of future generations. In fact the greatest value of such strategies may simply be the co-operation which they create among the voluntary sector agencies, the local authorities and the new NCC for Scotland.

However an even broader approach for ensuring environmental quality in towns is being fostered by Friends of the Earth in collaboration with a number of local authorities in Scotland, namely the creation of a Charter for the Environment. Such charters could have a dramatic effect on a council's policies relating to traffic, pollution, recycling and the conservation of green open spaces and wildlife in towns. Fife Regional Council, East Lothian, Dumbarton, Gordon, Ross and Cromarty and Orkney have already adopted their own environmental charters while many other district councils, such as Dundee and Aberdeen, are in the process of adopting them. Most of the regional councils are already involved in looking at these issues.

Fife Regional Council's Charter for the Environment Action Programme details at least sixteen major areas in which the Council proposes to change its own policies and methods of operation. These include initiatives on the recycling of wastes such as paper, glass and metals; the control of pollution of air, land and water from industrial and domestic sources; the conservation of wildlife through creative management of parks, open spaces and roadside verges; the development of environmentally friendly transport policies and the adop-

177

Arthur's Seat is a unique survival of an ancient landscape within a modern city.

4. HOLYROOD PARK: A MICROCOSM OF SCOTLAND'S ENVIRONMENT

Arthur's Seat and Holyrood Park represent a unique survival of a wildlife habitat within the heart of a major city, and the history of the area offers useful lessons about how we should manage our environment. The area was used as a royal hunting reserve by King David I (1124–53); at that time Edinburgh was evidently surrounded by thick woods of oak, birch, alder, hazel, gean and rowan. As late as the twelfth century these forests must have harboured red deer, wild boar and possibly wolves. During the Middle Ages the town of Edinburgh expanded and many oaks were felled to provide the great beams for the wooden houses of the Canongate.

This was a society in which almost every implement, every tool, every cart and every piece of furniture was made of wood, so deforestation must have been rapid. In fact it is evident that the area around Arthur's Seat had been totally cleared of trees by 1549, since a print of that era shows the area as treeless. In microcosm this reflects what happened throughout Scotland, but most Scots do not realise that their country has suffered a far greater loss of woodland than the Amazon has to date.

In 1541 King James V enclosed the entire area of Arthur's Seat and Holyrood Palace within a wall, creating the first Royal Park. Sheep were introduced to the park shortly afterwards; the court annals of 1556 record the conviction of one Thomas Bullerwell, who was banished for the 'steling of certane scheip fra the Quenis grace furthe of hir Park of Edinburgh'. As elsewhere in Scotland the grazing of sheep began a process of rapid environmental degradation. From the moment they were introduced into the park they would have destroyed all seedling trees, and the park rapidly became treeless and barren.

In 1966 more than 2,000 sheep were still grazing in the park which had remained treeless for over 300 years; to echo the words of John Muir when speaking of California's Yosemite Valley, the 'hoofed locusts' had swept everything away. In 1977 an ecological study by Napier College showed that the diversity and numbers of flowering plants, moths, butterflies and mammals had declined markedly over the previous century and there had been massive erosion of paths due to pressure from thousands of tourist feet.

The Napier study recommended that the sheep be removed entirely and that the original habitat should be restored by planting birch, oak, alder, ash and other trees in suitable areas. When the sheep were gone the grasses and flowering plants would be left to regenerate naturally while, at the same time, a serious look was taken at visitor management to guide people away from more sensitive sites and erosion areas.

Arthur's Seat remains a unique urban site and is designated as a Site of Special Scientific Interest (SSSI) because of its geological and botanical interest. It is home to the only known colony of urban fulmars, which have moved in from the coast to take advantage of the artificial sea cliffs afforded by Salisbury Crags. The effects of the new management of the park are already apparent and many thousands of visitors can look forward to a richer, more attractive landscape in coming years as the trees and shrubs mature and the birds, insects and animals return.

tion of an environmental enhancement strategy for all public open spaces.

EDUCATING FOR THE FUTURE

Perhaps the greatest hope for the future of both the urban and the rural environment in Scotland lies in the field of education in our primary and secondary schools, in the universities and colleges and in the community education sector. In the primary schools we have witnessed an environmental education revolution in the last decade; much of the primary curriculum has become focused on the local environment as children study the streets, the woods, streams and trees of their own neighbourhoods.

Centres of excellence and innovation have emerged at

Children from the 'Bellarmine Beasties' plant trees in Glasgow.

the Royal Botanic Garden in Edinburgh and at the National Museums of Scotland, where the educational programmes have earned high praise from teachers and children alike. The WATCH scheme, originated by the Royal Society for Nature Conservation (RSNC) in England and organised in Scotland by the Scottish Wildlife Trust, now involves many active groups of youngsters throughout Scotland on projects looking at everything from ozone pollution to acid rain in towns (see Chapter 14). The Bellarmine Environmental Resource Centre in Glasgow has also made great strides in promoting practical environmental education with city children and helping them to become actively involved

5. EDINBURGH WILDLIFE SURVEY

During the 1980s the Planning Department of Edinburgh District Council became concerned that they did not have an up to date survey of open green spaces within the city. As a result there was no overall strategy for the conservation of the birds, animals and plants which survive in the city's parks, gardens, disused railways and watercourses. Developers increasingly target these marginal spaces and gap sites for housing and for office space and the planners increasingly found that they had little information on which to judge the environmental value of proposed development sites.

In the spring of 1987 the Edinburgh Wildlife Survey was launched as a collaborative project. The aim of the project was to identify and survey every green open space within the City of Edinburgh. More than 965 sites were identified from aerial photographs and these were all mapped and surveyed by staff and volunteers from the Environment Centre and the Scottish Wildlife Trust. A report was produced which formed the basis for a city-wide Edinburgh Nature Conservation Strategy, similar to those of Dundee and Aberdeen. The recommendations from this strategy will be put into operation in the 1990s and should guarantee Edinburgh's reputation as having the richest urban environment in Britain.

Oystercatchers feed in the inner city areas of Pilton and West Granton, Edinburgh, and nest on the gravel-roofed tower blocks of Aberdeen.

in planting trees, clearing burns of litter and generally looking after their own community environment.

Scotland's major cities are among the greenest and most environmentally rich in Britain but the future environmental quality of our towns and cities depends on civic vigilance, education and the raising of general public awareness. The traditional nature conservation agencies must cast off their rural blinkers and begin to see the urban environment as a place worthy of conservation and environmental enhancement. They must also begin to accept that conservation is essentially a 'people-centred activity' and that we shall never involve the great mass of ordinary people in nature conservation unless we take an equally strong interest in our communal human environment.

Local authority planners should be encouraged to develop nature conservation strategies which protect the remaining green spaces of our towns and cities for the benefit of both the wild creatures which live there and the people who need such contact with common nature. District and regional councils must be lobbied to adopt environmental charters covering the entire range of services and duties which they carry out on behalf of the public. Schools and teachers must be supported in their use of the local environment as a source of environmental education materials, experiences and insights.

Above all the general public must be encouraged to bring pressure to bear on politicians, local authority departments, industry and commerce regarding the quality of the urban environment. The forces which can so easily destroy the quality of our lives in cities are rapidly growing in strength. The traffic choking our streets, the sewage fouling our streams and beaches, the pressure to build on every last square yard of playing field and green space – these are all symptoms of the developing urban environmental crisis of the 1990s.

This urban environmental crisis is real; it is happening right now in Scotland and none of us will remain immune to the effects of pollution, traffic congestion and aggressive building development which are blighting our towns. The forces creating this new urban crisis can be controlled, but only if enough people join relevant amenity and environmental groups and demand the rights for their children to breathe clean air; to drink clean, lead-free water; to swim from beaches that are not clogged with sewage; to walk in streets which are not grossly polluted by the noise and fumes of traffic; to have parks, playing fields, green spaces, ponds and canals which can be enjoyed by people and wildlife alike. 'Private affluence, public squalor' is an old adage, but it is one that will surely come to mar our towns and cities unless people unite in the struggle to make our cities green and pleasant places.

6. DUNDEE URBAN WILDLIFE PROJECT

Kestrels have adapted to city life by hunting along the verges of main roads.

Dundee was the first city in Scotland to undertake an urban wildlife survey and to publish a corresponding Nature Conservation Strategy. In 1987 the City of Dundee District Council and the NCC set up the Dundee Urban Wildlife Project, and within a year an Assessment of the City's Green Spaces had been produced. Fifty sites from the Derelict Land Register were mapped and surveyed; a list of all plant species for each site habitat was prepared and any interesting insect or bird species found were also recorded. The sites were rated for their amenity value, their educational potential and the general richness of the site in terms of habitat and rare species.

During the survey a site was rediscovered which had long been valued by local people but which had been largely ignored by the city planners. The site was called Shiell Street but local people always called the area 'Lovers Lawn'. It is a secluded area of ancient sand dunes which has somehow survived throughout the long period of Dundee's urban development, probably because it was sandwiched between two railway embankments. Local

people have walked there for over a century and it has long been used by courting couples. When the ecologists came to survey it they found it had a particularly rich of variety of habitats, with over 150 species of flowering plants and at least fifteen breeding bird species.

During the 1970s the Dundee Parks Department planned to pave some of the area and to provide tarmacadamed car parks on the site. However the Parks Department subsequently become involved with the Dundee Urban Wildlife Project, with the result that plans were radically altered and a much more environmentally sensitive approach has been adopted.

The Dundee Urban Conservation Officer discovered that a local resident was a keen botanist who had surveyed the area for at least eighteen years, providing a valuable scientific record. A group of local people is now involved in the practical management of the area, and projects have included the removal of invading gorse bushes as well as clearing litter from the area.

7. ABERDEEN URBAN WILDLIFE PROJECT

The Aberdeen Urban Wildlife Project is a collaboration between the City of Aberdeen District Council and the NCCS; it aims to promote a greater awareness and appreciation of Aberdeen's wildlife and green spaces. The project has pursued these aims by means of mobile exhibitions, leaflets, slide shows and the production of a superb document entitled *Aberdeen Wildlife and People* (1989) funded by the NCC and Texaco. The voluntary sector has also made a great contribution through the work of the Aberdeen Urban Studies Centre and the related Aberdeen Urban Wildlife Group, a purely voluntary body with no staff of its own. Its enthusiasts arrange an active programme of events, assist with the wildlife survey and arrange wildflower walks, birdwatching expeditions, visits to sewage works to discuss pollution, bat watches and educational talks on every aspect of urban conservation.

Aberdeen Wildlife and People identified 171 wildlife sites within the City of Aberdeen District and related these to their proximity to primary schools for educational purposes. The project aims to produce a nature conservation strategy for the city which will be written into the Local Plan.

Two sites, the Donmouth estuary and the Den of Maidencraig, have been selected to demonstrate how areas of land can be managed in a more creative and environmentally sensitive manner so as to benefit both people and wildlife.

Child at the opening of St Joseph's School wildlife garden, Aberdeen.

8. THE GREENING OF GLASGOW?

The environment of Glasgow has undergone dramatic changes in the last few decades, with the replacement of the 'merchant city' by the 'motorway city' and the slums of the Gorbals by high-rise tower blocks. In recent years there has been a growing recognition that the issue of green open space for people and wildlife is not just a cosmetic aspect of the city's future.

In 1989 the City of Glasgow District Council approved a Wildlife and Nature Conservation Policy Statement whose broad objectives were to protect the best wildlife sites and to enhance the ecological, recreational, educational and visual qualities of open spaces within the city; to provide a permanent network of natural green spaces with improved access to the countryside; and to increase the environmental attractiveness of the city for both visitors and investors, as well as improving the quality of life for its citizens.

The Policy Statement was based on an extensive survey which had been carried out by the Glasgow Urban Spaces Initiative. This project produced two vital reports: *Glasgow's Urban Spaces – An Ecological Perspective* (1987) and *Glasgow's Urban Spaces – A Directory of City Wildlife Sites* (1988).

The Policy Statement emphasised that nature conservation is not just about the protection of a few rare species in special rural areas, but about the creation, enhancement and conservation of habitats which encourage wildlife throughout the city.

Unofficial bathers in Pollok Park, Glasgow.

*Glean an Dubh Lochain,
Inverie, Knoydart.*

The Protection of the Land

JOHN ARNOTT

John Arnott is an amateur naturalist and a former editor and manager with BBC Scotland. As vice-chairman of the Countryside Commission for Scotland (CCS) he led the advisory panel that produced the important CCS report on the management and conservation of The Mountain Areas of Scotland (1990).

When we say 'protected areas', what do we mean? Protected from whom and from what? Is it the safeguarding of fine natural landscape from the development of factories and leisure complexes? Or are we protecting wildlife from disturbance? Perhaps we wish to protect mountains from the erosion caused by boots and bulldozed tracks? Or is it rural communities which must be defended against ever-decreasing employment and wealthy incoming house-buyers?

There is no model for an ideal countryside. It exists as we see it today as a result of a long process of competing claims on it, and of conflicting opinions on how to control this process. The pressures of change are accelerating: afforestation, housing, industry, road building, fish farming, recreation – they all make insistent demands on the countryside.

At the same time there is an increasing awareness that the countryside is the chief asset of a tourist industry which now has an annual turnover of more than £1.7 billion, and that the natural beauty of this landscape should be conserved in an ever more urbanised and developed Europe for enjoyment and recreation. The 1970s and 1980s have also seen a growing public interest in wildlife and in the importance on a global scale of protecting it 'for its own sake' as well as for its attractiveness.

But it is not only a matter of wildlife. The rural communities of Scotland with their rich cultural history peaked in the early nineteenth century. Since then there has been a steady decline, either through forced or voluntary emigration. Depopulation of the Highlands has now been stemmed, due partly to the Highlands and Islands Development Board (now Highland and Islands Enterprise), but the people who stay there and elsewhere in the countryside have the same aspirations for a higher standard of living as town-dwellers have.

Attempts by 'outsiders' to place amenity or conservation above jobs are understandably resented. It is sometimes said that it is people who are the most endangered species in the Highlands.

The problem of bringing together land-use management and protection of the environment is one of reconciling a host of conflicting demands on the land. Basically the problem is insoluble. We have a finite area of countryside and over the coming years a potentially infinite variety of pressures will be brought to bear to change it in somebody's interest, mostly by introducing man-made objects into a semi-natural landscape. Parts of the countryside are already in an ecologically impoverished condition because of heavy stocking with sheep and red deer.

In the end it is up to society to decide what it wants of its countryside, where its priorities lie, and how much it is prepared to pay for them. It has to place values on such unquantifiable assets as a magnificent view or a patch of alpine plants or a traditional rural way of life. These all have an intrinsic value. And simply because they exist they also have a value to the 95 per cent of the population who do not experience them most of the time.

AGRICULTURAL AREAS

Traditionally the stewards and protectors of the countryside have been the farmers and landowners who have a vested interest in a fully sustainable use of it. In the critical years of the Second World War they answered the call for more home-grown food by increasing production, and this was given a further post-war boost by the incentives offered by the European Community (EC) Common Agricultural Policy (CAP).

But increased output was not achieved without environmentally damaging effects: the wholesale removal of hedgerows and trees; the drainage of wetlands; the heavy use of artificial fertilisers, insecticides and herbicides; and loss of employment as expensive machinery took over. By the 1980s the pendulum had swung the other way, with over-production of food creating an embarrassment of riches. The resultant fall in farm incomes has created the need for support systems to secure the future of rural communities; it has also produced an opportunity to protect the country-

183

The Breadalbane hills Environmentally Sensitive Area (ESA)

Native pine wood at Coille na Glas Leitire, Beinn Eighe, Britain's first National Nature Reserve.

1. BEINN EIGHE

The National Nature Reserve of Beinn Eighe (pronounced 'Ben-Ay') in Ross and Cromarty, in the north-west of Scotland, was the very first to be established in Britain, in 1951.

The land was purchased by the Nature Conservancy Council to preserve Beinn Eighe, with its classic geological formations, as a splendid example of the mountain and moorland habitat of the northern Highlands, and in particular to conserve the fragment of native woodland, Coille na Glas Leitire ('wood of the grey slope'), overlooking the southern shores of Loch Maree.

This pinewood was recognised as an important remnant of the 'Great Wood of Caledon' which once clothed most of Highland Scotland (see Chapter 3). Beinn Eighe provides as good an idea of what a primeval forest was like as any other woodland scene in Britain; this was Scotland's original 'rain forest', one might say. The trees at Beinn Eighe are up to 350 years old, and to stand amongst them is to feel the nature of Scotland's past.

184

Native pine woods, the true woodland habitat of the red deer in Scotland.

side from the worst effects of intensive agriculture and to restore to it a greater diversity (see Chapter 10).

Both of these aims have been brought together in the Environmentally Sensitive Area (ESA) support system, which is designed to encourage conservation-friendly farming. As the system is voluntary it is also farmer-friendly conservation. EC Regulation 797/85 (Article 19) permits governments to make payments to farmers in designated areas of high conservation value to encourage farming practices favourable to the environment. After preparation of a farm conservation plan there is a flat-rate payment of up to £1,500, and then there are additional grants for drystane dyke and hedge repairs, protecting rough grazing from reclamation, limiting the use of herbicides and encouraging the natural regeneration of woodlands.

Other measures are grant-aided, including, in the Uists, traditional crofting and the use of seaweed as fertilisers. There are five of these ESAs in Scotland at present (see Chapter 10). By early 1990 the farmers of 45 per cent of the eligible 173,000 hectares (427,000 acres) in the five ESA areas had agreed to take part in the scheme; each project is to last for five years initially, and the system is to be reviewed in 1991. The possibility of a Mark II version of the ESA system, extending it to land-uses beyond agriculture-related work, is currently under discussion.

Similar in some respects to the ESA is the Agricultural Development Programme (ADP), though this has more emphasis on improving the quality of production. From 1988–93 it applies to all the islands except the Western Isles and, of the first 1,200 farm plans approved, over 50 per cent included environmental measures. Grants of £30–90 per hectare (£12–36 per acre) are provided.

Throughout most of the uplands hill sheep are the mainstay of farming and the Blackface sheep and its relatives can be encountered almost anywhere in the mountains. It is not an easy living for either the sheep or the shepherd. Over 90 per cent of Scotland (and 97 per cent of the Highlands) is designated as a Less Favoured Area (LFA) (see Chapter 10) under the accession agreement with the EC. Most of it is further labelled as a Severely Disadvantaged Area (SDA) or a Disadvantaged Area (DA). These classifications enable payments of Hill Livestock Compensatory Allowance (HLCA) which provide a subsidy for each ewe or cow. A stocking limit of six ewes per hectare in SDAs seeks to prevent overgrazing; the scheme has been criticised in the past for adverse effects on the environment because it has encouraged the reclamation of moorland for improved pasture and high stocking levels.

Without these subsidies and other support mechanisms most hill-sheep farming would be impossible. Lamb is one of the few agricultural products not in surplus in Europe, but as sheep-rearing moves down the hills and further south on to richer vacated land in the future, the prospects for hill sheep and their farmers become bleaker and their need for subsidy greater. Some people have argued that if hill sheep are uneconomic then there should be no more hill sheep and that it is futile to spend millions of pounds in this way. To stop doing so, however, would not only have a devastating effect on the upland communities but could also adversely affect the environment, since a degree of grazing encourages a wider variety of plants.

Growing trees as a farm crop is another way of protecting and enhancing the countryside. The Farm Woodland Scheme (FWS) is taking some faltering steps in this direction, but we do not have a tradition of integrated farming and forestry, unlike much of the rest of northern Europe with its attractive patterns of small, mixed-species woodlands.

GOVERNMENT AGENCIES

Attractive landscapes usually display a variety of land forms, land-uses, and plant and animal life. National policy for the conservation of the landscape has been divided between two government agencies, the Countryside Commission for Scotland (CCS) and the Nature Conservancy Council (NCC). The CCS answers to the Secretary of State for Scotland, whereas the NCC, until April 1991, answered to the Secretary of State for the Environment.

This created a curious division of responsibility, with one agency (the CCS) looking after the natural beauty of the countryside and another (the NCC) looking after the scientific conservation of its flora and fauna. New legislation in 1990 has created the new agency of the Nature Conservancy Council for Scotland by separating it from the original NCC; this will merge with the CCS in April 1992 to form a new agency, Scottish Natural Heritage (SNH), which will be required to take a more integrated view of nature conservation and countryside access and protection.

THE NATURE CONSERVANCY COUNCIL FOR SCOTLAND

The main site protection system operated by the NCCS is founded on the National Parks and Access to the Countryside Act 1949, and elaborated in the monumental NCC survey published in 1977, *A Nature Conservation Review* (NCR). This was an attempt to take stock of all the best plant and wildlife sites in Britain.

A similar review of geological sites is currently in production. The Wildlife and Countryside Act 1981, and the Environmental Protection Act 1990, require the NCCS to notify areas of special wildlife and geological importance. The NCCS calls these Sites of Special Scientific Interest (SSSIs); perhaps the 1990s will see the significance of these sites not as being exclusively scientific but in a wider cultural and heritage sense.

The principle behind this system is the protection of the most important areas for the range of habitats and diversity of wildlife occurring naturally in Britain, together with areas of national geological importance. Traditional land-uses such as farming and forestry continue in these SSSIs but, where any change of practice is proposed which was included in a list of notified operations likely to damage the features of special interest, the NCCS must be informed.

The 1981 Act introduced the novel and potentially expensive principle of compensation for profit foregone in cases where the NCC felt that the nature interest would be irreparably affected by a proposed change (see Chapter 10). However such compensation is seldom required. About 90 per cent of notified changes of practice are given consent; nine per cent result in agreed modification, and only one per cent end up with management agreements paying compensation either in a lump sum or annually. Even so this has resulted in capital payments in Scotland totalling £2.7 million up to 1990 and current annual payments amounting to £790,000.

The most costly agreements have been for afforestation proposals where the earning capacity of the land was greatly increased by tax concessions, although compensation is no longer paid for these. Notification (and renotification) of SSSIs has been going on throughout the 1980s and is now almost complete. Over 7,700 owners have been notified about some 1,200 sites, covering 770,000 hectares (1.9 million acres) or 9.6 per cent of Scotland. The SSSIs thus provide formal protection on a scale which has never previously been seen, but it is not complete protection. Damage to the nature conservation interest still happens, either deliberately or by accident. Major developments such as a new road may be allowed to go ahead after a ruling by the Secretary of State for Scotland. As a result of such damage a number of sites is de-notified each year.

Protection is always easier to promote when it is in the interest of the owners, and the NCCS owns, or manages under agreement with the owners, sixty-eight National Nature Reserves (NNRs) in Scotland. They range from the 26,000 hectares (64,000 acres) of reserve in the Cairngorms, the 10,000 hectares (25,000 acres) of the island of Rhum and 4,700 hectares (11,6000 acres) at Beinn Eighe in Torridon, down to a mere five hectares (12 acres) at the spectacular gorge of Corrieshalloch near Ullapool. Traditional land-uses may continue but the main object of the reserves is management for nature conservation, education and research. The NCCS can also create by-laws in them. There are also plans for a series of Marine Nature Reserves (MNRs), such as the one proposed for Loch Sween.

With its SSSIs and NNRs, Britain has an advanced system of nature protection by the standards of main-

land Europe where, for example, millions of migrating birds are killed each year for sport. The European Community is taking action on that issue, such as by its 1979 Directive on the Conservation of Wild Birds which, after agreement by the Council of Ministers, requires member-states to establish a general system of bird protection and to identify and protect particularly important areas for breeding and migrating birds. There are eighteen of these Special Protection Areas (SPAs) in Scotland, all protected by SSSI status.

These overlap with another protective designation devised by the Ramsar Convention (not another acronym but the place in Iran where it was drawn up in 1971) for safeguarding marshes and wetlands which are vulnerable to development. This was ratified by the UK in 1976. The nineteen Ramsar sites in Scotland are designated by the Secretary of State and eleven of them are also SPAs. Biosphere Reserves are a designation by the United Nations Educational, Scientific and Cultural Organisation (UNESCO) applied in Scotland to nine of the NNRs.

The 1981 Act which protects all of these areas provides the means of complying with two other international measures: the Bonn Convention on the conservation of migratory species of wild animals, ratified by the UK in 1985, and the Berne Convention on the Conservation of European Wildlife and Natural Habitats, ratified by the UK in 1982. The Act also extends throughout the whole of Scotland a general protection for almost all wild birds and plants and some

Creag Meagaidh National Nature Reserve where over 5,000 red deer have been culled in order to allow regeneration of the woodlands.

187

St Kilda carries a host of designations: SSSI, NNR, NSA, NTS inalienable, and World Heritage Sight.

mammals. It is perhaps not widely realised that uprooting any wild plant is an offence. Heavy penalties are provided for damage to specially protected plant and animal species, and these have recently been imposed in cases involving the theft of peregrines' and ospreys' eggs.

THE COUNTRYSIDE COMMISSION FOR SCOTLAND

The sight of a peregrine flashing past or an osprey taking fish from a loch, or the experience of the colours of an ancient pine-forest with its junipers and blaeberries and red squirrels, are very much part of the enjoyment of the natural beauty of the landscape; almost everything seen in the countryside consists of living things. The Countryside Commission for Scotland was founded by the Countryside (Scotland) Act 1967 which charged it with exercising functions for the improvement of facilities for the enjoyment of the countryside and for the conservation and enhancement of its natural beauty.

The CCS does this largely through enabling other agencies, by a mixture of grant aid and advice to local authorities, voluntary bodies and private landowners,

and by its own innovative projects. It provides most of the funding for the Countryside Ranger services, assisting the public and smoothing the relations between recreation and other land-uses. It grant-aids, among other things, native tree planting for amenity and much of the restoration work on mountain paths for walkers.

The CCS has identified forty National Scenic Areas (NSAs), a series of the most outstanding landscapes in the country. They range from St Kilda, the fantastical shapes of the Assynt mountains and the high semi-arctic plateau of the Cairngorms, to the more accessible scale of the Trossachs, the Kyles of Bute, and the Eildon Hills beside Melrose. Altogether they amount to over a million hectares (2.5 million acres or 3900 square miles), equivalent to 12.9 per cent of the country. Within these areas proposals for several types of development have to be notified to the CCS and if, contrary to the view of the planning authority, the CCS considers the development unsuitable for these special landscapes the decision is referred to the Secretary of State. The NSAs also have the general effect (some would say the insufficient effect) of drawing attention to the importance of protecting these exceptional areas.

The countryside around towns is less glamorous but just as important; it is the most accessible countryside for most people. The CCS has initiated a number of urban fringe management projects such as those at Clyde Calders and the Kilpatricks which are partnerships of local authorities and agencies east and west of Glasgow, rehabilitating land, planting trees, creating ponds and generally improving the area.

The Scottish Development Agency (SDA, now transformed into Scottish Enterprise) was also active in clearing up dereliction in many areas, and a measure of the success of its projects is that they tend to be overlooked. Anyone who remembers the doleful mounds of slate at Ballachulish now appreciates the view along Loch Leven all the more.

PARKS

Ballachulish lies in one of the five areas proposed by the Ramsay Committee in 1945 as a National Park. Scotland has no National Parks – one of the very few countries in the world without them. There was not the same organised pressure for access which brought about National Parks in England and Wales in the 1950s; and in Scotland the local authorities were not keen to give up any of their newly acquired powers.

In 1974 the CCS advocated what it called 'Special Parks', similar to National Parks, in its publication *A Park System for Scotland,* but this was not taken up by the government. After a review of the management and conservation of the mountain areas in 1990 it proposed the setting up of National Parks in four areas: the Cairngorms, Loch Lomond, Ben Nevis/Glen Coe, and Wester Ross, as part of a range of proposals to bring better stewardship to the high country.

Two of the other proposals in A Park System for Scotland were adopted, however: Country Parks and Regional Parks. There are now thirty-five Country Parks near towns and cities, mostly owned and run by district councils, giving townspeople a place to go in the country where they know they are welcome to walk or take part in informal sports. The parks are not very extensive, averaging 181 hectares (450 acres), and ranging from 675 hectares (1670 acres) at John Muir Country Park near Dunbar with its eight miles (13 km) of shoreline, to just 16 hectares (40 acres) at Clatto on the outskirts of Dundee which consists mostly of a reservoir with its water sports.

The Country Parks are among the few areas in the countryside where public recreation is acknowledged to be the primary land-use, but for that purpose they act as a protection in a double sense: by conserving their natural amenity, and by taking the pressure of people off more vulnerable areas. It is estimated that they receive 11 million out of the 44 million day-trips made to the Scottish countryside each year.

On a larger scale there are the Regional Parks, with four established since 1986. Run by regional councils, they are wide tracts of hill country extending to

Coire an Lochain in Cairngorms National Scenic Area (NSA)

thousands of hectares where existing land ownership and farming continues but where there is an extensive system of public access, aided by a Ranger service. The biggest of them, at 160 square miles (415 sq km), is at Loch Lomond; the others are at the north end of the Pentland Hills beside Edinburgh, in Fife centred on the Lomond Hills, and at Clyde Muirshiel in the hills between Greenock and Largs.

Some people argue that the protection and recreation afforded by the Regional Park concept should be extended to the green belts which, since the 1960s, have been designated round the four Scottish cities of Edinburgh, Glasgow, Dundee and Aberdeen, plus Falkirk and Grangemouth. They were set up to stop urban sprawl, restricting land-use to agriculture and horticulture, and on the whole they have served their purpose well on the negative side of preventing development.

The positive side – that of rehabilitating land which is highly marginal for farming and where farmers have in

Countryside Ranger with disabled visitor near Fort William.

189

Dawn over Loch Achtriochtan in Glencoe National Scenic Area.

Harvesting in the Lomond Hills Regional Park, Fife

some cases given up in the face of falling income, vandalism and litter – is not so easy to implement. There is little or no revenue to be obtained by protecting and improving the appearance of such countryside, and it requires the co-operation of many district councils, all of which have great pressure on their resources.

New initiatives are being set up to tackle this. In the Glasgow green belt, which extends for 100,000 hectares from Greenock to Cumbernauld and Carluke, the Strathclyde Green Belt Company has been set up to bring together a partnership of local authorities, government agencies, voluntary bodies and the private sector to set about the rehabilitation of derelict land. To the east a similar project has been set up under the Edinburgh Green Belt Initiative. Aberdeen does not have quite the same problem of blight, and Dundee abandoned the formal green belt designation in 1978 (although two major developments, the Ninewells Hospital and the Gowrie housing estate, were approved while the green belt was still in place). There are proposals to abandon the Falkirk/Grangemouth green belt which separates the two towns and replace it with countryside corridors.

Between the green belts of Edinburgh and Glasgow lies an area of high, bleak moorland with windswept marginal farms. The CCS initiated a pioneering project here which led to two million trees being planted, largely for amenity purposes. The project has now grown into the Central Scotland Countryside Trust, and the Central Scotland Woodlands Company (see Chapter 10, Box 4). The government has promised £50 million over twenty years to support further planting, which will include community woodlands and which should give this desolate 50,000 hectare (124,000 acres) area and its settlements a degree of positive protection and enhancement it has never previously seen.

LOCAL AUTHORITIES

In fifty years' time, perhaps, the Central Belt of Scotland may even be transformed into an Area of Great Landscape Value (AGLV). This designation derives from a Scottish Development Department (SDD, now Scottish Office Environment Department, SOEnD) Circular in 1962, and enables Regional and Islands Councils to identify particularly fine landscapes where they would apply a general presumption against development. The use made of this has varied among councils, but 178 such areas have been identified, covering 1.468 million hectares (3.63 million acres) or 18.6 per cent of the country. Variations include three Areas of Scenic Value (ASVs) in Orkney and nine Regional Scenic Coasts (RSCs) in Strathclyde.

Local authorities are also enabled by the 1949 National Parks and Access to the Countryside Act to set up Local Nature Reserves (LNRs), of which there are only six in Scotland. The first (and the first in Britain) was Aberlady Bay in East Lothian in 1952 (see Chapter 14, Box 1) and the latest is Montrose Basin (1981); since then there has not been the same call for them, with so many other organisations working in the field. The others are at Gartmorn Dam near Kincardine, Castle and Hightae Lochs at Lochmaben, the Eden estuary in Fife, and Gladhouse Reservoir, Lothian. Another protective mechanism is the Tree Preservation Order (TPO) for small areas of high amenity woodland.

In the larger sense local authorities have wide powers to affect the countryside and its amenities through their various physical planning and development control powers. But twenty-two classes of operation, including farming and forestry, are specifically excluded from the planning process through the 1981 General Development Order (GDO); so a very large part of the appearance of the countryside, and the wildlife habitats within it, lies outside this form of local scrutiny and potential protection.

Mass conifer planting in the Caithness Flow country.

FORESTRY

There are now moves to introduce more co-ordination and environmentally friendly practices in the basic land-uses, especially in forestry. The location of new forests is now being influenced by Indicative Forestry Strategies (IFSs). These arose from the outcry over the scale of afforestation in the Flow Country of Caithness and Sutherland in the 1980s (see Chapter 5).

When the NCC proposed notifying extensive areas of the Flow Country as SSSIs, the Highland Regional Council brought everyone concerned, including those who saw valuable job opportunities, round a table and together they worked out a strategy which indicated where forestry was more, or less, appropriate.

Strathclyde Region took up the idea and, with Scottish Office support, most regions are now devising Indicative Forestry Strategies. These divide countryside capable of growing trees into 'Preferred', 'Potential' and 'Sensitive' zones according to the number of constraints operating on them such as NSAs, SSSIs, or ancient monuments. They do not in themselves provide protection from inappropriate forestry; but they do give an indication of where most opposition is likely to arise and may well be helpful in reducing controversy over the location of new forests in future.

Scotland has about 13 per cent of its land under trees, compared with 27 per cent in France and 30 per cent in Germany. It has only one native conifer, the Scots pine, but its moist climate favours quick-growing North American conifers like Sitka spruce and lodgepole pine (see Chapter 10). They grow best when densely planted. The exclusion of red deer (which eat young trees) involves installing miles of expensive straight-running

Glen Affric Forest Nature Reserve (FNA)

fences, and there is a larger return if planting runs right up to the fence. The result throughout Scotland has been the hard geometrical blocks of so-called 'blanket forestry' of even-aged single-species plantations: man's handiwork writ large on the landscape.

Antipathy to this was compounded by a widespread feeling that fiscal advantages and doubtful economics were resulting in taxpayers subsidising landscape blight. An increasingly vocal and articulate lobby expressed this feeling. But complaints about serried rows of Sitka spruce are given a frosty reception by foresters. For generations they have been doing what they have been asked to do: produce timber. It is society which has moved the goalposts.

The Forestry Commission (FC) is both forest authority (grant-aiding private sector planting and issuing felling licences) and forest enterprise (growing its own trees). The public and private sectors each have about half a million hectares (1.2 million acres) of forest. The special fiscal arrangements for forestry ended with the

1988 Budget. Now the Woodland Grant Scheme (WGS) is the main engine in the drive towards the government target of 33,000 hectares (82,000 acres) a year of afforestation, the bulk of which will be in the private sector and in Scotland.

The Scheme gives planting grants of up to £1,005 per hectare (£407 per acre) for conifers and up to £1,575 (£637 per acre) for broadleaves, decreasing in larger areas. To qualify for grant the proposals must satisfy increasingly high FC standards of design, landscaping, and species mix (including a proportion of broadleaves among conifers), and safeguards for landscape and wildlife interest, archaeological sites and public access. Ancient and semi-natural ancient woodlands, registered by the NCC, are given special protection, and there are higher rates of grant for Native Pinewood Sites (NPS) in the hope of restoring more of the Caledonian Forest.

There is more consultation now with local authorities and others. Objections to planting proposals may be referred to the Forestry Commission's Regional Advisory Committees (RAC), and there are further appeals beyond that. Under a 1985 Act the FC is required to maintain a 'reasonable balance' between timber production and landscape and wildlife conservation. It is still too early to say how well the new arrangements will do that, and in the meantime we continue to live with the results of past practices. There will be a lot of scope for re-design in second rotations, but it could well be fifty years before we see the full benefits of the changes.

The Forestry Commission has long welcomed walkers in its forests. They have five Forest Parks (FP), the first dating back to l935 in Argyll, with others in the Trossachs, Glenmore, Glentrool and at Tummel, where marked paths and other facilities are provided for visitors. Some of the best wildlife sites have been designated as Forest Nature Reserves (FNRs), where conservation is the prime management objective. There are seventeen of them in Scotland, from the sand-dune forest of Culbin and the pine-forests of Glen Affric and the Black Wood of Rannoch, to smaller sites like the Dalavich oakwood at Loch Awe.

VOLUNTARY BODIES

Voluntary organisations too are widely involved throughout the country in managing reserves for protection and conservation objectives. There has been an enormous increase in their membership over the last decade, giving them clout in environmental lobbying. Some like the World Wide Fund for Nature (WWF), Friends of the Earth (FoE) and the Association for the Protection of Rural Scotland (APRS) work through fund-raising and education. Some, in addition to those primary objectives, have large land holdings bought with money raised by their members or by gifts, or by grants from government agencies and the National Heritage Memorial Fund (NHMF).

The largest of them is the National Trust for Scotland (NTS), which has 200,000 members. It holds over 100 properties covering 40,000 hectares (98,000 acres) across the country, from Fair Isle to Threave Castle beside the Solway, and from St Kilda to Provost Ross's House in Aberdeen. Some are huge, like Torridon with the beetling cliffs of Liathach; some are grand houses like Culzean with their imposing grounds; a few are domestic, like the crow-stepped houses of Culross.

The NTS is enabled by its legislation to hold property 'inalienably', meaning that it cannot be taken out of the Trust's care except by Act of Parliament. Its 1938 Act also enables it to enter into Conservation Agreements whereby owners of outstanding landscape voluntarily accept binding agreements, which are passed on to their successors, that nothing will be done to mar the property in future. Some 22,000 hectares (54,000 acres) of Scotland are protected in this way through more than 600 agreements.

For its wide tracts of mountain country the Trust's objectives are the same as for its other properties: to hand them on to the next generation in at least as good a condition as it found them. This has created some controversy about the extent to which access should be made easier by signposting and path building, as one of the Trust's many benefactors in the past, Percy Unna (see Chapter 17, Box 3), requested that the land should be kept as 'primitive' as possible, with unrestricted access but no new or improved paths. Little did he know the pressures that were to come and which have necessitated the elaborate and costly path building projects in Glen Coe and on Ben Lawers, but the Trust has done its best to maintain the wild quality of these areas, at least away from its visitor centres.

The Scottish Wildlife Trust (SWT), founded in l964, has a membership of nearly 10,000. It manages eighty-four reserves totalling about 17,000 hectares (42,000 acres), with a tenth of this owned and the rest leased or managed by agreement with the owners. They include Lochnagar and part of the island of Eigg, each at over 1,000 hectares (2,500 acres), with open access; and at the other extreme there is a tiny cave in the Trossachs used by hibernating bats which do not welcome any visitors.

Wildlife conservation is the primary objective of the reserves, most of which are SSSIs or NCR sites. Many of them require active management; without it, rhododendrons invade woodlands, thereby shading out the ground plants, and broken fences let in sheep and cattle. Members are encouraged to put on their wellington boots and help with the practical work, or explain to the public what can be seen from the visitor centres at, for example, the Falls of Clyde or the Loch of Lowes near Dunkeld.

The largest voluntary conservation body in Europe is the Royal Society for the Protection of Birds (RSPB), based at Sandy in Bedfordshire, which has over 830,000 members throughout the UK, including 40,000 north of the border. It manages forty-two reserves in Scotland totalling 30,000 hectares (74,000 acres), of which it owns about four-fifths. They range in size from a very extensive property in the Cairngorms running from Loch Garten with its ospreys through Glen Avon to the summit of Ben Macdui, down to the little island of Inchmickery in the Firth of Forth.

Although its emphasis is on birds the RSPB is interested nowadays in protecting whole habitats for nature conservation and brings a large professional staff to bear on the management of its property. Its reserve at Killiecrankie is probably more important for its plants than its birds. With the resources provided by its huge membership coupled with special appeals and grants from NHMF, the EC and government agencies, the RSPB has been able to deploy millions of pounds in land purchases and is likely to continue to do so whenever good bird areas come on to the market –

Native pinewoods in the Abernethy forest RSPB reserve.

although as the prices of sporting estates rise this may not be on the same scale as in recent years.

Operating on a much more modest scale are several trusts and societies devoted to safeguarding the natural beauty and wildlife of the countryside. Among them is the John Muir Trust which has 1,000 members and which takes its name from the Dunbar-born naturalist and writer who played a prominent part in the development of the United States National Parks at the turn of the century (see Dedication). The Trust owns more than 1,000 hectares (2,500 acres) in Knoydart which it aims to preserve in a wild state with no development and no promotion of access but with some rehabilitation of run-down countryside, including natural regeneration of trees.

Restoration of woodland lies at the heart of the work of the Lincolnshire-based Woodland Trust. It has fewer than 3,000 of its 65,000 members in Scotland where it owns twenty-five woods totalling 580 hectares (1,430 acres), the biggest of which is at Moncrieff Hill outside Perth. The Wildfowl and Wetlands Trust holds a 560–hectare (1,380 acres) Reserve at Caerlaverock on the Solway where 12,000 barnacle geese from Spitsbergen winter each year.

INTERNATIONAL PROTECTION

In addition to all these protective measures and systems operated within Scotland there are two designations which do not themselves add any safeguard except that, as an accolade, they give international recognition to the fact that an outstanding area has been adequately protected and can therefore cause opprobrium to be mobilised on a large scale if it is then unexpectedly threatened. World Heritage Sites (WHS) are designated by UNESCO; the St Kilda group of islands (NTS inalienable, NSA, NNR, SSSI) is the only site in Scotland so far, although others are being proposed.

European Diploma Sites are awarded by the Council of Europe and are not related solely to nature conservation. They are renewable every five years provided adequate protection still exists, and Scotland's two sites are Fair Isle (NTS) and Beinn Eighe (NCCS).

The international dimension is an important one,

Land at Torrin, Isle of Skye, purchased by the John Muir Trust.

reflecting as it does a greater world-wide understanding that life on earth is a fragile creation. We may all become affected by global warming and ozone depletion, but conservation of the nature around us – that is to say, the wise long-term management of all our natural resources in a sustainable way – starts at our front door, wherever we live on this planet. It is all inter-connected. As John Muir put it, 'Try to take anything out by itself and you find it hitched to everything else in the universe'.

*Glencoe: painting by
Horatio McCulloch—a
remote area that now has a
major road, a visitor centre
and millions of tourists each
year.*

196

The Playground of the Future

ROGER SMITH

Roger Smith is a freelance journalist who has specialised in environmental issues for many years and was the first editor of *Environment Now* magazine.

It was a glorious September day as the party climbed slowly up Carn a' Chlamain, above Glen Tilt, following a well-made path. Some were on ponies, some on foot. The men wore Highland dress or tweeds and most of them carried rifles. Bringing up the rear, two sturdy ponies carried essential provisions.

The lively young woman at the centre of the group was clearly enjoying herself. As every turn revealed a new view she exclaimed with delight, wishing that she had time to stop and sketch the beautiful landscape all around her. After a while they descended, eventually returning to Blair Castle by moonlight after a long but wonderfully rewarding day; and that evening the young woman recorded her impressions in purple prose in the diary that she kept for nearly seventy years.

The year was 1842 and the young woman was Queen Victoria, at the beginning of her long love affair with the Highlands of Scotland. On the way back from that first long trip she recorded that 'the English coast appeared terribly flat'. Further visits followed and in 1848 she and Prince Albert acquired Balmoral estate and built there the castle that we see today.

After Prince Albert died the Queen was persuaded to allow parts of her diaries to be published. The first volume, *Leaves from the Journal of Our Life in the Highlands*, appeared in 1867, with a further volume following in 1883. Both were bestsellers and both helped to draw still more people to Scotland to see the land that had so enchanted their sovereign.

Queen Victoria was thus a most definite influence on the development of the tourist industry, which she further encouraged by her regular attendance at the Braemar Highland Games. She was not, however, the first person to influence the development of the tourist industry.

In 1810 Sir Walter Scott published his epic poem, *The Lady of the Lake*. It was a tremendous success – the more so because it was set in a real landscape in the Trossachs which people could visit, thus bringing the characters closer to reality. *Rob Roy* (1817) and other novels had a similar effect. Scott's publisher, Robert Cadell, recorded that 'the whole country rang with praise of the poet. Crowds set off to view the scenery of Loch Katrine, and, as the book [*The Lady of the Lake*] came out just before the season for excursions, every house and inn was crammed with a constant succession of visitors.' It sounds like all of the Scottish Tourist Board's dreams come true!

Before Scott immortalised the area in prose and verse there had been other notable literary visitors, including William Wordsworth and his sister Dorothy, another inveterate diarist. They all swallowed the romantic legends of Rob Roy; I can't help wondering what the real Rob Roy MacGregor, who knew every cattle-thieving trick in the book, would have made of it all – or indeed of the newly opened Rob Roy Centre in Callander. I think the idea of taking as much money as possible from the tourists would have appealed to him.

There is no doubt in my mind that we can apply the word 'recreation' to the early tourists who followed Wordsworth, Scott and Queen Victoria to the Highlands. Until the coming of the railways in the latter part of the nineteenth century (see Chapter 11) their tours were adventurous and often quite strenuous. They wanted to experience 'rude Nature' and were prepared to rough it, to some extent, in order to do so. These early visitors were necessarily from the moneyed and leisured classes; the working-class folk got few holidays and would never have thought of using that time to visit the Trossachs or Deeside. But a pattern was being set, and into that pattern fell, quite neatly, inns and hostelries established long before on cattle-droving routes or as change-houses. Many of them still welcome visitors today.

Recreation can mean many things. To most people it probably means visiting, touring, seeing and enjoying. To others it means more active pursuits and we shall look closely at some of these later in this chapter. To a few, often accorded the epithet 'privileged', it means the pursuit of game on land, in the water and in the air.

'IF IT RUNS OR FLIES, SHOOT IT!'

The nineteenth century saw changes in both land

Queen Victoria and her Highland retainer John Brown, Balmoral 1863 by George Washington Wilson.

'Dead Stag and Eagles', sketch by Charles St John from a 'Tour of Sutherland'.

ownership and land-use in Scotland. The arrival of royalty on Deeside meant that the Highlands were 'in', as rich industrialists from the south found that they could buy land cheaply. At the same time, influenced by continental trends and by Prince Albert's German background, wild animals which had always been hunted for food were transformed into 'game' to be hunted for sport and trophies, with any food thus provided being only a secondary benefit.

There was no thought of profit in this. Landowners, whether of the aristocracy or the nouveau riche, invited their relatives, friends and associates to their estates to stalk and shoot almost anything that ran, flew or swam. In this they were aided by the knowledge, hillcraft and skill of their staff: the stalkers, keepers and ghillies who managed the game under the guidance of the estate factor.

Major landowners, such as the Duke of Sutherland, had their own private railway stations built as a condition of allowing the lines to cross their land. Many of these people took a keen interest in wildlife and would have been taken aback if you had suggested that

by their sporting efforts they were hastening the decline of a species (Box 1).

The obsession with hunting game led to many estates being completely barred to the public. Sir George Bullough and his family, for example, purchased the Inner Hebridean island of Rhum and ran it as a sealed estate with no uninvited visitors allowed for many years. He built there the extraordinary and extravagant Kinloch Castle and paid his workers (many of whom came from Lancashire) extra to wear the kilt.

Right up to 1945 there were problems of access to the land on the big sporting estates. In more recent years there has been a slightly uneasy truce with mountaineers and ramblers over access, but there are signs that this relationship is now breaking down (see below FREEDOM TO ROAM). Faced with the problem of remaining financially viable many estates are diversifying into different types of game shooting and are consequently starting to try to restrict public access for longer periods of the year.

The reasons for this are self-evident. Sportsmen from other countries, notably Germany and Belgium, will

1. CHARLES ST JOHN (1809–56)

Charles St John typifies the Victorian sportsman/ naturalist. We know more about him than about most of his contemporaries because of three fine books he wrote, of which the best known is *The Wild Sports and Natural History of the Highlands*. The title gives a clue to the approach favoured in those days, a century and a half ago.

St John lived in Scotland from 1833 to 1853; during that time he toured the Highlands extensively, recording what he saw in his detailed notebooks which give us an accurate picture of the natural history of the Highlands in the mid nineteenth century.

But, in common with others of his time, St John saw nothing wrong in pursuing wildlife as well as recording and writing about it. Any bird of prey was fair game for the gun. Both golden and white-tailed eagles were especially prized, as were the osprey and peregrine. Eggs of all these birds were commonly taken for collections.

It is fascinating to imagine what Charles St John might think if he returned today. He would probably be dismayed by the loss of species from the Highlands and surprised at the measures required to protect those that remain. If he and his fellow hunters of the nineteenth century had been equipped with cameras instead of guns we might enjoy a much richer wildlife today.

pay large sums of money for the right 'bag'. On some estates it is said that a fine stag will now fetch up to £30,000 – an almost tenfold increase over the last decade. According to one report, in 1989 a million pheasants, 300,000 grouse and over 60,000 deer were shot as part of an industry that is worth about £30 million to the estates. Fishing is also extremely valuable to many estates and choice 'beats' on salmon and trout rivers change hands for very large sums.

Without this income large estates would struggle to survive. They are charged rates for shooting and have had to pay the community charge for their employees. Nevertheless the increased amount that sportsmen are willing to pay has led to estate land values rocketing by 200 per cent in under five years. We have come full circle: a Highland estate is once again 'the thing to have', but the new owners are much more varied than previously.

They may be pop stars, sportsmen (of other kinds), businessmen or rich people from abroad. Scotland is one of the very few countries with no restrictions on land purchase by foreign nationals and we have seen large areas bought by Arab royalty, European aristocrats and companies registered in Liechtenstein, the Virgin Islands or other tax havens. Many of these people have no knowledge of Scottish culture or traditions of public access and, although they may bring money in, they also want to keep the public out.

Those who shoot, hunt and fish certainly see themselves as taking their recreation in the Scottish countryside. Whether you regard it as sport to shoot driven birds reared for the purpose or wild deer bred on the hill is a matter of individual taste. I personally find it strange that this sport is valued so highly in monetary terms. While it is, much of Highland Scotland will continue to be dominated by large sporting estates and those estates will want to ensure that the profits derived from the recreation of their owners and clients is paramount; this aim is sure to come into conflict with other, more passive, recreational pursuits.

UPWARDLY MOBILE

Mountaineering in Scotland will always be associated

2. SIR HUGH MUNRO (1856–1919)

Sir Hugh Thomas Munro, Bart, the man who gave his name to Scotland's 3,000 ft (914 m) mountains, was born into a comfortable life as the son of Sir Campbell Munro of Lindertis, the eldest of nine children. He was a great traveller and collector from childhood and began mountaineering while still a student at Stuttgart in Germany. After a spell in business in London he went to Africa and saw action in the Basuto war. He then returned to manage and, in time, inherit the family estates at Kirriemuir in Angus.

Munro was a founder member of the Scottish Mountaineering Club in 1889, by which time he was already familiar with the Scottish hills; he was also aware that there were far more hills over the 3,000 foot mark than had previously been recognised. His list of 'Munros' (some 277) appeared in the second edition of the SMC journal in 1891.

He has given us all a century of fun in trying to climb all the hills he listed – a list which many people feel should never have been amended, as it has been over the years. The difficulty presented by the challenge of climbing all the Munros is shown by the fact that he failed in this goal himself, never managing to scale the 'Inaccessible Pinnacle' on Skye, despite several attempts. He died of pneumonia at the age of sixty-three and is buried on the family estate.

Sir Hugh Munro (1856–1919)

199

Mountaineers on Beinn Eighe look across to Liathac

with the name of Sir Hugh Munro – the man who, in 1891, gave his name to the list of Scottish mountains which top 3,000 feet (914 metres) in height (Box 2).

The first 'Munroist' was the Revd Aeneas Robertson, who completed the list with the ascent of the summit of Meall Dearg above Glencoe in 1901. Robertson was a fine all-round mountaineer and a great hill man. He spoke Gaelic and often stayed with shepherds and keepers in remote areas. He was also an accomplished photographer at a time when cameras were heavy and difficult to use in the mountains, and he was very knowledgeable about old tracks, drove roads and the like.

In the days of Munro and Robertson mountaineering was a gentleman's pursuit. The Scottish Mountaineering Club, founded in 1889, organised yachting trips to Skye for its early meetings. Most of its early members were professional people and some, like Hugh Munro, were titled. These were people with leisure time at their disposal – Aeneas Robertson could take two months off from his Rannoch parish, time which he used to the full in the hills.

Things began to change after the First World War; the youth hostels movement arrived in Scotland in 1931, providing inexpensive accommodation in the mountain areas, and there were hiking clubs as well. But it was the Depression which brought the most profound change. The hills became not just a hobby but a way of escaping the poverty and slums of the cities. By that time many of the 'classic' routes on Scottish mountains had been climbed by great pioneers such as W. W. Naismith, Harold Raeburn and Norman Collie; Shadbolt and McLaren traversed the Cuillin ridge on Skye in 1911, taking fifteen hours.

But the new breed of climbers were less interested in first ascents than in simply being outdoors, almost regardless of the location.

Since 1945 mountaineering and hillwalking in Scotland have become totally egalitarian pastimes, enjoyed by countless thousands of people from all over Britain and abroad. Modern road and rail communications are vastly better than they were and today few areas can be classed as 'remote'. The Munros have remained under assault, with almost a thousand people now claiming to have completed ascents of all of them.

Climbing has also reached out to new frontiers; climbs of ever greater severity have been put up in Glencoe, in the Cairngorms, on Ben Nevis and elsewhere, with completely new faces such as Sron Ulladale on Harris being opened up. However, the vast majority of hill-goers are content with humbler achievements. They may climb ten or twenty Scottish hills; they may climb one or indeed none at all, being content with walking the superb rights of way through the glens. The West Highland Way and the Southern Upland Way attract large numbers of walkers – as well as competitive races and erosion! Scotland has thus far proved capable of accommodating them all, whatever their desires or aspirations.

Scotland is a country which, despite its relatively small size, truly has something for everyone. People have come to expect that they can take their recreation in Scotland's hills and glens at most times of the year, untrammelled by restrictions. But that situation is at present showing signs of coming under stress. As ever, economics are the root of the problem. Hillwalkers and climbers do not pay directly for their recreation (although it can be argued that through their taxation they contribute via such bodies as the Countryside Commission for Scotland). Many put something back in voluntary labour or through schemes financed by bodies of which they are members, such as the Mountaineering Council for Scotland, the National Trust for Scotland, Scottish Conservation Projects and so on. There have been suggestions of a 'boot tax'; indeed the purchase of Ladhar Bheinn, the fine west coast Munro, by the John Muir Trust was partly funded through equipment sales.

In the 1980s extensive research and survey work on mountain footpaths in Scotland was carried out, principally by Dr Bob Aitken on a contract awarded by the CCS. His report, *Scottish Mountain Footpaths*, is a classic document which starkly outlines the problems before us. As a result of this pioneering work, for which the CCS must take much credit, we have seen the creation of 'Pathcraft', Scotland's first full-time professional pathwork specialists. There is talk of £2 million being needed for essential path maintenance. Within the CCS there is a belief that many more Pathcraft-type operations are needed, even to hold the problem at its present level.

Restrictions on access, not for shooting or stalking but for conservation purposes, are being seriously considered for certain areas. It is all a far cry from the days of Hugh Munro and Aeneas Robertson, but it is a reflection on the very heavy recreational use of our hills today – a use which has arisen from their relative ease of access.

FREEDOM TO ROAM

The idea of free and open access to the mountains is relatively new, born of the egalitarianism of post-war Britain in the 1940s. Before the Second World War there had been considerable obstacles to freedom of

Rock climbing continues to grow in popularity

access in Scotland. Such incidents as the Battle of Glen Tilt in 1847 and the lawsuit over Jock's Road in Angus in 1886 are well documented. The Jock's Road case arose after a visit by a deputation from the Scottish Rights of Way Society, a body founded in 1845 as the Edinburgh Association for the Protection of Public Rights of Roadway in Scotland.

This society has done much to ensure that ancient rights of way have remained open and freely walkable and still pursues the same objectives today. It was especially active in the 1880s, the decade which also saw the first attempt to legislate for 'freedom to roam'. This came in the shape of a parliamentary Bill introduced by James Bryce, Liberal MP for South Aberdeen, a very capable mountaineer with world-wide experience and the first president of the Cairngorm Club. For twenty years Bryce repeatedly strove to press the case for free access to the hills. He never succeeded in gaining sufficient Parliamentary time, not least because the opposition was strong and well organised. The access movement in England and Wales finally achieved limited success with the National Parks Act 1949, but

A climber heads for the Skye ridge.

the issue of Scotland was put to one side (see Chapter 16).

In the absence of legislation however a complementary atmosphere of mutual understanding and tolerance developed between walkers and landowners. This itself was a substantial step forward from the atmosphere of the 1920s, when stalwarts such as Ernest Baker risked prosecution or even worse in their widespread 'stravaiging'. Baker's book, *The Highlands with Rope and Rucksack* (republished in 1942 as *The Forbidden Land*), clearly shows what a grip the great sporting estates had at that time. Mountaineers and walkers were barely tolerated and some areas were effectively closed off to all access.

After 1945 public opinion would not accept such a situation. National Parks were being set up in England and Wales and many more people wanted the simple free recreation of walking the hills and glens, which after all represented what they had fought and risked their lives for in six years of war. The National Trust for Scotland, established only in 1931, had within six years acquired Glencoe, largely through the efforts of Arthur Russell, their law agent (who was also secretary of the Scottish Rights of Way Society for many years), and of

Percy Unna, president of the Scottish Mountaineering Club, who organised the donation of funds by the mountaineering fraternity and also gave substantial sums himself to aid the acquisition not just of Glencoe but later of Kintail, Ben Lawers and Torridon (Box 3).

Unlike England and Wales, where the situation regarding access is closely controlled by the law, the mutual tolerance evident in Scotland in recent years is based on the *de facto* not the *de jure* position. Contrary to popular belief there is a law of trespass in Scotland; but trespass itself – the act of going on to another person's land – carries no penalty. Either damage or persistent nuisance must be proved legally and, as far as hillwalkers or others taking informal recreation are concerned, the position is largely untested in the courts.

Those who regularly walk the hills of Scotland have accepted the need for restraint during the peak shooting season from mid-August to mid-October. Outwith that period it has been generally felt that access should be given. This is the basis on which *Heading for the Scottish Hills*, a book published jointly by the Mountaineering Council of Scotland and the Scottish Landowners' Federation, was prepared. During the peak shooting season, it asks people going to the hills to check with the estate first to see if shooting is in progress or is planned and to be prepared to alter their route if necessary. Most landowners have, in turn, recognised that many people legitimately wish to take their recreation in the countryside and have placed few obstacles in their way.

Regrettably there are currently signs that the situation is deteriorating; there have been attempts to restrict access during the deer-calving season from mid-May to late June – one of the very best times of the year for walking. It is a development deeply resented by hill-walkers. There is no real evidence of walkers causing significant disturbance to calving hinds.

On some estates, notices have been put up asking people to keep off the land from 1 July through to February because of shooting. The number of notices which could be described as intimidatory, rather than informative, is certainly increasing. Many of these are wrongly worded and deliberately misleading, claiming a false legal status by using phrases such as 'Official Route', which are meaningless in law.

Most people would prefer the present situation of mutual tolerance and understanding to continue. Few want legislation, although this is the declared aim of the Ramblers' Association, both nationally and in Scotland. The Scottish Landowners' Federation is against such legislation, fearing it would lead to greater confrontation. The Federation's convenor, Patrick Gordon-Duff-Pennington, has said that 'on the day that the people of Scotland do not feel free to go to the hills, seas and islands, Scotland is finished'. It will be sad indeed if the 1990s turn out to be a decade of conflict on Scotland's hills – especially as the diversity of recreational use is increasing steadily.

SKISTERS TO PISTERS

Skiing in Scotland is far from being a new sport. The Scottish Ski Club (SSC) was formed as far back as November 1907, although at that time and for some years thereafter cross-country skiing was simply used as a practical means of getting about in the mountains during winter. Downhill or 'piste' skiing for recreational purposes and competitive sport had to await the development of reliable ski-tows. The Scottish Ski Club lay dormant from 1918 to 1929 when it was reformed. As with walking and climbing, access had been transformed by the advent of the popular motor car and ways were soon found of attaching skis to the roof or running board. Equipment too was much improved, with better and lighter skis and clothing being developed in the Alps.

There was still much ski-touring but informal races were soon introduced, using a mass start system which became known as 'the geschmozzle' because of the frequent collisions and mix-ups which occurred on the way down the hill. A hut was erected in 1932 on the

Skiers queue for the lift at Aonach Mor, Fort William.

flanks of Beinn Ghlas above Loch Tay at a height of 2,300 ft (690 m) and there, two years later, the SSC organised its first slalom race.

After the war, demand for uplift facilities grew steadily. The hut on Beinn Ghlas was renovated and expanded and by 1953 there were rope-tows running there and at Cairnwell. The Killin skiers also had the use of a 'weasel', a tracked vehicle which took them uphill for the ski down. But the focus was shifting away from Killin to three other areas where energetic people were preparing the ground for the commercial skiing which we know today – although they could not have foreseen either the huge commercial growth which occurred or the environmental problems which have resulted.

By the beginning of the 1960s there were tows in Glencoe, Glenshee (Cairnwell and Carn an Tuirc) and on Cairngorm; the last named was the result of many years of work behind the scenes leading to the formation of the Cairngorm Winter Sports Development Board. At this time the ski clubs were still the prime movers, but things were beginning to change as the numbers wanting to ski grew and the sport changed from being the province of enthusiasts to becoming a commercial winter sports operation. Companies were set up and an important development was the creation of the Highlands and Islands Development Board (HIDB) in 1965. The HIDB was able to grant-aid skiing developments and became even more closely involved when it took over the ownership of ground at Cairngorm from the Forestry Commission in the early 1970s.

The effort put in by those developing skiing in Scotland was truly heroic and the obstacles they had to overcome were formidable. In the early days however, there was little or no attention paid to environmental considerations. The environmental movement in Scot-

Skiers on Aonach Mor summit, Ben Nevis range, Fort William.

land was small and the overriding drive was for the provision of facilities for skiers. This was also seen at the Hillend artificial ski slope in the Pentland Hills just outside Edinburgh. When it was opened in 1966 it was the longest artificial ski slope in Europe. In the twenty-five years since then it has provided tremendous enjoyment and excellent training for thousands of youngsters, but close examination of the area reveals a serious lack of attention to good housekeeping in the environmental sense.

The same applied at Cairngorm and Glenshee in particular (the other developments at Glencoe and later at the Lecht are smaller in scale and have had less impact). By the end of the 1970s there was growing concern over the erosion and scarring of the landscape, the spread of mechanical facilities and buildings and the increased ease of access into sensitive nature areas provided by ski-roads and chairlifts.

Matters came to a head with the application for a very large-scale development into the northern corries of Cairngorm in 1981. Uplift facilities were proposed for Coire an t'Sneachda, Coire an Lochain and Lurcher's Gully, with either a road or chairlifts across the mouths of these superb corries. For almost the first time the environmental movement in Scotland united in opposition. The case went to a public inquiry at which the developers were surprised to find the conservationists so well organised. The inquiry reporter came down firmly on the side of conservation and in December 1982 the then Secretary of State for Scotland, George Younger, confirmed the reporter's decision: the development proposals were rejected.

The last year of the decade saw two significant developments. A new ski centre opened on Aonach Mor, near Fort William. For the first time environmental considerations were fully taken into account and it is generally agreed that the developers, Nevis Range, have done all they could to minimise the environmental impact of the scheme. Cables and power lines have all been buried, and during construction everything was taken up by helicopter, no vehicles being allowed on the hill. The car park is low down in a forest setting and access to the main slopes and the restaurant is by gondola, another first for Scotland. The Aonach Mor development has set the standard which must now be followed by all other ski centres in Scotland.

At the end of 1989 there was a fresh proposal for skiing development and road access into Lurcher's Gully. Once again the environmental movement came together forcefully; a 'Save the Cairngorms Campaign' was set up and both government agencies, the NCC and the CCS, objected to the development. During the period available for public consultation over 7,000 letters of objection were received. In June 1990 the then Secretary of State, Malcolm Rifkind, turned the project down.

In many ways Lurcher's Gully highlights the dilemma which faces skiing in Scotland today. The sport has enjoyed rapid growth and has brought considerable economic income into areas which previously lacked it, Strathspey in particular. However skiing faces two major problems; it is always going to demand development in environmentally sensitive areas and it relies on an increasingly unreliable snow fall. In recent winters, snow fall has been erratic and the regular intrusion of warm periods into the normal pattern of winter weather has prevented the consolidation of the snowpack. Some ski centres have only been able to operate at anything like full capacity for six weeks, which is not enough to ensure commercial survival. It could be said, with some truth, that people ski in Scotland despite the climate not because of it.

It is essential that skiing organisations and environmental bodies get together and work something out. Both sides may have to compromise but it would be worth it to see an end to the bitterness and entrenched positions of the last decade. There have undoubtedly been ski developments which should not have been permitted (Glas Maol for one) and there have been others which were perhaps unnecessarily opposed. Skiing brings benefits but skiers are still only a minority of those who take their recreation in the Scottish hills and they should moderate their demands accordingly.

OTHER RECREATIONS

Hill running has grown in Scotland from very small beginnings to a sport with a full calendar and a wide variety of races – over seventy a year; these range from Black Meldon (just one mile or 1.6 km long, taking about eight minutes) to the West Highland Way Race (from Milngavie to Fort William, a distance of 95 miles (152 km), for which the winning record stands at fifteen hours).

Ski mountaineering on Mamore mountains, Glen Nevis.

An offshoot of hill running is 'mountain marathoning' which developed out of orienteering, the competitive navigational sport which started in Scandinavia between the wars. The first attempts to develop the sport in Scotland were in the 1960s, led by the universities and athletic clubs. There is now a full calendar of events at every level from club to championship every year.

There are many charity walks and climbs in Scotland each year. The question of mass participation events arouses mixed feelings, for while the aim is often admirable the impact of large numbers of people crossing sensitive ground within a concentrated period of time can be serious. The National Trust for Scotland has now decided that the annual climb of Ben Lomond, held to benefit the Royal Commonwealth Society for

Mountain bikers walking into a steep, pathless area of mountainside.

the Blind, can no longer take place. This is part of a policy to discourage such events on mountains owned by the Trust because of the path erosion and wildlife disturbance which may result.

There are also pastimes where considerable motive power is required; people now use wings, engines, paddles, paws or hooves. There seems to be no end to the ingenuity that people have shown in their determined pursuit of recreation. Paragliding, where a parachute is used to rise up over the hills, is a newcomer to the scene, as is hang gliding, where a fixed wing sail is used to ride the wind thermals. One of the big centres for hang gliding is at the Cairnwell near Braemar, where the chairlift for skiers is much appreciated by the gliders.

WHEEL POWER

Two-wheeled recreation is the sport that is making greatest inroads into the hills at present and causing the most concern. There is a long tradition of 'rough stuff' cycling in Scotland, using routes such as the Lairig Ghru through the Cairngorms; this pass rises to 2,700 ft (820 m) and gets pretty rough in places. The Scottish

Rights of Way Society signs at either end of the pass do say 'unsuitable for cycles' but this doesn't deter real rough-stuff enthusiasts for one minute. This hardy fellowship of riders go into the hills alone or in small groups; they enjoy and respect the solitude and wildness of the hills and expect no favours or facilities.

The same cannot be said for their newest cousins, the mountain-bike fraternity. This new sport is posing very real problems for the countryside, for landowners and for the conservation agencies. When these bikes are used on good tracks or forest roads they present few problems; but when they are used on the paths and grassy slopes of the open hill, especially in numbers, then there is a genuine cause for concern over the erosion damage they can cause. There are also issues related to disturbance of stock, to estate work and to other countryside users.

A recent book called *Mountain Biking in the Scottish Highlands* listed a number of routes, including a ride through Glen Nevis, which is certainly not a place nor environment where mountain bikes should be allowed in any numbers. The stretch between the road end and Steall through the gorge is a narrow and well-used footpath which is to my mind totally unsuitable for

Mountain biker on eroded footpath, Ben Nevis.

bikes of any kind. The guide itself describes the route as 'rocky, steep and almost totally unrideable'. So why encourage its use?

There is a warning for us from the USA where mountain bikes are the centre of great controversy. In California routes have been closed and radar guns have been brought in to try to curb reckless riding and to protect walkers and horse riders. There have been calls to ban these bikes altogether from some parts of the American countryside.

BIG BUSINESS IN THE PLAYGROUND

Tourism is big business in Scotland. According to the Scottish Tourist Board it is now 'Scotland's largest industry, sustaining 150,000 jobs and generating £1.7 billion in the economy'. But is that all good news? Is the expansion of tourism something we can afford to sustain indefinitely? How much more can, or should, Scotland take?

There are more large developments being planned in the Scottish countryside than ever before. Most have at least some recreational aspect built into them; golf in particular is experiencing a boom. A survey by the Association for the Protection of Rural Scotland revealed the startling total of 91 new golf courses in various stages of planning or development.

All these proposals use substantial amounts of land. In some cases the land was lying fallow, waiting to be used. In many cases however the proposed developments would take out land presently zoned for agriculture, and – as at Archerfield in East Lothian, St Cyrus on the east coast, and the Kilpatrick Hills west of Glasgow – there has been considerable local opposition.

Many of these developments have an element of housing attached, usually highly priced, and most are aimed at the top end of the market. Naturally such developments require large investments and frequently the capital is sourced abroad, from people who have little or no knowledge of Scotland, its heritage or traditions.

Does that matter? It need not, provided that quality is maintained and the developments provide facilities that are genuinely needed and which fit into the local economy. Sadly, too many of them fail to meet these standards. Developments are out of scale with their surroundings – sometimes grossly so – or are so highly priced as to be out of reach of local people. Several have

Salmon fisherman on the river Spey, Grantown on Spey.

been found to rest on flimsy financial support which has disappeared when objections were raised.

Such objections come from well-organised local pressure groups, from established environmental bodies, from local councils: but very rarely from the Scottish Tourist Board whose role in all this presents curious anomalies. The Board's remit is to promote and encourage tourism in Scotland, which it has done so successfully that it can proclaim tourism as 'Scotland's largest industry'.

But should the STB not have an equal role in helping to conserve the scenery, landscape, wildlife and history which is the very basis of the industry that it promotes? Tourism is important to Scotland, but Scotland is far more important to tourism. Untrammelled development – much of it enthusiastically supported by STB – is biting into the very resource that tourism needs most. We must have better central planning and the STB must surely adopt a broader environmental stance.

Let it contemplate the wise words of the Prince of Wales:

I am sure that future generations will not measure our success by the number of visitors who can be encouraged to pass through such an area, but by the state of health of these special parts of our Scottish heritage.

CONCLUSION

No one can predict what will happen to recreation in Scotland over the next twenty-five years, but we should certainly be thinking about it and deciding what we want the future to hold for our children and grandchildren. Do we want them to know the joy of walking the wild places without another soul in sight? Do we want them to be able to fish for trout and salmon in clear unpolluted lochs, enjoying the view of hills which are unmarked by bulldozed tracks, ski-tows or any other intrusive developments? Or will we leave to them only a regimented countryside, formalised into 'recreation areas' where they may have to apply for a permit to climb, walk, ski or fish? It would be foolish to think that this could not happen in Scotland; it has already started to happen in other places.

In the American National Parks permits for wild camping and even for 'off-trail' walking have been required for years. In England the huge SSSI of Rainham Marshes in Essex may be sacrificed for the development of a film studio complex and associated theme park development.

There is an even worse case happening in Spain right now: the Coto Donana, long acknowledged as one of the world's great wildlife areas, is under severe threat from tourist development. It is home to thousands of flamingos, to Spanish imperial eagles, to deer, wild boar, herons, spoonbills and avocets. If the development goes ahead the demand for water to service the tourist complexes will lower the water table and cause the drainage and destruction of the irreplaceable wetlands which form the heart of the area.

Disasters on this scale have not yet happened in Scotland, although some would argue that the losses sustained in the Flow Country come close to it (see Chapter 5). The vital lesson is that it need not happen here. We must learn from our own mistakes and those of other countries, and we must plan the future of our

own land using the wisest heads that we have.

We must not let vast areas of Scotland be closed off for months of the year for the 'sporting pursuits' of a selfish and mostly wealthy few. We must not let the lure of short-term profit and the blandishments of 'planning gain' blind us to the long-term consequences of in-

Canoeing on the West coast of Scotland.

3. PERCY UNNA (1878–1950)

Mountaineers and all those who love the grandeur of the Scottish hills owe a great debt to Percy Unna, a civil servant of Danish parentage; but the debt has only come to light in recent years. In 1937 he was President of the Scottish Mountaineering Club (SMC) when it was learned that the 11,600 acres (4,700 ha) of Dalness Forest, in Glencoe, was for sale. Unna took the initiative and organised an appeal among all the mountaineering clubs in Britain to raise the purchase price of £9,000 so that the National Trust for Scotland (NTS) could acquire the land. He gave most of the money anonymously himself.

In providing the funds to purchase Glencoe, Unna also put before the Trust a set of management guidelines which both he and the SMC wished to be followed. These stipulated that there should be no new paths made, no shooting for sport, and the very minimum of man-made structures; and that generally the hills were not to be made easier or safer in any way. Unna also provided most of the funds for the NTS to purchase Kintail in 1943, and money from the Mountainous Country Fund went towards the purchases of Ben Lawers, Torridon and Goatfell on Arran.

Many people feel that Unna was a true visionary who foresaw the great increase in recreational pressure which was to come and wished to conserve some areas in as natural a state as possible by laying down guidelines for their future management. The National Trust for Scotland has interpreted these guidelines somewhat liberally in the years since Unna's death, making paths and building bridges in Glencoe and putting up visitor centres, both in Glencoe and on the flanks of Ben Lawers, and it has been strongly criticised for doing so.

The arguments will surely continue but there can be no doubt that without Percy Unna's farsightedness and generosity it would have been extremely difficult, if not impossible, for these magnificent mountain areas to have been acquired and safeguarded for the benefit of the nation.

Percy Unna (1878–1950) laid down the 'Unna Rules' in order to preserve the wildness of the mountain land which he donated to the nation.

*Sailing off the coast of Mull
in the Western Isles*

appropriate development, whether it be in a city green belt or in the heart of the Cairngorms.

We must develop more effective ways of planning on a national as well as a local scale. Our present jumble of countryside designations and protected areas is a misunderstood and mistrusted mess (see Chapter 16). It must be simplified and applied selectively, but rigorously when necessary.

The next decade will be critical for the future of recreation in Scotland. The new Scottish Natural Heritage agency, to be formed in 1992, will combine the roles of the Nature Conservancy Council for Scotland and the Countryside Commission for Scotland and will have a very important role to play. But it is only one player on a stage where there are already rather too many agencies taking bit-parts and confusing the plot.

The number of agencies and organisations with some say in what goes on in the countryside is alarming (see Chapter 16). There are development agencies, enterprise boards, tourist boards, agricultural bodies, local authorities, conservation groups, recreational bodies, fisheries boards, forestry organisations, water authorities, parks, councils for this and that, and dozens more. Nobody is pulling them all together – yet there is a desperate need for them all to work together towards the common good. How often in recent years have we seen two government agencies with different agendas fighting each other over this or that development – and using taxpayers' money to do so? It is rarely necessary and far too often what is at stake is entrenched pride or self-esteem rather than any real issue.

The solution must lie in partnership and co-operation rather than separatism and conflict; a balanced

approach and not rampant development or rigid sterilisation or the slapping of designations on every green area in the land. The countryside belongs to us all and we must work together to ensure its healthy future – not just for our unparalleled richness of wildlife but also for the people who live and work in the countryside and for those of us who wish to take peaceful recreation there. In Scotland we have a majestic and magnificent country of which we should all be proud; it deserves the highest standards of wise conservation and long-term planning that we can give it.

Above all, we must all become less selfish. Whether our chosen recreation is walking, climbing, skiing, sailing, paragliding, shooting, fishing or dog sledging, we cannot expect exclusive use of any part of the Scottish countryside. We must all be prepared to give up a little in order to gain a lot. We all need recreation in the best sense of the word, be we the humblest in the land or the highest born. Prince Charles clearly has the same feel for the land as did his great-great-grandmother, Queen Victoria. Speaking of tourism in Scotland, he said recently:

> We need to spend a bit more time thinking about the long term and about what our grandchildren will feel about what we do. You see so many results of rapid development, taking the cheapest option, which turn out to be disastrous or leave behind an appalling legacy which we have to clear up. In the future, we should be thinking many years ahead.

For the sake of Scotland's countryside and all those who wish to take recreation there, that thinking about the future must start now.

*The view from Bonnie
Prince Charlie's Cairn,
Arisaig, Lochaber.*

Bibliography
Books for further reading

Bass, Rick, *Oil Notes*, London, Fontana, 1989.

Baxter, Colin and Goodier, Rawdon, *The Cairngorms*, Lanark, Colin Baxter Photography, 1990.

Blamey, Marjorie and Grey-Wilson, Christopher, *The Illustrated Flora of Britain and Northern Europe*, London, Hodder and Stoughton, 1989.

Boyd, J. Morton, *The Hebrides: a natural history*, London, Collins, 1990.

Burnett, John H., *The Vegetation of Scotland*, Edinburgh, Oliver and Boyd, 1964.

Cameron, A. D., *Go listen to the crofters*, Stornoway, Acair, 1986.

Clapperton, C. M. (ed), *Scotland: A New Study*, Newton Abbot, David and Charles, 1983.

Coppock, J. T., *An Agricultural Atlas of Scotland*, Edinburgh, John Donald, 1976.

Corbet, G. B. and Harris, S. (eds), *The Handbook of British Mammals*, 3rd edn, Oxford, Blackwell, 1990.

Craig, G. Y. (ed), *The Geology of Scotland*, 3rd edn, Edinburgh, Scottish Academic Press, 1990.

Cramp, S. (ed), *Handbook of the Birds of Europe, the Middle East and North Africa, the Birds of the Western Paleartic*, Oxford University Press, 1988.

Crawford, B. E., *Scandinavian Scotland*, Leicester University Press, 1987.

Donaldson, Gordon, *Scotland: the making of the kingdom*, In: Duncan, A. A. M. (ed), *The Edinburgh History of Scotland, Vol 1*, Edinburgh, Mercat Press, 1978.

Emery, Malcolm, *Promoting Nature in Cities and Towns*, London, Croom Helm, 1986.

Emmet, A., Maitland and Heath, John (eds), *The Moths and Butterflies of Great Britain and Ireland* vol 7, part 1 – The Butterflies, Colchester, Harley Books, 1987.

Fenton, A., *Scottish Country Life*, Edinburgh, John Donald, 1989.

Fraser Darling, F. and Boyd, J. Morton, *Natural History in the Highlands and Islands*, London, Collins, 1964.

Gordon, George and Dicks, Brian (eds), *Scottish Urban History*, Aberdeen, Aberdeen University Press, 1983.

Grant, J. S., *The Part-time holding – an island experience*, Coulnakyle, Nethy Bridge, Inverness-shire, The Arkleton Trust, 1983.

Grigor, I. F., *Mightier than a lord*, Stonoway, Acair, 1979.

Haldane, A. R. B., *New Ways Through the Glen*, Edinburgh, Nelson, 1962.

Halliday, Fred (ed), *Wildlife of Scotland*, London, Macmillan/SWT, 1979.

Halliday, Geoffrey and Malloch, Andrew (eds), *Wild Flowers and their Habitats in Britain and Northern Europe*, London, Peter Lowe, 1981.

Hawthorn, J., Reid, J. M. and Wyllie, G. A. P., *Scotland's Energy Future*, Royal Society of Edinburgh, 1987.

Hetherington, Alastair, *Highlands and Islands: a Generation of Progress*, Aberdeen University Press, 1990.

Hume, John R., *The Industrial Archaeology of Scotland*, vols 1 and 2, London, B. T. Batsford, 1976 and 1977.

Lindsay, Jean, *The Canals of Scotland*, Newton Abbot, David and Charles, 1968.

Lister-Kaye, John, *The Seeing Eye: Notes of a Highland Naturalist*, London, Allen Lane, 1980.

Lythe, S. G. E. and Butt, J., *An Economic History, 1100–1939*, London, 1975.

MacLean, M. and Carrell, C. (eds), *As an fhearann (From the Land): Clearance, Conflict and Crofting*, Stornoway, An Lanntair/Third Eye, 1986.

MacPhail, I. M. M., *The Crofters' Wars*, Stornoway, Acair, 1989.

Maitland, Peter S., *The Ecology of Scotland's Largest Lochs: Lomond, Awe, Ness, Morar and Shiel*, The Hague, Junk, 1981.

Morrison, Ian, *Landscape with Lake Dwellings*, Edinburgh University Press, 1985.

Murray, W. H., *Scotland's Mountains*, Glasgow, Scottish Mountaineering Trust, 1987.

Nature Conservancy Council, *Nature Conservation in Great Britain*, Northminster House, Peterborough, 1984.

Nature Conservancy Council, *Nature Conservation and Afforestation in Britain*, Northminster House, Peterborough, 1986.

Nethersole-Thompson, D. and Watson, A., *The Cairngorms: Their Natural History and Scenery*, Perth, Melven Press, 1981.

Payne, Madge, *Gardening for Butterflies*, Loughborough, British Butterfly Conservation Society, 1987.

Piggott, S., *Scotland Before History*, Edinburgh, Polygon, 1990.

Ratcliffe, Derek, *The Peregrine Falcon*, Calton, Poyser, 1980.

Ratcliffe, Derek, *Highland Flora*, Inverness, Highlands and Islands Development Board, 1977.

Raven, John and Walters, Max, (*New Naturalist* series) *Mountain Flowers*, 2nd edn, London, Collins, 1984.

Ritchie, G. and A., *Scotland: Archaeology and Early History*, Edinburgh University Press, 1991.

Scroggie, Sydney, *The Cairngorms Scene and Unseen*, Glasgow, Scottish Mountaineering Trust, 1989.

Simpson, Myrtle, *Skisters: The Story of Scottish Skiing*, Carrbridge, Landmark Press, 1982.

Sissons, J. B., *The Evolution of Scotland's Scenery*, Edinburgh, Oliver and Boyd, 1967.

Stephen, David, *Living with Wildlife*, Edinburgh, Canongate Publishing, 1989.

Steven, Campbell, *The Story of Scotland's Hills*, London, Robert Hale, 1975.

Steven, H. M. and Carlisle, A., *The Native Pinewoods of Scotland*, Edinburgh, Oliver and Boyd, 1959.

Sutcliffe, A. J., *On the Track of Ice Age Mammals*, London, British Museum (Natural History), 1985.

Thom, V. M., *Birds in Scotland*, Calton, Poyser, 1986.

Thomas, Jeremy A., *The Hamlyn Guide to Butterflies of the British Isles*, London, Hamlyn Publishing Group Ltd, 1986.

Thomson, George, *The Butterflies of Scotland*, London, Croom Helm Ltd, 1980.

Timperley, L. R., *Directory of Landownership in Scotland c.1700*, Edinburgh, Scottish Record Society, 1976.

Twidell, J. W., *et al*, *Energy for Rural and Island Communities*, a series of Proceedings in four volumes, Oxford, Pergammon Press, 1981, 1983, 1985, 1987 and In: *Journal of Wind and Solar Technology*, January, Oxford, Pergammon Press, 1990.

White, Graham, (ed), *The Scottish Environmental Handbook*, Edinburgh, Environment Centre, 1990.

Whitten, D. G. A. and Brooks, J. R. V., *The Penguin Dictionary of Geology*, Harmondsworth, Penguin, 1972.

Index

Aberdeen, 155
  fishing, 34
  Urban Wildlife Project, 181
Aberdeenshire Canal, 129
Aberlady Bay, *160*, 191
Abernethy Forest, *46*, 47, 194
Achray, 148
Acid rain, 143
Agricultural Development Programme, 112, 185
Algal blooms, 38, 143
Almond Viaduct, 130
Altnabreac, 148
Aluminium smelting, 150
Antonine Wall, *91*
Aonach Mor, *203*, 204–5
Arctic-alpines, 43–4
Ardnamurchan, 48
Areas of Scenic Value, 191
Argus butterfly, *79, 84*
Arisaig, *210*
Arthur's Seat, 12, *22*, 61, *178*
Association for the Protection of Rural Scotland, 193
Assynt, 188
Atlantic Ocean, formation, 19
Auchindrain, 103
Auk, 67
Avens, Mountain, *44*
Aviation, 134

Ballachulish, 189
Ballantrae, 24
Balmoral, 197
Balranald, 65
Bartsia, alpine, 44
Bass Rock, 22
Bathgate, 22, 154
Bawsinch reserve, 163
Beaker people, 89
Bears, extinction, 58
Bearsden, Romans in, 92
Beavers, 58
Beinn Eighe, *184*, 186
Bellarmine Environmental Resource Centre, 179
Bell, Henry, 131–2
Ben Eighe, 194
Ben Lawers, 43–4, 193, 202
Ben Lomond, 17
Ben Lui, 43–4
Ben Macdui, 193
Ben Nevis, 189, 200
Bettyhill, 44
Biological Recording in Scotland Campaign, 160
Biosphere reserves, 187
Birch forest, 45, *55*, 162

Birds,
  populations, *65*
  reintroductions, 70
Black Wood of Rannoch, 47, 193
Blackhouses, 103, *107*
Blacksmith, *104*
Bloomeries, 147
Blue, butterfly, *80*, 82
Bluebells, *48, 123*
Blyth, James, 151–2
Boar, wild, 59
Bogbean, *52*
Bonawe, 148
Breadalbane, 43–4
Bridge of Weir, 131
British Butterfly Conservation Society, 83
British Trust for Ornithology, 70
Britons, 92
Broch of Mousa, *91*
Bronze Age, 89
Brooklime, *175*
Brough of Birsay, *93, 94*
Bunessan, 19
Burt, Edward, 104
Butterfly farm, *85*

Caerlaverock, 194
Cairngorms, 44, 186, 188, *189*, 200, 203–4
Cairnwell, 203, 206
Caledonian Canal, 129, 138, 141, *175*
Caledonian forest, 45, 120, *158*, 192
Calgacus, 91
Callanish stone circle, *90*
Cameron of Lochiel, 148
Campsie Fells, 17
Canisp, 25
Canoeing, *209*
Capercaillie, 72–3, *74*
Carluke, 151
Cattle-raising, 111, *118*
Celtic peoples, 89–91
Central Scotland Countryside Trust, 191
Central Scotland Woodlands, 122, 191
Cereal crops, 101–2
Charcoal, 90, 148
Charity walks, 205–6
Charr, Arctic, 139–41
Chequered Skipper, *82*
Clearances, 13, 101–2, 107
Clyde, 17, 138

Clyde Muirshiel, 189
Clyde steamers, 131, *132–3*
Coal, 12–13, 149, 153–4
Coastline habitats, 49
Coatbridge, 154
Cockenzie, 130
Cod, 35–6
Comet, 131, 132
Common Agricultural Policy, 118, 183
Coppicing, 90, 148
Corncockle, 47, 49
Corncockle Muir, *20*
Corncrake, *68*
Coulnakyle, 148
Country Parks, 189
Countryside Commission for Scotland, 186, 188, 210
Cowlairs, 131
Craigellachie, 128
Craig, James, 172–3
Crannogs, 90, 94–5, 139
Creag Meagaidh, *187*
Crested tit, 73
Crinan Canal, *129*
Crofting, 103, *106*, 114–15
Crop markings, 91
Crossbill, *73*
Cruachan, 142
Crustaceans, 30–1
Culbin Forest, 193
Culbin Sands, 51
Culross, 149, 193
Cunningsburgh, 94
Cycling, 135, 206

Dalavich oakwood, 193
Dale, David, 149
Dalriada, kingdom of, 92–3
Dams, 37, 143
Damselflies, 139
Darling, Sir Frank Fraser, 166
DDT, 69–70, 164
Deer,
  fallow, *58*
  red, 52, 59, 63
Deforestation, 45–6, 88–9
De-stoning, 97
Diapensia, 45
Diver,
  black throated, *75*
  red throated, 66
Diving, 30
Dolphins, 62, *63*
Dounreay, 156
Dragonflies, 139
Drainage, 100, 110
Droving, 98

Drumnadrochit, 113
Drymen, 17
Dunadd fortress, *93*
Dunbar, British fort, 92
Dunblane, glaciation, 17
Dundee Urban Wildlife Project, 180
Dunoon, 133
Durness, 139

Earthquakes, 20, 24
Eden estuary, 191
Edinburgh, *168, 170*, 172
Edinburgh Wildlife Survey, 179
Edzell, 148
Eelgrass, 51
Eigg, *115*, 193
Eildon Hills, *125*, 188
Elk, Irish, *55, 56*
Enclosures, 98, 100
Environmental charters, 177
Environmental education, 164
Environmental Impact Assessment, 164
Environmentally Sensitive Areas, 111, 125, 185
Erosion, 51, 121
European Diploma Sites, 194

Fabricius, Johan, 78, 84
Fair Isle, 152, 193–4
Falkirk, 154
Falls of Clyde, 193
Farm buildings, 102–3
Farm Woodland Scheme, 186
Farming,
  effects on wild plants, 48–9
  Norse, 94
Ferm-touns, 99–100
Ferns, 48
Fife coast, fishing, 35
Fingal's Cave, *19*
Firth of Clyde, 133
Fish farming, 37–9, 142, 162
Fishing, 30, 35–6, *112*, 164, *208*
Flag Iris, *52*
Flow Country, 45, 65–6, 161, 191, 209
Footpaths, mountain, 201
Forest clearance, 88–9
Forest Parks, 193
Forestry, 66, 119–21, 162
Forestry Commission, 73, 82, 120, 192–3
Fort William, 150
Forteviot, Pictish centre, 92
Forth, 138

salmon fishing, 36
Forth and Clyde Canal, 129, 138, 174
Forth estuary, Ice Age, 17
Fossil Grove, *21*
Fossil sharks, *23*
Foxes, 169, 170
Foyers, 142, 150
Fraserburgh, *34*
Friends of the Earth, 193
Fritillary, Marsh, *80*
Frog, *163*
Fulmars, 60–1

Galson, 107, 112
Gamekeeping, 59–62, 68–9
Gannets, *66*
Gartmorn Dam, 191
Gas industry, 154–5
Geddes, Sir Patrick, 174
Geese, 67, *69*
Gentian, alpine, 43
Girvan, 24
Glaciers, 17
Gladhouse Reservoir, 191
Glas Maol, 205
Glasgow,
    parks, *176*
    wildlife policies, 181
Glasgow Bridge, 129
Glen Affric, 47, *167, 192*
Glen Avon, 193
Glen Tanar, 47
Glen Tilt, 197
Glencoe, *16, 190,* 193, *196,* 200, 202–3
Glenkinglass, 148
Glenshee, 203–4
Gododdin, kingdom of, 92
Golden eagle, *70*
Golf courses, 207
Grain trade, 97–8
Grangemouth, *164*
Grazing, effects of, 47, 82–3, 110
Great Glen, 24, 138
Green belts, 190
Greenhouse effect, 19, 41
Greenshank, 67
Grouse moors, 47
Gullane, 131
Gunpowder manufacture, 148

Haddock, 35–6
Hairstreak, Green, 82, *83*
Hamilton, Duke of, 133
Hang gliding, 206
Hares, *54, 55*
Hay, Sir George, 148
Hay-making, *109, 116*
Heathlands, *50*
Helmsdale Fault, 20
Herbicides, 49
Heron, *159*
Herring, 33–5, *34*
Highland cattle, *96*
Highland farming, 103

Highlands and Islands Development Board, 113
Highlands and Islands Enterprise, 183
Hightae Loch, 191
Hill forts, 90
Hillwalking, 200–1
Hogweed, 49, *50*
Holyrood Park, 178
Hopetoun House, 98
Horses, wild, *56*
Housing, *174*
Hunterston, 156
Hutton, James, 24, 27
Hydro-electricity, 141, 150–1

Ice Age, 12, 17–18, 43
Improvers, 100
Inchmickery, 193
Indicative Forestry Strategies, 191
Integrated Development Programme, 112–13
Iron Age, 90
Iron-making, 147–8
Irrigation, 142
Isbister, *88*
Islay, geese on, 67–8

Jacobite Rising, 127
Jedburgh, 24
Jenny's Linn, *136*
John Muir Country Park, 189
John Muir Trust, 194, 201
Johnson, Samuel, 104

Kelp, 30
Kelvin, Lord, 150–1
Kelvin, River, 149
Kestrels, 169
Kettle-holes, *137*
Killin, 203
Kilmacolm, 131
Kilmartin Valley, *95*
Kilpatrick Hills, 141
Kinloch Castle, 198
Kinross House, 98
Kintail, 202
Knoydart, *182,* 194
Kyles of Bute, 188

Ladhar Bheinn, 201
Lairig Ghru, 206
Lammas Drave, 34–5
Land,
    ownership, 52–3
    tenure, 112
    use, 67, 164, 183
    values, 118
Lazy-beds, 101
Lead-mining, 149
Leadhills, 149, 151
Lecht, 148, 204
Less Favoured Area status, 108, 118, 185
Letterewe, 148
Leverhulme, Lord, 107

Lewis, 25, 107, 112, 114–15
Liathach, *42,* 193
Lichens, 48
Lime kilns, *99*
Limpets, *35*
Linlithgow Loch, *144*
Linn Dean, 82
Lismore, 139
Liverworts, 48
Local Nature Reserves, 191
Loch Awe, 137, 142, 151
Loch Duntelchaig, 144
Loch Fyne, 34
Loch Garten, *136,* 193
Loch Katrine, 141
Loch Leven, 143–4, 189
Loch Lomond, *17,* 48, 137–8, 141, 144, 189
Loch of Lowes, 193
Loch Maree, 148
Loch Morar, 137
Loch Ness, 137, *139,* 150–1
Loch Rannoch, 47
Loch Sunart, 48
Loch Sween, 48, 186
Lochnagar, 193
Lomond Hills, 189, *190*
Lomond Readvance, 17, *55*
Lorne Furnace Company, 148
Lothian, kingdom of, 92
Lurcher's Gully, 163, 165, 204–5
Lyell, Sir Charles, 18

McAdam, John, 128
MacDiarmid, Hugh, 11
Machair, 51, 53, 65, *108*
Maes Howe, *88*
Malcolm II, King, 37
Mallaig, 36
Mammals, human effects on, 56
Mamores, *205*
Marine life, *30–1,* 40–1, 62
Marine Nature Reserves, 186
Mauchline, quarry, 20
Meadow Brown butterfly, 77
Meadowland, 49, 161
Meikle, Andrew, 100
Metallurgy, 88–9
Miller, Hugh, 23, 25
Mills, 139, 149
Mining, 154
Mink, 60
Monasteries, 92
Moncrieff Hill, 194
Monkland Canal, 129
Mons Graupius, 91
Montrose, 152
Montrose Basin, 191
Mosses, 48
Mossmorran, 155
Motor vehicles, 133–4
Mottes, *94*
Mountain Avens, 44
Mountain-bikes, 206–7
Mountaineering, 199–201

Mountaineering Council of Scotland, 201–2
Mouse, St Kilda, 57
Mull, 19
Munro, Sir Hugh, 199–200
Musk rat, 60

National Heritage Memorial Fund, 193
National Museums of Scotland, 179
National Nature Reserves, 82, 110, 159, 164, 186
National Parks, 189, 201–2, 209
National Scenic Areas, 188
National Trust for Scotland, 193, 202
Native pine wood, *185*
Nature Conservancy Council for Scotland, 61, 70, 82, 109–10, 159–60, 163, 176–7, 186, 191, 210
Nature corridors, 163
New Lanark, 149
New Red Sandstone, 20
'New Town', 172–3
Newts, *175*
Norse settlements, 93–4
North Atlantic Drift, 29, 162
North Berwick, 131
North Minch, 20
North Uist, birds, 65
Nuclear power, 156–7

Oak woodland, 45, 48
Ochil Hills, 23, 141
Oil, 12–13, 154–5
Oilseed rape, 119
Old Red Sandstone, 20–1, 23
Opencast mining, 163
Orange Tip butterfly, *81,* 160
Orchids, 161
Orkney, fishing, 35
Ospreys, 70, *71,* 188, 193
Otter, 60
Owen, Robert, 149
Oxford Ragwort, 169, *170,* 171
Oxytropis, 43–4
Oystercatcher, *179*
Ozone pollution, 162

Painted Lady, 79
Paisley Canal, 129
Pathhead Bridge, 129
Peacock butterfly, 76
Pearls, Tay, 140, 160
Peat, 45, 89, 94, 103, 105, *147,* 148
Peebles, 131
Pentland Hills, 204
Peregrine falcon, 69–70, *71,* 188
Perth, 149
Pesticides, 13, 38, 62–3, 69–70, 164
Peterhead, 34, *155*

Picts, 92–3
Pigs, husbandry, 101
Pine, 45, 46, 55, 171–2, 191
Pine marten, *60*
Plankton, 29–33, 38, 41
Ploughing, 100
Poisoning, birds of prey, 68–9
Polecats, 60
Pollution,
    air, 143, 164
    effects on mammals, 63
    effects on salmon, 37
    marine, 41
    water, 37, 143, 164
Poppies, 49
Post Office, 135
Potatoes, 101, *105*, 107, *109*
Powan, 141
Preston Mill, 149
Primrose, Scots, *51*
Princes Street, 173, *177*
Puffins, 32, *64*

Quarrying, 20, 94

Rabbits, 58
Railways, 33, 130–2, 134, 175
Raised beaches, 18–19
Ramsar Convention, 187
Ranger services, 188–9
Rats, *57*
Red Admiral, 79, 169, 174
Red Deer Commission, 52
Red kite, 71, *171*
Regional Scenic Coasts, 191
Reindeer, *55*, 57
Rheged, kingdom of, 92
Rhinns of Galloway, 92
Rhododendrons, 161, 174
Rhum, *14*, 70, *115*, 186, 198
Rights of way, 201
Ring of Brodgar, *90*
Ringlet butterfly, 79
Road transport, *128*, 129, 134
Rockall, 29
Rodents, 56–7
Romans, 55, 91
Rosebay Willowherb, 169, *170*, 171
Rothesay, 133
Rothiemurchus, 47
Roy Bridge, 151
Royal Botanic Garden, 172, 179
Royal Mile, 172–3
Royal Society for Nature Conservation, 159
Royal Society for the Protection of Birds, 61, *65*, 68, 70, 159, 163, 193
Run-rig system, 98–9
Rural life, 104

Sailing, *210*
St Abbs Head, *165*
St Andrews, 18, *19*
St Columba, 92

St Cyrus, 51
St John, Charles, 198
St Kilda, 29, *188*, 193–4
St Monans, 151
St Ninian, 92
Salisbury Crags, 22, 61
Salmon, 36–7, 139, *143*
Salt-marshes, 50–1
Saltcoats Canal, 129
Sand-dunes, 51
Sand eels, 32–3, *33*, 65
Sands of Forvie, 51
Satellite photograph, *161*
Saxifrages, 44
Scots, arrival of, 92
Scott, Sir Walter, 104, 197
Scottish Conservation Projects Trust, 162
Scottish Enterprise, 189
Scottish Landowners' Federation, 202–3
Scottish Natural Heritage, 11, 186, 210
Scottish Ski Club, 203
Scottish Tourist Board, 207–8
Scottish Wildlife and Country-side Link, 163
Scottish Wildlife Trust, 54, 82, 159, 161, 163, 179, 193
Sea eagle, 70, 72
Sea of the Hebrides, 20
Sea lochs, 30, 38, 162
Sea-level changes, 19, *55*
Seals, *41*, *62*, 162
Severely Disadvantaged Area status, 185
Sewers, Edinburgh, 172
Shale-oil, 154
Sheep-farming, *117*, 119, 185
Sheep-shearing, *110*
Shetland Bird Club, 65
Shielings, 98, *101*
Shooting, 198–9
Siccar Point, 24, 27
Silverweed, *50*
Sites of Special Scientific Inter-est, 47, 67–8, 82, 109–10, 123, 159–61, 163, 186, 191, 193
Sitka spruce, 120, *121–2*, 161, 191
Skara Brae, *87*
Skiing, 163, 203–5
Skye, 44, *202*
Snowy owl, 72
Soil formation, 43
Southern Upland Way, 201
Sparrowhawks, 63
Speyside, 37, 47
Squirrels, *58*
Standing stones, 86
Starlings, 170
Stew ponds, 142
Stirling Castle, *126*
Stone-carving, 92–4
Strathbeg, 151
Strathclyde, kingdom of, 92

Suilven, 25
Sundew, *165*
Sustainable development, 11, 164
Sutherland, Duke of, 198

Tacksmen, 107
Talladale, 148
Tay, River, 37, 137, 140, 144
Taynish, 82
Telford, Thomas, 128
Tentsmuir, 51
Threave, 193
Thrift, 50, *51*
Tomb of the Eagles, 88–9
Torness, *156*
Torridon, 25, 193, 202
Torrin, *195*
Torrs Warren, 51
Tourism, 197, 207
Town growth, 131
Tramways, 132, 135
Tranent, 130
Trawling, 35–6
Tree Preservation Orders, 191
Troon, 131
Trossachs, 188, 193
Trout, 139, *145*
Turf, in construction, 94
Turnips, 97, 101
Tweed, salmon fishing, 37

Union Canal, 129, 174
Unna, Percy, 193, 202, 209
Unst, 94
Urban wildlife conservation, 175–6

Victoria, Queen, 197
Vikings, 57, 93–5
Volcanoes, 19, 22
Voles, Orkney, 56–7

Wade, General, *127*
Walkways, 135
Wanlockhead, 149
Waste disposal, 163–4
WATCH scheme, 162, 179
Water of Leith, 149
Water power, 149
Watt, James, 153
Weasels, 55
West Highland Way, 201
Wester Ross, 189
Wetlands Trust, 194
Whaling, 39, *40*
Whisky, 133
White fish, 35–6
White Fish Authority, 38
Wildcat, 60, *61*
Wildlife and Countryside Act, 160, 186
Wind power, 151–2
Windmills, 151
Wolves, extinction of, 59
Woodland Grant Scheme, 192
Woodlands Trust, 194

Wood, Stan, 22, 24
World Conservation Strategy, 11, 160
World Heritage Sites, 194
World Wide Fund for Nature, 163, 193

Young, James "Paraffin", 154, 157